John Grierson

John Grierson

John Grierson

FILM MASTER

by *James Beveridge*

Macmillan Publishing Co., Inc.
NEW YORK
Collier Macmillan Publishers
LONDON

All photographs are from the National Film Board of Canada, except those on pages 12, 48, 49, 50, 66, 68, 69, 72 and 73, from the Central Office of Information; page 22, copyright The Roy Export Company Establishment; page 23, from the Flaherty Study Center; page 24, from Famous Players/Lasky for Paramount Pictures; page 25, from the National Film Archive; pages 36 and 37, from Metro-Goldwyn-Mayer; page 45, from United Artists; pages 42, 43 and 67, from National Film Archive/Sovexportfilm; page 71, from Ceylon Tea Centre; pages 113 and 116, from Time-Life Inc.; page 229, from EMI Elstree Studios Limited; and pages 306 and 307, from Liberation Films.

Macmillan Publishing Co., Inc.
866 Third Avenue, New York, N.Y. 10022
Collier Macmillan Canada, Ltd.

Library of Congress Cataloging in Publication Data

Main entry under title:

John Grierson, film master.
Interviews and essays, most of which were done for the film, Grierson.
1. Grierson, John, 1898–1972. 2. Moving-picture producers and directors—Great Britain—Biography. 3. Grierson. [Motion picture] I. Beveridge, James A. II. Title.
PN1998.A3G7135 791.43′023′0924 [B] 77-17799
ISBN 0-02-510530-2

FIRST PRINTING 1978

Printed in the United States of America

To Margaret

We operate in a new world, but are not yet possessed of it. We have given ourselves a new kind of society, but have not yet given ourselves the new kind of imagination or the new conception of citizenship which makes it tolerable.

We have given away our capacity for self-sufficiency, but still want to be free individuals, so-called free to go our own gait and let the devil take the hindmost. Now, when we ought more than at any other time in history to be talking about responsibility and discipline and duties, we are talking most about freedom from controls and self-restraints, even when they are only our own necessary self-controls and self-restraints.

A mirror held up to nature is not so important in a dynamic and fast-changing society as the hammer which shapes it—it is as a hammer, not a mirror, that I have sought to use the medium that came to my somewhat restive hand.

I look on cinema as a pulpit, and use it as a propagandist.

JOHN GRIERSON

Contents

Acknowledgments

I would like to acknowledge the assistance in various ways, all valuable to the project, of the following:

SUSAN SCHOUTEN, researcher and librarian of the collected Grierson materials at the National Film Board of Canada, Montreal.

ROGER BLAIS, film director, my colleague and companion during location work on the film.

LES HALMAN and JOHN KRAMER, film editors, who helped greatly with co-ordinating transcript materials from the film interviews.

SYDNEY NEWMAN, former Chairman of the National Film Board, Montreal, for making available production stills, textual and research materials pertaining to the film.

MICHELE SNAPES of the National Film Archive, British Film Institute, for helpfulness in providing still pictures.

ROSS MCLEAN, for reading the manuscript and supplying valuable background concerning the formation and early work of the National Film Board of Canada.

GEORGE and MARY FERGUSON, Montreal, for access to personal correspondence and for helpful guidance.

EDGAR ANSTEY, London, for much good counsel.

LADY MARGARET ELTON, for providing the illuminating document "Answers to a Cambridge Questionnaire."

FORSYTH HARDY, Edinburgh, for great helpfulness in the original film project plus subsequent assistance and goodwill in respect of this book; also for permission to reprint certain items from his well-known *Grierson on Documentary* (Collins, London, 1946).

DR. JACK ELLIS, Northwestern University, for generous permission to reprint a letter of personal reminiscence from Charles Dand, "Grierson at University."

ELIZABETH SUSSEX and the late ERNEST BETTS, for kind permission to reprint interview material which each had obtained from John Grierson shortly before his death.

GERALD GROSS, for initial encouragement and assistance in launching this project for a book about the film of Grierson.

RAY ROBERTS, Macmillan Publishing Co., Inc., for great patience and forbearance.

To all these and numerous others who have helped with materials or encouragement, my grateful thanks.

J B
Poona, India
December 1976

Foreword

John Grierson was a great theorist and a great activist in communications. His lifetime was the span of this century up to 1972. He came out of a rigorous ethical and intellectual tradition in Scotland, with a full awareness of the mounting tensions of these times—an age of labor unrest, of social imbalance, of rival imperialisms, of two world wars, of many revolutions in the areas of science, philosophy, technology, education, and communication (to which last he added his own significant contribution).

Like most human beings he was not without weaknesses, lusts, contradictions, and vanities. But his energies and thought flowed powerfully in a steady stream. He influenced many individuals and whole areas of teaching and communication. He galvanized pupils and colleagues in such numbers and with such energy that his concepts have spread far and wide.

What all did he do in his lifetime? He is not very widely known beyond a fairly limited circle of educators, civil servants, men in public life, media people, film-makers, and students. But it seems very clear that his insights, concepts, intuitions, and judgments have had a potent influence not only on the techniques of communication (especially film), but in philosophical areas.

Grierson saw the world whole. He believed with a passion that modern man had an overriding duty to his fellow-man, to the community, the state, the commonweal. Coming out of the nineteenth century and its concerns with science and rationality, and coming from Calvinist forebears, he believed strongly in the duty and capacity of humankind to learn, to act, to progress. He was outraged at the thought of wasted talent, of defeatism, of personal vanity. He saw life as a series of great challenges—mental, moral, political, and technical. He believed in organization, rationality, and duty; yet together with this he believed deeply in the role of the artist with his special gifts of inspired intuition. All of this makes for a turbulent spirit and a turbulent life.

One of Grierson's most concrete achievements was the founding of the National Film Board of Canada, which is an agency of the Canadian government empowered to produce films of many kinds. In 1971 the Film Board, after thirty years of activity and with a very solid and prestigious reputation, requested that Grierson take part in a film document about his life and work. He was quite naturally pleased at this prospect. However, it was not to be, since Grierson, not long after a period of travel in India, died at Bath in England in February 1972.

The film project initially intended to be a document made with Grierson's full participation therefore became a biographical piece, a "tribute." This was specifically what he had *not* wanted, "not a personality piece." But circumstances and the feelings of his old pupils and associates inevitably combined to produce a memorial film.

As one of his first Canadian recruits and pupils, I was involved with a production group of the Film Board in making the film about Grierson shortly after his death. I had talked with him about the proposed film on three occasions, and knew pretty well the values he had hoped the film would project. But now Grierson had irrevocably left the scene. His presence seemed strong and vivid to us all, yet now the record had to be researched rather than recounted by its maker, had to be compiled and assessed by others. The film was put into production, and a friend and colleague Roger Blais was assigned as director of the film crews who would undertake the Grierson project. He and I, as adviser, were occupied with the design and planning of the film. Blais would also interview in French for the proposed French-language version, which would necessarily involve the filming of several additional French-speaking spokesmen in Montreal and Paris. Location shooting and the compilation of archive materials took some four months. Editing was done through the following winter, and the film completed early in 1973.

Many people were involved with the making of the film during 1972. Much money was spent; three different camera and sound crews were engaged in various regions; Blais and I traveled from Montreal to Los Angeles, New York, Toronto, London, Edinburgh, Glasgow, the Scottish Highlands, Amsterdam, Paris, and Florence. Film material was researched and obtained from archives and spokesmen in Ottawa, London, Peking, New Delhi, Sydney, and New York. We filmed interviews with forty former colleagues or associates of Grierson. A number of his own talks and broadcasts on tape and film were obtained, and luckily it proved possible to convey his character and temperament by using actual footage, photographs, and sound tapes taken at different times in his life.

The final film conveys something to those who knew him, and something to those who didn't, who have no prior knowledge of him and no special interest in him. It is surely worthwhile as a record. But were we correct in summing up his life, in stating as we did what Grierson meant to us, and what his value was? Of course a good deal of film footage is of Grierson himself, recorded directly. But there is always the film editor's role in deciding what to include, what to omit. The work was done under pressure to meet deadlines—in this case, air dates in Canada on national television, through the Canadian Broadcasting Corporation.

Any film is a corporate enterprise, as all film people know. This one in particular was such. A score of people were directly and intimately concerned with the making of the film; another fifty appeared in it. Several of Grierson's British colleagues interviewed for the film have died since it was made; already in that short interval, the film has become perforce historical.

This book deals primarily with the content of the film that we made, the experience, research, and personal contact of that involvement. I had the responsibility of selecting and interviewing the people who appeared in it, most of whom I had known earlier, some ten, twenty, or thirty years before. By 1972 few of them were still in touch with one another. Our common meeting ground was Grierson, our respective recollections and interpretations of what he said, what he meant, how it happened—perhaps a long time ago. Yet neither the film nor this book is a "definitive biography." Mr. Forsyth Hardy, Grierson's good friend from Edinburgh days, has the primary responsibility as his biographer, and other writers have published books about Grierson or have books in preparation.

This therefore is a version of an experience in film-making, the goal of which was to create a fair and accurate account, in film, of the life of John Grierson. I felt him to be very close to us while we worked, and indeed still feel so as I prepare this material.

Withal, these pages will give a composite account, largely in terms of personal memories and assessments by a number of individuals, of those particular media developments in Britain and Canada that have resulted from Grierson's efforts. I must mention that a number of spokesmen who appear in the film of Grierson are not among those interviewed in these pages. Of forty persons whom we filmed, only twenty-five are quoted here; while some others who have given taped interviews or written statements for the book were not interviewed in film.

The objective has been to give a rounded picture of Grierson, as representative as possible both in the documentary and in the book. This presents problems of balance and selection in each case. The choice of images, visuals, to tell a story on film is of course a different process from the choice of words, quotations, and statements to compose a book.

I feel a special sensitivity about the fact that several of Grierson's close associates, including senior colleagues from the great first flowering of documentary film in Britain, are not quoted here. These eminent filmmakers and communicators, all of whom we filmed, include Edgar Anstey, Lord Ritchie Calder, the late Sir Arthur Elton, Mary Losey Field, Bert Haanstra, Stanley Hawes, Pierre Juneau, Philip Leacock, John Marshall, Professor Marshall McLuhan, Paul Rotha, and John Taylor. It is an embarrassment that persons of this distinction should become either faces on the cutting-room floor or pages of copy edited out. However, as stated earlier, this book is not a complete biography or an exact history, but an interpretation of Grierson. It is largely the extension of a process in which a group of film researchers and film-makers, myself included, prepared

Paul Rotha, long-established film critic and writer, a major contributor to the expansion of the documentary idea in film.

under some pressure a film for public audiences about John Grierson and his work.

The growth in the range and power of the media—press, radio, film, television—is part of our recent social history around the world, and affects that history in an interpenetrating process. In Britain and Canada, specific models or patterns for spreading information and education have derived from Grierson's activity. In some cases these models have not endured; in others they have grown into wide-ranging instruments of information policy, or (put another way) powerful instruments of education. The role of such systems of information is not simply to increase the quantity of information, but also to help us cope with the appalling number of messages, facts, and stimuli which fill our waking days. But what of the content, the message, the policy, the philosophy of communication itself? Grierson's life was wholly taken up with such questions. This book contains perspectives on his work and its impact from a number of people who shared in the effort, over many years and in several countries.

Youth

DEANSTON is a small, quiet village laid along a narrow wooded valley, near Stirling in Scotland. This was Grierson's birthplace. The family moved when the children were very young to Cambus Barron, a nearby village on the outskirts of Stirling, that beautiful Scottish town with its majestic castle towering on a rocky bluff. At Cambus Barron, Grierson's father was headmaster of the school. Here the children—two brothers and three sisters—grew up.

Doubtless Grierson loved Scotland, whence his first perceptions and experience came—the winding narrow roads along the shores of Highland lochs, on which in his youth, as a sometime lay preacher, he would racket off on a motorbike to tiny halls in isolated rural parishes. Grierson's roots were in Scottish and British culture, studies, and philosophy. His models, he has said, were H. G. Wells, George Bernard Shaw, Bertrand Russell, and the British philosopher A. D. Lindsay. He studied English literature and moral philosophy at Glasgow and Durham universities. At home the members of his family were always concerned with moral and religious principle, not as dogma or theory but in terms of social responsibility and social action; this was the turbulent time in which the Clydeside movement of militant labor organizations and protest grew to political strength. From this background he gained a kind of classical insistence upon values more closely associated with Europe than America: a strong sense of the fabric of civilization; the desire for excellence in all fields; the paramount importance of intellectual integrity; above all, the sense of responsibility to one's fellow-man.

Grierson grew into a world readying for World War I. At seventeen he, like so many millions of his generation, was swept into it, in the naval reserve, on mine-sweeping duty in a converted trawler in the channels and ocean reaches off the Western Isles and up to Scapa Flow. His first adult experience was therefore in time of war, the war that marked the end of nineteenth-century power and rule, the end of empires.

Amid times of change, young men and women born into the early twentieth century had to evolve their own philosophies, take their positions, make their own interpretations of and judgments concerning the meaning of events. The century of mass man, of great industries, great concentrations of power and technology, had begun. Not least, the art and science of communication would undergo tremendous expansion of scale and influence. People would be in contact as never before, among the continents and nations. How could they be equipped to cope with the new situations and concepts? How would the modern citizen conceive his duties to the state? What were his duties to the future? How could he grasp, mentally and philosophically, the new developments and potentialities in science, or the effects of new technologies upon the future condition of his society?

Such questions filled and occupied John Grierson's mind for the whole of his lifetime. His role in part was to mull these questions over and to make others aware of them. All of Grierson's pupils, disciples, and associates attest to the urgency which he infused into discussion of these matters. He felt the overwhelming importance of and the need to make known and clarify contemporary problems and challenges.

At the same time, the beauties of the world cannot be lost sight of either, for they are civilization. For Grierson, these aesthetic considerations were the proper ground for the artist. Moreover, the artist and the poet could, in their own special ways, illuminate the future—foresee the direction of our movements, the shape of things to come. The artists and the arts must therefore take their proper place in the great process of interpretation, foreshadowing the future. This had been their role in history, and now the artist's role took on redoubled importance. The artist must be part of education, part of communication in the widest sense.

Young Grierson's task upon leaving the university would be to find the ways and means, the effective processes, whereby people could be reached with these ideas. Should the fullest resources of education be reserved to select schools and universities? Should not the rank and file of the citizens have equal access to these resources? But how then to make them available? Libraries? Adult education? How could the real masses, the great number of human beings in modern industrial society, learn about the true nature of the modern world and its problems? This would require methods, channels, techniques, resources, more than the conventional means at hand —the conventional structures of school and university, newspapers and journals. The times were now too turbulent, too fast-moving to be served adequately by the traditional means of communication. Something new was needed. Pursuing a solution to this general problem, Grierson set out upon his professional life, a seeker.

James Reid

A two-story gray stone house with steep Victorian gables and tall narrow windows stands in a neat garden. Behind the house is the Cambus Barron Schoolhouse, a bleak architectural breath of the nineteenth century. Plainly visible on the skyline is Stirling Castle.

Mr. Reid is headmaster at the school where Grierson's father in his day was headmaster and where the Grierson children had their early education. Mr. Reid is handsome, sturdy, and youthful and speaks with a distinctive, musical, high-pitched and totally Caledonian cadence. He showed us the school, which smelled of floor oil, disinfectant, and chalk dust. The big, high-ceilinged rooms with austere desks and forms were softened by bright new paint. On the Honour Roll, wooden shields lettered in gold hung on the walls of the assembly hall, were listed the prizewinners of years gone by, the Grierson girls among them. The old floorboards creaked as we walked through the rooms, and sunshine flooded in through the narrow windows.

Mr. Reid gave us tea in his house, in a comfortable Victorian parlor with antique furniture and a fine fireplace. Though Stirling was nearby, and Edinburgh and Glasgow were less than an hour away, here there was still a feeling of village life—in touch with the world but not oppressed by big-city considerations.

We had not arranged to interview Mr. Reid on-camera, but the school and the headmaster's house are shown briefly in the film.

Reid: Grierson was two years old when he came to Cambus Barron; his father was appointed headmaster. He was born in the village of Deanston in 1898. He came to live in the schoolhouse that I occupy now, and there his family dwelt for twenty-five years during the time his father was head-master in this school. His was a large family, and the house was extended quite considerably to accommodate them all. The children were all good pupils. Two of Dr. Grierson's sisters were medalists in Cambus Barron School, Dorothy in 1914 and Ruby in '16. In 1908, after five years at Cambus Barron School, John Grierson went to Stirling High School.

It is quite possible that in Cambus Barron School with Grierson's father, they had the first movie picture to be shown in any Scottish school. They had also a school garden, and it is quite probable that this was among the first school gardens as well. There was a soup kitchen, which meant that the people in Cambus Barron were not very rich. Dr. Grierson himself referred to this when he said he knew the people of Cambus Barron were poor people, and he remembered the time when there were open sewers and middens. In fact, the school had a midden of its own at the bottom of the garden. The workers on the land were paid about thirteen shillings a week, and the lad who worked in his father's school received only twelve shillings.

One of the most precious things to him was the fact that he had grown up with nature at his doorstep. He remembered well a day in the woods in search of wild flowers to enter in the children's section of the flower show, which has taken place every year to this day. Happy is the child, he said, who grows up in the presence of nature and with the seasons. And this he did at Cambus Barron.

In Dr. Grierson's own words, the real grain thrown into the good earth was the children. And the teachers were the most important people in the midst of the community.

John Amess

At the edge of Stirling not far from the great gray castle, we went through a garden gate to a low stone cottage half covered with red climbing roses. Here we called on John Amess, a sprightly gentleman in his late eighties, keen of eye and hearing, lively in mind and manner. He received us amid the many books in his study, a room frugally furnished but comfortable.

John Amess was Grierson's teacher at the Stirling High School. He took us there, to a Victorian building with large windows and cupolas, and with a solid air of majestic ugliness. In front of the school we talked with Mr. Amess about Grierson and other pupils; his memories went back over some sixty years. The schoolmaster recalled accomplished students who had gone on to greater scholarship and to distinctions both civil and military throughout the Empire and Commonwealth. He conveyed to us a sense of continuity, of high standards in teaching and in deportment, of civic responsibility and patriotic dedication. Many boys and girls had moved through this somber building and now lived in places scattered across the world. The teacher remained here, recalling the names and faces and grades and distinctions of many he had taught in years gone by.

Amess knew that Grierson was bright, but he had not expected him to be "all that bright." Grierson had kept in touch over the years. With great glee Mr. Amess produced a cable that Grierson had sent him a year or two before. The cable was eloquent of the bond between teacher and student; eloquent, too, of the strength of that Scottish tradition which values scholarship, diligence, and a strong sense of duty to the commonweal.

Mr. Amess read out to us, for the film, part of the message: "It begins, DEAR MAESTRO—AM NOW PROFESSING AT MCGILL UNIVERSITY. Then Grierson talks about his studies here at school, and he says, YOU YOURSELF, WHAT DID YOU DO BUT CREATE A SORT OF SNOBBERY AROUND CONSTITUTIONAL HISTORY, WHICH WAS BOUND TO DRIVE YOUR INNOCENTS TO MACHIAVELLI AND THE CONSIDERATION OF POWER AND THE NATURE OF PROPAGANDA, AND THEREBY MYTH-MAKING ITSELF—I AM YOUR WITNESS."

Amess: It's sixty-three years ago next month since I came to Stirling to join the staff of the high school—that was in 1909. One of the pupils who enrolled for the first year was John Grierson from Cambus Barron school-

John Amess, Grierson's teacher in high school, lively and cheerful when interviewed in Stirling, Scotland.

house. I already knew something of the family and his two older sisters. Of course I expected quite good work from Jack Grierson, but I didn't expect that he would turn out to be so brilliant as he did. There were twenty-five boys in that section, and three of them got the mark "excellent" on the report cards. One of them was Jack Grierson. His father was a headmaster, his mother was a teacher. In fact, Grierson told me later on in life that his mother was a better teacher than his father was.

I was assistant in the English Department with a special responsibility for History. You see, I had had History with Sir Richard Lodge in Edinburgh. It was History more than English that I taught Grierson at first, but I taught English classes as well. Then the war came in 1914 and 1915; after he was six years at school, he went into the Royal Naval Reserve. And afterward to the university. I don't remember much about his career at the university because at that time I was away in the army myself. He did philosophy—yes, Moral Philosophy and English.

After that, our lives separated and we had no correspondence for years until the point at which some enthusiasts decided to form a film society in Stirling. One of the ladies invited me to be chairman at the inaugural meeting. And the Stirling Film Society was founded. Of course it was

Grierson's influence that inspired people in Stirling to take an interest in films.

Question: Many, many hundreds of students have graduated from your classes. There must have been a good number of quite distinguished men.

Amess: Well, yes, John Ferguson was a brilliant boy, ultimately one of the directors of ICI; he traveled all over the world and took part in the research that led to the atomic bomb, he told me, out in America. He drew up his car one day, opened the door and invited me in. I stepped in, and he said, "You won't know who I am." I confessed I didn't, and he said, "I'm John Ferguson." I said. "Oh, I remember you well. You were always first in your class and Jeannie Bain was always second." So he invited me up to dinner in the Golden Lion, and we renewed the old days. Then Norman McLaren, a very likable boy, very humble boy but original, very original. I knew his films well. And Muir Matheson, of course—his mother was a violinist and his father was a well-known artist, so he inherited the talents from both his parents.

Question: Over these long years there must have been a big change in the climate of study. Have you noticed that in your lifetime?

Amess: Not so much while I was teaching, but I have seen it since. My son-in-law is a headmaster and is very conscious of all these changes that have taken place; some he approves of, and some he deplores. Discipline,

Grierson at 17.

for example. Then in the old days we were given grammar, spelling, punctuation, they don't bother about those things now. My son-in-law'll correct essays, and if he finds one very interesting, he'll pass it on to his wife, my daughter, to read. And she'll agree that it is a very good essay, but will note that the spelling is very bad. Oh, he'll say, we don't bother about that. We are losing something in the process, but on the whole I think the changes are really quite good.

Marion Taylor

Glasgow in 1972 presented the impression of a large city in the midst of a colossal upheaval of demolition and rebuilding. The valley of the Clyde seems very wide and spacious and open to the sky. The new suburbs along the crest of the low hills are very modern-looking. The long, long central streets with their tall, grim smoke-stained buildings conform more closely to the nineteenth-century image. There are clusters of spidery-looking cranes in the shipyards, which seem to be embedded in the heart of the city itself.

On a windy stretch of elevated sidewalk across an intricate traffic interchange, we filmed Grierson's sister, Marion Taylor. A forthright, easy-mannered person, she has dark keen eyes and a musical Scottish burr, and evokes a strong impression of Grierson without literally resembling him. She has worked in films and was married to an eminent documentary film producer. She now lives in Glasgow, close to the place of her birth and upbringing, and does social work.

Leaning on the railing, we talked and watched the activity in Glasgow below. Afterwards, quite red-cheeked and chilled, we all repaired to a dark mahogany pub and drank neat Scotch whiskey in large wineglasses until circulation was restored. Marion Taylor seemed to have much of the directness, liveliness, and self-assurance of her older brother. She and another sister living in Edinburgh are the only ones now who can recall the early family life of the Grierson household.

Question: When did actual involvement in film-making start for you?
Taylor: My first introduction to it, though I didn't do any work, was while my brother was working on *Drifters* [1929] in his little flat in Hampstead. It was a rather primitive attempt at a cutting room he had there, and as far as I remember, the films were all suspended from the mantelpiece in strips. He had wastepaper baskets to hold most of it. But I didn't have anything to do with film-making at that time, and went, as you know, to Canada for two years.
Question: So, when you came back to Scotland?
Taylor: Grierson wanted me to come and help him with a thing we called the *Empire Journal*, a film that went out monthly and was shown to the public at the Imperial Institute in London. This contained items from

Grierson at work on *Drifters*.

Canada and other countries; I think it ran for two or three years. That was my first introduction, when I did the editing. In those days we didn't really have very much live film to spend money on; the whole thing was done on a shoestring, and the films came from all sorts of sources. I think one of the main sources was a film made for a royal tour through the Empire. We simply cut it up and used little bits here and there, and made up these edited items for the Imperial Institute showings.

My mother was of course very keen on education as such. She herself had been a teacher of teachers: she was a rector at the training college here in Glasgow. My father was a schoolmaster. Yes, there was a big emphasis on teaching as such, on education, but I think the main subject of conversation in the home was deeper than that, really. I think our conversation had more of a philosophical nature, with much talk on religion and social conditions. For example, my brother was terribly interested in the condition of the Clydesiders; that was in the 1920s, when there was a great deal of life in the political movement here in Glasgow. My mother was a socialist and a suffragette, which at that time was really quite brave. Their politics were not really party politics, but more politics from a social point of view. I think that both my brother and my mother were terribly interested in improving the condition of the people they lived with, the miners in the village we were in. It was obvious that a great deal of help was needed there, and of course the condition of the Clydesider is the same as it always has been. It's always been difficult for a man to know whether he was going to work for long or not on the Clyde.

Question: What about religion? Is it true that Grierson was at one time a lay preacher?

Taylor: I think he was interested in writing, so much so that when he had an opportunity to take a post in one of the little Highland churches, he seized the opportunity as a means of speaking and writing. He spent a lot of trouble on sermons and prayers and so on, and I think some of these still exist, but that really was for a very short period, just until he went to Durham University as a lecturer.

Question: What about his studies at Glasgow in Moral Philosophy?

Taylor: Yes, philosophy—I think he always described himself as a Kantian. I don't know what a Kantian is, but I suppose other Kantians would know! His great master was Kant. He also was a great admirer of John Stuart Mill and Adam Smith, of course, and quoted them a lot.

Question: Was there a particular wing of the church, or a group within the Scottish church, that your family came from?

Taylor: Well, the family two generations back had certainly been connected to, or had been members of, the very narrow sect of the Wee Frees in the Highlands, and although my father was a member of the established Church of Scotland, in his youth he must have had a great deal of association with the narrow way of life of the Wee Frees—their Calvinistic attitude, their rigidity, and so on. I think a lot of his feeling was in rebellion from this. I think the rigidity and the narrowness offended him, and I think this still exists in Scotland.

Question: There seem to be two things: a rigorous sense of discipline and obligation, and at the same time a revulsion or turning away from orthodoxy.

Taylor: That's right. Yes, a sense of duty to the community is inculcated.

Question: And yet there's a refusal to be bound by the forms.

Taylor: Oh, a tremendous freedom. The forms certainly weren't respected in the cult. Churches were not used in many parts of the Highlands, because the people wouldn't sit in churches. They sat and worshiped in their own homes, many of them, but they had services several times a day, you know, two or three services each day.

Question: What is your own work?

Taylor: I was connected with social work with adolescents for a while. I am doing some research work, in association with a team in Glasgow, trying to find out ways of stimulating the people in a locality to improve their own conditions—you know, to get busy and complain and get their situation improved.

Question: Is there a lot of unemployment?

Taylor: Just in the last year or two there's been a great deal of unemployment, especially on the Clydeside. I think with some of the new industries coming up here and with a little bit of hope on the Clyde again, we'll just go on and hope things will improve. Certainly the new face of Glasgow that's being created all around us has made people a little bit more excited about their city. I think they're taking a greater pride in it.

Question: In Scottish life and in your family life, what do you think creates this social awareness? What pushes people like your parents toward this sense of society and its problems?

Taylor: I think it was being closely associated with people who needed help. The miners in the village in which we lived—their problems were constantly in front of both my parents. My father was always consulted about problems in the village. In fact, he considered this as much his duty as being a schoolmaster—to help people when he could. My mother was politically conscious and certainly was all for the suffragette ideals; she did in fact chair many of the socialist meetings in our area. My father was very quiet, but my mother was very articulate indeed and could express opinions very forcefully. I don't think my brothers were particularly reserved. It was a bit difficult to find a voice in the household, for there were too many voices all at once.

Question: Do you remember much of Grierson as a young child?

Taylor: Of course he was older than I. One of my first recollections of him was of his interest in finding some medium for combining all the arts into one. I think he was in his early twenties when this conversation between himself and me happened. I think he must have thought of films at this time, though he didn't mention films in the conversation I'm speaking of. Of course, it was the time of *The Covered Wagon* and the *Iron Horse* and the early Chaplins, and he spoke about combining music, art, all the media together. I think this is in fact what he did try to do: he found a medium that could do it.

Charles Dand—Grierson at University

An impression of the young Grierson, returned from war service at age twenty-one, at Glasgow University is given by his fellow student Charles Dand, later a civil servant and senior director of film distribution for the Central Office of Information. This sketch of an imperious young intellectual already commanding special gifts of preachment pinpoints those qualities which made Grierson in later life such an effective prime mover of new policies and programs.

Mr. Dand's account is excerpted from a 1967 letter to Professor Jack Ellis of Northwestern University, published in *Cinema Journal* XII, Spring 1973, and kindly made available by Professor Ellis.

When I enrolled as a student at Glasgow University, the first thing I did was to set about becoming a member of the University Fabian Society. I had read myself into socialism at school but had been too diffident to join any organisation in my home town. The meetings of the society were held in the women students' union, and when I turned up at the first one of the term, there were about a dozen men and women present in a small room with a large fireplace and only one comfortable chair which no one seemed to want to occupy, contenting themselves with upright wooden chairs arranged in a semicircle facing the comfortable chair. For about fifteen minutes nothing happened. It wasn't the chairman they were waiting for, since she had spoken to me. Suddenly the door was thrown open and there strode in a small man in a bowler hat, a military trench coat rather too large for him and reaching right down to his ankles, and wearing a small moustache. One's first thought was of the suggestion of Charlie Chaplin in the size, the hat, the moustache, and something in the gait as he crossed the room, threw off the coat, and sank deep into the comfortable chair. The expression on his face was grim and he spoke no word, giving nobody a greeting, merely settled back in the chair and stared fixedly at the ceiling.

There was no doubt it was he whom we had all been waiting for. Hastily the chairman introduced the subject of the evening and somebody began to speak. I have no recollection of the subject and probably paid it scant attention, being fascinated by the figure in the chair who in the course of the talk swung himself around, elevated his feet to the mantelpiece, and closed his eyes. His expression relaxed and I wondered if he had gone to sleep. When the speaker had finished the chairwoman asked for discussion and some desultory talk began. There wasn't much heart in it, however, and I got the feeling that the participants were addressing their remarks primarily to the recumbent figure in the chair and hoping it would come to life. Suddenly it did. It rose to its feet, took a long churchwarden clay pipe from the mantelshelf, filled it with tobacco, applied a long wax taper to the fire, and puffed clouds of smoke into the air. The talk languished into an expectant silence. The figure sank down into the chair again and began to speak.

I sat transfixed, as did we all. Never in my schoolboy life had I encountered anything like that flow of analysis and authoritative exposition. It was not just the eloquence. A great new light was being shed. Man and subject had blended into an effulgence at which I gazed in rapt admiration and wonder. He spoke for perhaps fifteen or twenty minutes and stopped, resuming his pipe. An animated discussion ensued. There was no deference about it. Everybody spoke freely, and not all were in agreement with the man in the chair, who debated with vigour and a skill that stunned me. I left the meeting feeling I had had the most exhilarating experience of my young life.

The ritual was more or less repeated at subsequent meetings. It was not that all the members were sitting at the feet of a god as I unquestionably was. I was younger than most of them, having come straight from school while a majority of the others, including my god, had delayed their university education to serve in various ways in the 1914–1918 war and were consequently several years older and maturer and by this time (1920) were nearing their final examinations or even post-graduates and I was a freshman. Among them were D. T. Jack, who became a distinguished economist, Lothian, later a professor of literature, Alexander Werth, prolific commentator on international politics, and William Barclay, for long parliamentary reporter of the *London Daily Express*. All of these could readily hold their own with John Grierson and could disagree with him. But for some reason it had become the accepted thing that until he had made his position clear they should hold their sharpest fire. They waited, as it were, for him to raise the target and call the numbers.

My open-mouthed admiration continued for three or four meetings until one day I was browsing in the library and picked up a copy of *New Age*, a periodical edited by A. R. Orage, a brilliant left-wing journalist of those days but up to then outside my ken. I started to read an article by Orage on the Middle East crisis of the day in which (if I remember rightly) British gunboat diplomacy was being threatened against Turkey. Words, phrases, arguments sounded familiar. Then I realised, with shock: it was these words and arguments Grierson had been so impressive with in the last Fabian discussion. So this was where it all came from. I hunted through back numbers. Yes, there it all was. My venerated oracle was an echo. But not, as I happily had the sense to appreciate, on that account a sham.

I have not related this anecdote to suggest that there was nothing original about Grierson in those days. On the contrary, wherever he got his facts and whoever influenced his opinions, the personality of the man which gave him such persuasive and dominating influence in the documentary film world was already highly developed. We waited for his views in the Fabian Society because we recognised him as a leader. It might be Orage he was giving us, but it was Orage presented with the racy speech, the analytical penetration, the thrusting logic, and the visionary enthusiasm of Grierson.

The University Fabian Society was dissolved in the following year on Grierson's suggestion. We were, of course, nothing more than intellectual socialists. Some were not socialists at all, only intellectuals seeking fellows with whom to argue. Moreover, Glasgow was not Oxford or Cambridge. There was no retreat from the coal, steel and shipbuilding by which we were surrounded. These industries were suffering post-war troubles. Strikes and lock-outs were frequent. A great new politically conscious labour movement was struggling to its feet. In these circumstances Grierson had lost patience with discussion for discussion's sake. Teaming up with members of the Independent Labour Party—the left-wing of the fast-growing political body in the industrial area—he decided that our society should be merged in a New University Labour Club to stand alongside the established Conservative and Liberal Clubs which were very active propagandist bodies within the university. Intellectualism was not to die, however. Those of us who were interested could become members of a Critics Club which he was founding to meet regularly to consider developments in literature and the arts. So the meetings in the small room in the women's union continued much as before, but now it was not Orage Grierson expounded to us but Benedetto Croce.

He was equally active on the political side. An election for the Lord Rectorship was due that year. In Scottish universities the Lord Rector is a person of some note elected by the students to represent them on the university governing body. At that time it had become customary to invite leading politicians to stand as candidates on the understanding that if elected they could appoint a substitute to act for them in university affairs. The Tory candidate was Lord Birkenhead, great advocate and (to our minds) notorious die-hard conservative. I can't recall the Liberal, but no doubt he was equally eminent in his time. There was as yet no Labour politician who stood a chance against them. Ramsay Macdonald was the hero within the movement but would cut little ice with the student body. The New Labour Club decided to ask H. G. Wells, who agreed.

Electioneering was by meetings in the students' unions and the publication of literature. The meetings were riotous, speeches being punctuated by fireworks, eggs, and bad fruit. Speakers were showered with flour and soot. The literature had to be produced in great secrecy to avoid destruction by the opposing clubs. Grierson was a leading speaker at our meetings and a formidable heckler at our opponents'. Traditionally the literature was humorous, satirical, scurrilous, and ours was not less so than our opponents'. Grierson wrote articles and poems. We lost the election but we put the New Labour Club on the map and introduced some notes of an altogether new "protest" type into the university writing. We had no illusions that we were doing anything for the working classes. Our aim was within the set terms of the election to take up a revolutionary posture in support of more serious revolutions outside, and, in all this, again we got our leadership from Grierson.

This rectorial election was a short interlude, of course, in more serious things. Grierson worked hard and brilliantly on the academic side. His industry was prodigious. He seemed to read everything. I have used the word "revolutionary." He was a great admirer of Lenin and Trotsky, more of the latter. He was more interested than most of us in the tremendous social experiment then starting in Russia. None of us, however, ever thought of labelling him as a Communist. He was too individual, too catholic in his interests. It was not the methods of organisation and government that seemed to draw him, but the hopes the Russian experiment raised of a power-house of reconstruction, a new release and orientation of human energies. It was this conception of revolutionary possibilities that he found in Trotsky, and it was one of the inspirations of his approach to documentary film. Another was his feeling of kinship with the miners and farm-workers among whom he had grown up as a boy and the sailors and fishermen with whom he had lived and worked during his war service and which was also evident in his student days. An intellectual himself, he was fascinated by the rhythms, skills, and wisdoms of the men who worked with their hands and drew its harvests out of the earth. These men deserved a new respect from us, a life worthy of their own integrities, and it was by them and for them that whatever revolution was needed to release suppressed and depressed human energies should be organised. Add to these his interest in all experiments in expression and communication, verbal and visual, and you have Grierson the revolutionary, at least as far as I understood him.

U. S. A.
—the Twenties

THROUGH a Rockefeller scholarship, Grierson came in 1924 to the United States, ostensibly to study at the University of Chicago. The record of his studies is somewhat elusive, but clearly what he in fact studied was the United States. Of course the twenties is now legendary as a period of exuberance and exhilaration combined with lawlessness, inflation, and Prohibition. At the end of the period came the Crash.

At that point in American history, the people of the United States were closer to their European antecedents, to the great flood tide of immigration that had poured into North America for over a century, than they are today. Many citizens still spoke an imperfect English and remained close in feeling and tradition to the lands of their birth. Though many first-generation immigrants could not read or write English, there theoretically was no limit upon their prospects, or more particularly upon their children's prospects.

American society in the 1920s was converting from primarily rural to primarily urban as the number of factories, offices, corporations, assembly lines, mines, foundries, and smelters steadily grew. The population was increasingly a working-class, industrialized one; mass methods, mass marketing, mass housing, mass education, and mass attitudes were being developed in a very large and wealthy territory.

Against this background, old forms of communication began to change and new ones arose. Tabloids and popular magazines proliferated, drawing their readers from groups other than the literate and educated middle class. Radio broadcasting had begun and would swiftly and enormously widen the audience for already popular music and entertainment. Above all, the great mass entertainment of the age was the movies.

In the 1920s the movies had a fresh appeal, that of novelty itself, plus the appeal of comedy, action, and drama. They provided entertainment for the literate and the illiterate—entertainment that seized upon music-hall comedy, slapstick, and acrobatics; upon the suspense, heroism, and high emotions of popular literature; and in particular, upon the special dynamics, optical marvels, and potentialities of film itself. The early screen comedies with their zany energy; the universal delight in Chaplin; the action of the cowboy movies, expanded and ennobled bit by bit into the epic Western; the throng of real-life characters, everyday heroes and heroines, who peopled many American films—all these brought vitality and universality to the screen.

America in 1924 was colorful and restless—mayors Jimmy Walker and "Big Bill" Thompson, Chicago gangsters, New York's bulls and bears, Dixieland, Babe Ruth and Jack Dempsey, the new mobility of men leaving the fields for mines and factories, of Southern blacks going North—a hustling, seeking, striving nation. Grierson dived into this world. In Chicago he explored a turbulent urban society. In New York he reviewed films

Charlie Chaplin—a universal image,
by means of cinema.

and talked with journalists and critics. He traveled widely—exactly where is difficult to trace, but to many states and up into Canada. He met publishers and editors, learned about local politics and attitudes, and scanned the whole map of North American society. He was (as we will read in his own words) greatly stimulated by the popular press—the Hearst press; its sensationalism, its direct contact with readers having scant education. By comparison, the British press seemed labored and lethargic.

Concluding that the press would not ever be able to provide for a truly informed and educated citizenry, Grierson looked to Hollywood and the films. The scale of the movies and the new distribution and exhibition systems for them excited him, but their content was something else again, mostly froth and fantasy. Then he met Robert Flaherty, a poet of cinema whose works were so fresh and conveyed such a striking and beauteous

Nanook of the North, by Flaherty: natural man on film.

view of the natural world that the movie industry in those early years was fully prepared to buy them and distribute them as widely as first-line dramatic story films. Flaherty's view of reality, of natural life in other climates and continents, struck the fancy of American audiences at the time; *Nannook of the North* and *Moana,* gave them a totally different point of view, opened a different kind of window into the world of cinema. For Grierson, Flaherty's method was full of promise; they made contact and began what was to be a long and stormy friendship.

As far as Grierson was concerned, the point of Flaherty's films was that they showed real human beings in the real world—albeit Flaherty saw this world with a poet's rather than a journalist's eye. But the essential beauty and dignity of man as seen in the Flaherty films was striking, especially when opposed to the tinsel and champagne of the standard 1920s Hollywood output. Grierson felt that film could perform a far more valuable function than simple entertainment. He imagined that it could serve as a marvelous means of informing, exciting, educating, revealing—in short, communicating the essence of modern life, with all its problems and possibilities, to the mass audience.

With this in mind he returned to Britain from America to find a way whereby the vision could be realized. The realization clearly called for large amounts of money; support from large interests; some system or systems of distribution. This all had to be organized and implemented.

Grierson had in effect turned from the spoken and printed word to the visual image. This brought him to a concern with many visual fields— graphic arts, typography, posters, exhibitions, design, photography. To a concern, in short, with motion pictures and all that they involved in terms of "cinema"—the special laws and dynamics of the motion-picture narrative necessarily taking account of image itself, the impact of the single image; the effect of movement; the effect of continuity, "montage," the fluid sequence of movements and connections which enable the film to tell its story in a unique way. Grierson would now become involved not only

Moana by Flaherty.

Robert Flaherty—mining engineer, surveyor and explorer who became a poet of humanist cinema and brought to the commercial screen a sense of the wide-ranging world of human beings in exotic cultures.

with a new medium, but with "cinema," with "movie," with the subtle art of the film. This would in turn bring him into future conflicts with his associates. Inevitably there would be clashes over the matter of form versus function, artistic expression as opposed to forceful exposition. Out of it all would emerge new potentialities for film itself, as an almost limitless medium condensing all manner of information, emotion, insight, within a single viewing experience. With no clear foresight of how this could be organized, Grierson dropped his study of America to return to Britain and new realities.

Revolution in the Arts

North Carolina, 1962

America always excited John Grierson. Its energy, scale, and confidence
stimulated and delighted him. Part of his excitement was due to the new,
technological, mass-society aspects of an American aesthetic. In a speech
given in 1962 at the University of North Carolina at the invitation of Terry
Sanford, then governor of the state, Grierson reviews the elements that
constitute this American aesthetic with its special significance in the contemporary world.

I am glad to be with Dr. Gilbert Seldes on this talk, very glad. I owe him
a lot: in fact a lot more than he suspects. Now that we are here together in
North Carolina I shall remind him that he gave me my first real introduction to this state. I was going about my business in a faraway country some
forty years ago when, in a historical moment for me, he pointed out that
there was nothing quite like "walking with your girlie when the dew was
pearly early in the morning," and that it was in Carolina only in all this
wide, wide world where "butterflies they fluttered up to kiss each little
buttercup at dawning."

I had of course other, more academic reasons to know about the Carolinas. There was a certain association with Sir Walter Raleigh. There was
another reason which must especially interest you in this university. In that
faraway country—and I mean my native Scotland—my own city of Glasgow was founded on the fortunes we made in the Carolinas; and the
modern development of my own ancient university drew its resources from
the economy of the Carolinas long before you did. But if anything brought
me to America it was this vision, however improbably, of "walking with
your girlie when the dew was pearly early." I have been grateful to Dr.
Seldes ever since.

All this was in the early twenties. We were just out of the war. We were,
of course, conscious of our own adventures in the arts and our own innovations in the arts. The painters, postimpressionist and post-postimpression-
ist, were exciting. We had the carvings of Modigliani and Brzeska and
Brancusi to give us a fresh vision of plastic forms. There were sporting
innovations in the use of words all along the line, from the Dada boys to
James Joyce and *Ulysses*.

But what was our principal guide to all these innovations and stirring new influences? It was an American journal called *The Dial*, financed to his ever-lasting honor by Dr. Sibley Watson of Rochester, New York. T. S. Eliot may be thought very much of an Englishman today, with an O.M. [Order of Merit] and all that, but the first appearance of *The Waste Land* was in that self-same *Dial* in America. In fact, it was from America that we there in Glasgow, Scotland, got our first sight of most things new in the arts. . . .

Now this business of Revolution in the Arts is a large subject, which can be approached from many angles; but I will put to you first a simple proposition which I think will take you quite a way—not all the way but quite a way. The proposition is this—and I merely put it to you as a primary exercise: that *while you may consider Russia as the great homeland of political revolutionaries in our time, you may well consider America as the great homeland of aesthetic revolutionaries in our time*. And it's an odd thing: you may not breed all the revolutionaries yourselves, but a lot of them, wherever they come from, tend to finish up under your protection.

If this is true, or even only half true, I think it would be interesting to wonder why. Now, as some of you may know, I have spent some years of my working life in North America and, as a foreigner, I have certainly been very much influenced by it. I think, therefore, it would be very proper to our argument if I told you something of the America which imposed its image on me and on my work as I first came face to face with it in 1924.

I had a perfectly good degree in philosophy at the time and a perfectly good fellowship; but against all academic advices I elected for the maelstrom of Chicago. Well, first of all, there were the attractions of people like [Carl] Sandburg and Vachel Lindsay and Sherwood Anderson. Here, too, was where Upton Sinclair had roared his head off and the Shame of the Cities was supposed to be most manifest.

I am afraid I approached the Shame of the Cities with no great moral fervor, but rather with a sense of dramatic anticipation; I certainly wanted a sight of the yellow press at its yellowest. There was too, of course, the great giant figure of Frank Lloyd Wright in the Midwestern background. In a sense he meant more to me than anyone, and still (in that same sense) does.

But what decided me was another kind of reality, and in fact the kind of reality from which, as I shall maintain in this talk, aesthetic form finally derives. It was the long immigrant length of Halstead Street. Here was the melting pot. Here was where the people of many lands were made over into Americans in three generations. I wanted to know. In fact I not only elected for Chicago but elected to come there as I thought an earnest student of the real America should: in a bootlegger ship charged with the solemn duty of delivering thirty thousand cases of Scotch whiskey to these eager, all-absorbing shores. "Give us your poor," you asked on the Statue of Liberty. I brought you the whiskey.

This Chicago of 1924 was certainly an exciting place to a young man. The gang wars were, of course, only one aspect of the growing pains of a fast-growing immigrant town. It was the sort of thing you might expect in a city where the foreign origins and loyalties were not yet resolved. The first generation of immigrants was caught up in foreign-speaking households with their own European loyalties, and the new community had its very different loyalties. As a result, the new generation often grew up in the streets without real benefit of either.

Yet the desperate effort to become American had its own crude influence on the approach to the arts. I am thinking of the mental habit which developed, of thinking old things bad and new things necessarily good. In the circle I knew best, the word "modern" had a sanctity which it never had in the Europe I had left. "What's new?" they cried. One year when "Big Bill" Thompson had a big city exposition, he was reminded that he had better do something about the arts. "Okay," said Big Bill, "but none of your old stuff, nothing but the new, nothing but the modern for this, the greatest of all possible cities of the future." And modern it was, under the direct influence and auspices of a mayor who, to say the least, didn't know Picasso from a hole in the ground.

I'm sure that much of the American interest in modern aesthetic movements, and America's creation of them, derives from this American desire to be forward-looking at all costs; but there were other aspects of the life in Chicago which even more directly dictated drastic new approaches to the arts.

I myself came out of Chicago with a theory about film-making which has in its day been regarded as a novel and even dynamic contribution to cinematic art. I want to take you back for a moment to Halstead Street and to the problem of making over the immigrants from the European way of life to the American way of life. My natural interest in the yellow press didn't turn out to be altogether useless because I quickly came to the conclusion that the yellow press, for all its sensationalism, was the most important factor in this revolutionary educational exercise. It was the only English press the immigrants read because it was, in fact, the only one they could read, with its simple headline-stories and its pictures. What fascinated me as a European was the way the Hearst press and its imitators on every level of journalism had turned into a *"story"* what we in Europe called a *"report."* They had in fact made the *story*—that is to say, a dramatic form—the basis of their means of communication.

This seemed to me a highly logical way of approaching the problem of mass communication. What was most significant was that the story line was a peculiarly American story line. The contemplative headline was as dead as the dodo. The active verb had become the hallmark of every worthwhile story. Something had to *do* something to something else. Some*one* had to do something to someone else. In fact, the world the newspapers reflected was a world on the move, a world going places.

All I did in my theory of the documentary film was to transfer that concept to film-making, and declare that in the actual world of our observation there was always a dramatic form to be found, if you would only look for it enough. Something was always *doing* something to something else, some*one* was always doing something to someone else. I saw in it a necessary instrument not only of education and illumination in our highly complex modern world, but an instrument necessary to a democratic society.

Of course, I saw it not only as a cinematic way of revealing the *dramatic* nature of the actual, but also as a means of revealing the *poetry* of the actual. And this I could not help noting because already in America, in the pioneer work of Robert Flaherty, you had shown the way to the combination of the dramatic and the poetic in describing the actual lives of the people of the Arctic and of Polynesia. What Chicago and the journalistic approaches of America gave was the vital thought that there, tucked away potentially in the cinema, was a medium of illumination and persuasion to be put in the hands of democratic forces everywhere. In fact, the reality was creating its own necessary medium.

There were other forces at work in the Chicago I speak of, and other fresh contributions to the arts of expression. I was not long there when I first heard a young man called Louis Armstrong blow his horn. In fact, these were the pioneer days of Chicago jazz. Much came from that, as you know.

Here again the origins were very real ones to which Americans can readily give a habitation and a place. But when you talk of the Negro's racial memories, the Negro's peculiar attachment to religious feelings, the Negro's reason for sadness and sorrow and consequent power to express the melancholy of a people, you must think, too, that it was the triumphant beat and the triumphant blast of the horn which made jazz all-American, and one of the great images of the all-American in the world today. In that matter, it may be that the Negro American has been as sensitive to the positive aspect of the American vision as any other of America's constituent citizens.

At this point I should mention a basic source of change in the arts. *Art changes as society changes, as new economic forces and widening horizons establish new habits of thought and new values among men; and as these, in turn, suggest new dramatic patterns and images of beauty.* This I shall have to return to as one of the fundamental laws governing aesthetics; but here let me speak of a man I met in Chicago who taught me much. He was Rudolph Weisenborn, the painter. I spent a lot of time with him, and much of that time we spent just wandering round the city looking and looking at its sprawling growth, sprawling outward and sprawling upward, building and boiling. I never knew a man so dedicated to his hometown; but not as William Allen White was, in the case of Emporia, Kansas, because of the worthiness of its citizens and their devotion to the ultimate cultural decencies. Weisenborn was excited by the thing *in itself*: the images of action everywhere, the visual dynamics that went with this city on the build; images, many of them, that had never been seen or seeable before: the vast volumes of the buildings, the extraordinary relationship between the volumes of the buildings and the bridges and the overhead railroads and the swinging curves that connected them. And above all there were the extraordinary effects of light on the new materials the builders and engineers disposed of. An asphalt surface could look brighter than the bright sky above. The concrete and the glass and the aluminum and the steel and the synthetic materials the architects were now using were catching the light in a new way—as, indeed, by all the laws of science they had to. You were a world away from the light on satins and silks and velvets, and all the substances of ancient interiors. You were a world away from the natural surfaces of nature itself.

There was another powerful shift in our visual attitudes. We were no longer seeing a prairie stretching away to the horizon; we were no longer seeing a man against the sky. Our world of space was no longer that kind of space at all. Wherever we were, we were seeing up, and seeing down; we were at the *center* of seeing. This was in simple fact what our man-built metropolitan world necessarily imposed on us.

At that time the cinema was growing up, and some of us, when we put our minds to it, immediately realized that the eye level of the camera could be anywhere at all, that it was not necessarily tied to the human eye level of a man moving around on his feet in space. We pioneers of movie criticism were supposed to be very bright when we announced the new visual logic of the kino eye. But there we were in Chicago actually seeing with the kino eye, simply because the shapes and sizes of our modern city imposed the kino eye upon us.

By that illustration I am suggesting to you that our sense of relationship with the world of modern art can come to us as quite a natural phenomenon, even as an inevitable result of the new world we have built to live in

In Canada (1942); painting is by Weisenborn.

and do actually observe. I am suggesting to you that what some people think of as *abstract* art may be in fact the most *naturalistic* and the most *realistic* description of what we see, consciously or unconsciously, as we move about in our metropolitan world. And so constant must the impact be that this new way of looking, this new way of seeing from every angle and in terms of dynamic whole, is in fact becoming a natural and necessary habit of vision; so that when we come to landscape or even portraits, we must see them likewise. And again I suggest for your thought that there is no country in which this new way of seeing can be so naively and naturally come by as America. If this rule is valid, the shift in the habit of vision will affect your appreciation in all the arts of expression.

I have seen it repeated over and over that the significance of *Moby Dick* was first noted in Europe: and that would be no wonder, because the power of evil is something *we* traditionally know about. Naturally and natively we allow for the permanence of tragedy. Even Trotsky, you may remember, found that he had to break all the Marxist rules and allow for the permanence of tragedy. For Europeans, certainly, it is a remarkable phenomenon in the history of your arts, that you alone of all peoples actually went through the process of rediscovering the permanence of tragedy, as though it were a new revelation. It accounts possibly for the sometimes violence of your approach to the tragic in literature; it accounts certainly for some of the sense of disillusionment, and even bitter and brutal disillusionment, which has to some extent informed your arts in general. When I say that there is something in you so deeply rooted in Romanticism that you do not really accept the permanence of tragedy even now—that in fact you *refuse* in your hearts to accept it—it explains a great deal in your arts. It certainly explains Hemingway.

As I keep on reminding you, the changes in the reality dictate the changes in the arts. What I think we have most surely to do as observers of the arts is to realize the great shapes of change in the reality, which drive the arts historically forward. . . .

I will remind you that the march of science and the impact of scientific thought and scientific images have been among the most powerful facts of life in the last century. The new images which the architecture of Chicago imposed on me, as I noted, were after all only made possible because of certain scientific developments. Think, too, that the study of light which became a passion with the impressionists arose from the new scientific understanding of the *nature* of light. Think, too, that postimpressionism and cubism after that, and many of the experiments associated with the Bauhaus, were a reflection of the new world of shapes which science was revealing to us or making possible for us. It is my own habit to see films shot on many of the frontiers of human observation, and that of course includes the world of physics, the world of biology, and the worlds of scientific inquiry in general. The shapes that are now common to my observation are bewildering in their variety. And they must mean an intensive visual enrichment for every man with any appreciation of shapes. I don't think you will find it difficult to see the impact of that rich new world of observation on both our architecture and our painting.

Here I would refer you to yet another of the basic changes in our era. It is the change in ourselves. I have talked of how we are bombarded with the new images, of the new world which our scientific discoveries have created —and I can't think of any atom bombardment more intense than this constant bombardment of our minds with the actualities of our widening horizons—and the fact that we have not altogether been blinded by our own sciences demonstrates a remarkable resilience of the human spirit.

But this same development has created a new world for us as social beings. We are no longer the citizens of the feudal village or a walled city. Our immediate community is tied inalienably to a wider community, and in the last resort, as Wendell Willkie said, we are citizens of one world. This again must have its effect on our aesthetic perception just as it has a profound effect on our lives. Our ever-widening contacts with other peoples, other religions and points of view, must inevitably affect our valuations and therefore our sense of appreciation.

First of all, there are negative reactions. The new world can be felt as so large and so complex that it seems to overwhelm our capacity to find the harmonies within it, which the human spirit forever seeks and must seek. One tendency may be to see only the disorder. There may be a certain feeling of hopelessness about finding order within that seeming disorder. You will, therefore, expect some pessimism and even some despair in our present aesthetic expression. I refer you to Beckett's *Waiting for Godot* as a remarkable account of this modern dilemma. Waiting for Godot we are, all of us, but what, of course, is hopeful in the situation is that in merely waiting for Godot, we find him.

There is even an element of mental breakdown in the individual to be taken account of. Brought up in old-time individualistic expectations, we have come face to face with the fact that we are expected to be organization men, subject increasingly as individuals to responsibilities determined by corporate ends and not individualistic ones. The very presence of these psychological problems must affect the arts. I don't think I am wrong in seeing a certain relationship between the modern psychological dilemma and, say, some of your own American experiments in ballet and music and comedy. I don't wonder that the words "beat" and "sick" and "black" now belong to the aesthetic vocabulary. They are the marks of much that is personally unresolved in our experience as citizens. And why do we like it *sick*? Because it is a true reflection of a very deep reality indeed, even if it is only a temporary one.

Fashions of expression will change as they must do, but the arts must continue to be rooted finally in the traditional absolutes of human destiny. Macbeth will still be Macbeth even when he turns up as a First Secretary of the Party in Moscow, or for that matter as an ambitious baron of General Motors. One can still see Hamlet dithering, not the less so when, as now, there is so much to dither about. Nor can I see Bach and all he represents in music beaten out of his place in our minds, for the simple reason that the will to order is an absolute of the human spirit at all times. I personally, excited as I am about all the changes in the arts, intrigued as I am by the changing habits of thought which cause them, do not feel under any duty to deny the majesty of Michelangelo's images of human splendor. Nor do I find the 19th Psalm out of date, for all the discoveries of the scientists. "The Heavens declare the glory of God," it says. One might conceivably think that the scientists have simply given us more to declare glorious.

Perhaps we don't yet match the arts of other times when they arrived at their particular peaks of expression. That would be too much to ask. But there is much we have in our midst that comes out of the same spiritual force, the same aesthetic drive which informed the master poets and master dramatists and master painters and master architects of history. I for one would not trade the blossoming architecture of America for any other architecture I know. That is where we live and have our being. The arts of older times we can admire, but it is in these even now unfinished and incomplete arts of our own time that we must draw our immediate strength, as present and sentient beings. So I say to you finally *Circumspice, Circumspice*—look around you, look around you. And by the recurrent lights of all our Broadways, in the crowded, the broken and the unfinished, see the infinite potentiality.

Richard Watts, Jr.

During the time of his studies in the United States, beginning in 1924, Grierson had visited New York and had met the few film critics who were then writing for the New York papers—few because film was not yet taken seriously as a respectable art form. This was still the heyday of the legitimate theatre, vaudeville, and the live stage show. A young film critic of the time was Richard Watts, Jr., of the *Herald Tribune.* Up until 1976 he was a drama critic with the *New York Post.* We called on Mr. Watts in Manhattan and arranged to film him at Sardi's Restaurant. In the famous after-theatre gathering place hung with cartoons of all the stars of Broadway, the great names and faces of show business, we talked with him at the bar amid the rattle and babble of a cocktail-hour crowd. The atmosphere was rich and evocative; the sound—too much. Proud as we were of our new directional microphone, sophisticated, sensitive, discriminating, selective as it was, it was not up to the task. The background sound of voices and music overwhelmed Mr. Watts' soft-spoken recollections. His interview, regrettably, does not appear in the finished film.

Watts: My own interest had been the stage. Then I got a job as assistant film critic with the *New York Herald Tribune* in 1924. The papers didn't take films very seriously then. There was a young man of my age then, named John S. Cohen, Jr., who was a movie critic with the *New York Sun.* We took the movies seriously, became interested in them, saw the possibility to pioneer in a new art form. We were laughed at quite frequently, but we did form this little block of serious-minded critics and reviewers, and then John Grierson came over. I don't remember the exact circumstances, but I do remember that when we did find this man who took films seriously the way we did, he scared us a little bit because he was such an intellectual. Grierson at the time was young, but he seemed older than us. We were a little bit awed by him, but then we found that not only did he like to discuss the cinema, but he also didn't mind sitting in speakeasies and drinking with us. So we got extremely friendly.

Question: Was Grierson himself then writing about film?

Watts: Yes, he was. That's why Paramount was interested in him and had such respect for him. They wanted him to do a rather elaborate study of their product and their methods, and they published it. It was a kind of market research, and it was artistic research also. Paramount and all the film producers had a very wistful ambition to be artists as well as makers of fortunes. Grierson went out to Hollywood, studied their product, and wrote a long, detailed account with advice that he had suggested to them. I did see it at the time—either he or Paramount showed me a copy of it—but I don't remember it very vividly, except that it obviously was a very thoroughgoing study.

As far as New York went, that was the heyday of the theatre, 1925–26–27. There were many theatres, people went to theatres, and the young people were there in the audience. Now young people have lost that interest in theatre and are entirely interested in the screen. But *we* were concerned with the screen, and we decided that the directors were more interesting than the stars. I got to know all of the famous film directors.

I got to know Flaherty quite well, and then later he made *Man of Aran*. I was interested in that movie particularly because I'd been out to the Aran Islands, though I hadn't contributed anything to the film. He was, of course, one of the most endearing men I've ever met. My recollection is that *Nanook* was superb and that I was a little disappointed with *Moana*.

One of the first things to excite me and my friend Cohen as reviewers was the Russian film *Potemkin*. We thought it was magnificent. The late Robert Sherwood, who was then a movie critic and loved being a movie

King Vidor's *The Crowd*—ordinary people in ordinary life; moving closer to reality.

Cimarron—the Western story moving towards an epic form.

critic, didn't like *Potemkin*. I wrote that the procession had passed Sherwood by, that he was over the hill. Later we became great friends, and he told me that really hit him because he was then thirty-five years old.

The thought of exploring a new medium was interesting critically. There were other fine films; some of the best things were coming along at the very end of the silent-picture era. One that seemed to me the best film that France had ever produced was *The Trial of Joan of Arc*, directed by Carl Dreyer. I was reactionary and objected to the coming of sound. I thought we were developing the film medium and doing quite a good job of it, so why should we now do an imitation-stage job? And for a long time that is all talking films were. Studios would get stage directors out to Hollywood, stage directors who knew nothing about the medium of the silent film. So both silent pictures and talking pictures were really very bad for a long time after sound began. As to critical opinion, I think in general Grierson and ourselves were pretty much in agreement, though we certainly disagreed in detail. Some of the American films he really admired we were not so enthusiastic about. He seemed to be an austere man, rather austere in his verdicts. But on the whole we did see eye to eye to a rather remarkable extent, considering we were all very opinionated young men.

Britain
—the Thirties

IN the early 1930s in Britain some elements of the government were actively concerned about the situation of the Empire and Commonwealth. World War I had fatally flawed the fabric and structure of the Empire. The desire for independence was clearly a powerful sentiment, and various territories could be expected to pull away. Above all it was important to Britain to retain the support and loyalty of the great Dominions—Canada, Australia, New Zealand, and South Africa. This necessitated some changes of attitude on the part of imperial ministries, which after a century of immense authority tended to be a bit smug and self-satisfied in their dealings with lesser states and nations. Some of these elements in government felt that World War I was in fact only the first phase of a greater conflict. Against the dangers of an unforeseeable future, they sought to strengthen by every means possible the bonds of common allegiance and sentiment that still held the Commonwealth, and some parts of the Empire, strongly together despite the rising tide of feeling for national independence all around the world.

Grierson, returning from America in 1928 with his new awareness of the possibilities of film as a valuable information tool, set about finding support for the development of his ideas. The full account of this chapter in his career must await a more detailed biography than this one, but in short he became associated with that body known as the Empire Marketing Board. This was an agency designed to promote and strengthen intercommonwealth and empire trading with the mother country. This agency felt that in order to create an awareness of and interest in empire products, it had to make the British public itself aware of the diversity and richness of resources throughout the imperial territories; it was the first to commission, from Grierson, the making and use of films by the British government for functional purposes that might be called broadly educational.

Grierson busied himself with explaining and promoting his film ideas to certain ministers and senior civil servants, and for this purpose organized programs for viewing new films of many kinds from different sources. Some of Flaherty's films were shown, and some European films representing new modes of film-making, exhibiting the striking possibilities of film form. These included the dynamic—in those days, startling—Soviet films being produced by Eisenstein and Pudovkin, not yet generally known outside a small circle of admirers in Europe.

Among the films shown were a number produced by agencies that were already at work in Canada, agencies that had been active since shortly after World War I. Chief among these were the Motion Picture Bureau of the Department of Trade and Commerce in Ottawa and the film production unit of the Province of Ontario at Trenton. This film output will be described more fully later; it is sufficient here to say that a surprisingly extensive production of short, descriptive silent films for educational, agricultural-training, and trade-promotion purposes had already been begun by these departments of government; and active use of such film programs was maintained in Canada throughout the 1920s.

Grierson made use of these films to show how such a functional use of film could be organized. Indeed, with these and some few others he began at the Imperial Institute in London the first free-loan educational film library in Britain provided for public use. The Imperial Institute became a showcase for these short educational films that displayed the resources and activities of Commonwealth countries overseas.

There were many problems to resolve, apart from the primary one of creating interest and dispelling inertia on the government side. There was the art of film-making to consider: clearly, film by its very nature must entertain as well as edify, or its use may well be counterproductive. Film in

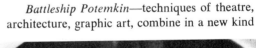

Battleship Potemkin—techniques of theatre, architecture, graphic art, combine in a new kind

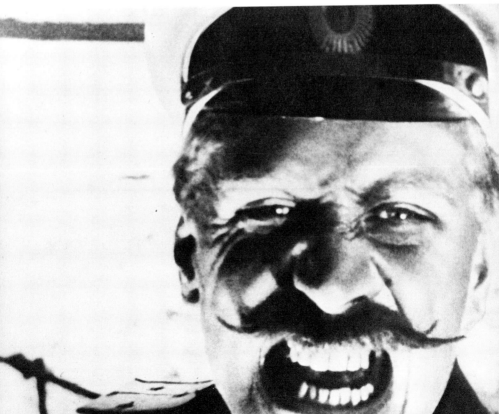

1929 and 1930 was itself undergoing great technical and aesthetic development. In Germany the powerful expressionist films of F. W. Murnau and Carl Mayer excited artists and intellectuals. In Holland, Belgium, and France the avant-garde had seized upon the medium of film as another avenue of expression and experiment, and films by Henri Storck, Joris Ivens, Luis Buñuel, Man Ray, René Clair, and others were beginning to reach the newly formed film societies in London and elsewhere. Sound films had not yet entered into commercial film distribution, though experiments with sound were numerous.

The film associated with Grierson's name most directly, which he himself directed and produced (*Drifters*, 1929), clearly reflects the new creative currents in the film-making of the time. *Drifters* was shown in company with *The Battleship Potemkin* at the premier presentation of the Soviet film in London, and the occasion was one of true artistic and intellectual excitement. Looking back, one can imagine the impact—or to be more precise, the shock—of two such films with their harsh percussive styles set against the context of contemporary commercial feature films of 1929, sugary fantasies from a world of pure escapism.

By energetic persuasion, by screenings of imported films, and by the

of cinema characterized by dynamic compositions
and rhythms of editing.

prestigious success of his own film, Grierson was able to inaugurate the first production programs for the British government. This development would occupy a full decade, 1929 to 1939.

Conditions were favorable for the use of any new medium that would serve effectively as a means of informing and persuading *numerous* audiences, whether small or large, of all kinds and in all kinds of locations—schools, clubrooms, meeting halls, church halls. Distribution—effective circulation and use of the film prints themselves—would always be central to this film activity. But the films themselves had to be effective: lucid and able to hold the viewer's interest, imaginative enough to strike the viewer's fancy and stick in his memory. The documentary also had to display as much inherent interest, beauty, and fluidity of movement as any feature film. Moreover, it had to be far more concentrated and focused in its message.

What was British life like during this period? Both the coalition government of Ramsay MacDonald and the Conservative government of Stanley Baldwin that succeeded it had to deal with increasing unemployment and social unrest. Britain, long secure in her overseas wealth and raw materials, was beginning to deteriorate industrially, her industrial plant obsolete and her technology old-fashioned. The glittering worlds reflected by such writers as Evelyn Waugh, Virginia Woolf, and the Bloomsbury group represented a small segment of British society, the upper class. Below it, working-class Britain, mass man, labored at great social and economic disadvantage.

Under Grierson's energetic leadership in Britain in the 1930s the medium of film entered a new phase. Film became a means of defining and clarifying issues of the day. It took on some of the functions of a newspaper editorial or an essay in a journal of opinion. At first this new kind of film was used to describe or explain various functions of government service, and was therefore a cinema of exposition. But subtly, it consciously began to take the point of view of the film-maker, and the film-maker in this context was a person of a certain philosophy. In Grierson's group, the film-maker was by instinct a reformer. He or she was informed and impelled by a feeling of obligation to "put things right"—the "things" being problems such as social and economic injustice, those wrongs within society the continuing existence of which became more and more galling and dangerous as frustrations grew at home and fascism grew on the continent of Europe and elsewhere.

Yet this film group was not primarily political. They were humanists, intelligent young men and women moved and motivated by the obvious wrongs of their society. The forms of society had fallen behind the times;

orthodox education and opinion were irrelevant to contemporary needs. The community of nation-states was being brought closer together (though not in legal or in spiritual terms), by technology, trade, and communications, to speak only of those areas.

The young Jimmy Cagney—natural man
in an urban setting.

In the Soviet Union, film had been officially built into the educational and informational apparatus from the start. Lenin's famous dictum concerning film and its essential social role was embodied in news-film, in information films of a strongly hortatory, nation-building type, and in feature films produced in all the languages of the republics, films involving ideological themes and archetypal revolutionary heroes and heroines. The distribution of such films would become an immense network, integrated throughout the whole tremendous society, finally supervised and invigilated by the policy-makers of the Politburo.

In the first phase of revolutionary Soviet idealism, there were great developments in communication and the arts—dynamic experiments in theatre, in new film forms, in graphic art, in the techniques of Agitprop. The Soviet goal was simply to ensure that the revolutionary program and imperatives would reach the masses—the industrial workers, the intellectuals and bureaucrats, the peasants. Literacy was a prime goal, for communication largely depends upon literate citizens. Posters, primers, banners, ceremonial occasions, and rituals for large and small events, both local and national—all were part of the Soviet program of communication and remain so to this day.

In contrast, the British press, apart from its traditional reticence on certain privileged matters, was by and large a free press. BBC radio broadcasting was becoming a vital news medium. Up to this point films had been wholly a business—commercial and speculative, as is their nature. British feature films of the 1920s and 30s were for the most part meager, minor, bloodless, and bland, with only a few distinguished exceptions to brighten the record. At that point it seemed as if Britain had little or no native gift for the film medium, despite important innovations in the early days of cinema.

Russian films—their dynamic montage and strong social and political content—powerfully affected Grierson and those members of the government and civil service to whom he showed them. American films, with their energy and gusto, their concentration on the commonplace and the real stuff of human behavior, their showmanship and sure instinct for the audience, had equally impressed Grierson. How could the humanity and energy of American film-making, and the radical techniques of Soviet film, be combined for effective social communication in the films of Britain?

As it happened, the next substantial sponsor for Grierson's innovative short films was the General Post Office. These films were to describe the work of the GPO, which in Britain involves many fields, including telecommunication and meteorology, beside the mails. Logically, communication was the main theme—communication over long distances, between countries and continents, ultimately to satisfy the daily needs of the citizen. The people shown in the films were everyday people, post-office workers, butchers and bakers, the citizens of modern Britain. In documentary films produced during the 1930s and thereafter, ordinary people, the rank and file of British citizens, took their place upon the screen. Today modern film-makers are still investigating the daily life, work, attitudes, feelings, and pleasures of ordinary people, of humankind in every country.

Basil Wright, one of the pioneer film-makers of the British documentary

Sir Arthur Elton brought to British documentary his own special gift of lucid scientific and technical exposition, notably displayed in the work of the Shell Film Unit.

group, outlines in the following pages the shift in subject matter and mode of film treatment as the decade of the thirties moved toward its end. Striking among his comments is the observation that during the first phase of the thirties these films set out to explain, to inform, to give a sense of pride in national achievement, while during the second phase, the films began to warn of the pressing nature of Britain's social problems and to urge government and citizen alike to take stock, take heed of these problems, and then take action. This phase developed as World War II began to loom on the horizon.

The increase in the number of noncommercial, interpretive, documentary films during this decade did not depend solely upon government. Grierson thought that all great corporations and businesses should undertake film programs of their own to explain their functions, to provide training, and to give "an account of stewardship" of their service to the community at large. He promoted tirelessly among such large organizations as Shell-Mex, the BBC, the Orient Line, the Ceylon Tea Propaganda Board, the Gas Council, and Imperial Airways, in addition to the ministries and agencies of government. Indeed, Shell established its own sizable film unit in London and under the late Sir Arthur Elton produced over a thirty-year span perhaps the most lucid films of science and technology that have been made in any country.

As this work developed in London during the thirties, small independent film units began to spring up around Film Centre, Grierson's own coordinating and development unit in Soho Square. In these units, young men and women from the universities came to learn the new craft of documentary film. Film Centre devoted itself to promotion, to new sponsorship, and to tireless contact work among industries and ministries. In order to develop the field and expand the possibilities for the new medium, Grierson had given up his own film-making, at which he had made such a promising

Night Mail—the young rookie nervous about his new responsibility.

start. Here and there among the ministries were some civil servants with authority and foresight who saw the point of Grierson's propositions. Important among these was Sir Stephen Tallents,* a career man in government public relations, who gave important support and sponsorship to the lively, unstoppable Grierson.

As the work increased, a group of new film talents and film theorists also developed. Their center was Soho Square, with its convenient cluster of friendly nearby pubs—the Highlander, the Pillars of Hercules, the Fox and Grapes, the Dog and Duck. The talk was fervid and intense among these visionaries of the film—"the dirty jersey boys," as their detractors sometimes labeled them. Political theory, the arts, films, the Spanish civil war, Europe and America, and of course films above all were the topics of discussion. There were Americans and Canadians among them—Irving Jacoby, a New York film-maker, and Evelyn Spice, a Saskatchewan schoolteacher, both joined the circle in 1936.

Always there were two important areas of development—the promotion

* Widely experienced in the field of governmental public relations, Tallents was secretary to the Empire Marketing Board, 1926–33, and later public relations director for the GPO. He helped greatly to introduce the young Grierson into the higher levels of the governmental and intellectual establishment.

Night Mail—the mail pouch slung outboard from the speeding train; brilliantly orchestrated sound effects and rhythms characterize this sequence.

Night Mail—the poetry of reality.

of new sponsorship and the innovative development of the film medium itself. Grierson had the overwhelming weight of responsibility in the first area, but as producer and adviser played a highly influential role in the second as well. When sound engineering at length provided a talking picture for the world's commercial screen, documentary film-makers immediately had to catch up with this new dimension in film-making. A new set of technical and organizational problems arose—how to cope with sound in nonfeature films of short length, made in most cases outside the studios by film crews often unfamiliar with studio methods and recording technology.

At this point an influential new recruit came to join the group—Alberto Cavalcanti. This seasoned film-maker from France was a native Brazilian who had made feature films and worked in the avant-garde. To the stern and sharply focused purposes of documentary Cavalcanti added not just the touch of studio professionalism and expertise in sound film that he had learned in France, but also a preoccupation with film form and film aesthetic.

In working as an experienced film professional with the young students and artists lately come into documentary, Cavalcanti in effect functioned like a training officer. One might guess that a tension between form and function would develop in this tight-knit and purposive community of highly motivated film-makers. To a degree perhaps this was so, and inevitable. European art and style and thought were persuasive and seductive to young English intellectuals. Cavalcanti brought a strong whiff of that European world into the British group, and indeed modified and perhaps enriched their work. Some maintain that Grierson's functionalism and Cavalcanti's aestheticism clashed, that there was a genuine tension between their views. The films from this period would seem to serve as evidence that there was more of a fusion and synthesis than of an opposition. Consider *Song of Ceylon, Coal Face,* and *Night Mail,* three of the early classic documentaries marked by poetic quality as well as by forceful realism and authenticity in their use of real people (nonactors) and real-life activity. The fact is that these films demonstrate both lucidity of exposition on the one hand, and lyrical elegance on the other. It is this synthesis that has ultimately given documentary its bite, its force and persuasiveness as a vehicle of information.

As a student in Vancouver in 1936, I saw *Night Mail* at a screening of the film society. It must have been very soon after its completion, for we knew nothing of the film or its origin. There on the large screen of the Stanley Theatre was displayed an entirely new world: some other Britain, a foreign land having little or no resemblance to the casements and battlements of those British feature films that occupied such a meager space on the screens of Canada in those years. In this new, strange film, there was a sense of the intimate presence of human beings, not actors, disturbingly near—one could see almost into their pores. They spoke a strange language, that of working-class England—a language not readily understood by the North American ear. Underlying the terse, straightforward progress of the film was a rhythm, a natural, hypnotic, powerful sound—the train clacking over the rails as it rushed northward toward Scotland. There was this excitement about the leather mail pouch snapped with a vicious *whack* into the outstretched net along the line; and the simple fellow, the young postal clerk, counting on his fingers the beat of the clicks on the rail until he should sling the pouch outward on its bracket and *whack* again, into the net. Then the poetry—*poetry* in a film!

NIGHT MAIL*

This is the night mail crossing the border,
Bringing the cheque and the postal order,

* Verse by W. H. Auden from the sound track of the GPO documentary film *Night Mail.*

Letters for the rich, letters for the poor,
The shop at the corner and the girl next door.
Pulling up Beattock, a steady climb—
The gradient's against her but she's on time.
Past cotton grass and moorland boulder,
Shovelling white steam over her shoulder,
Snorting noisily as she passes
Silent miles of wind-bent grasses;
Birds turn their heads as she approaches,
Stare from the bushes at her blank-faced coaches;
Sheep dogs cannot turn her course,
They slumber on with paws across.
In the farm she passes no one wakes,
But a jug in the bedroom gently shakes.
Dawn freshens, the climb is done.
Down towards Glasgow she descends
Towards the steam tugs, yelping down the glade of cranes
Towards the fields of apparatus, the furnaces
Set on the dark plain like gigantic chessmen.
All Scotland waits for her;
In the dark glens, beside the pale-green sea lochs,
Men long for news.

Thrilling, that rhythm, those orchestrated sounds, voices, percussion—a new experience of film. We were stunned. To a generation reared on silent cowboy movies every Saturday afternoon throughout the late 1920s, *Night Mail* seemed a message from another planet.

In Paris in 1969 at the Cinémathèque Nationale, Henri Langlois, the distinguished director of the French national film archive, presented a retrospective tribute to the films produced by the General Post Office in the 1930s—his *Hommage à GPO*. These films, seen thirty years later, were a revelation of British life and of the swift movement of events. The Britain they depicted not only evoked Victorian and early industrial Britain, but seemed almost as remote as the Plantagenets and Tudors. Here indeed was shown the British workingman—and what a revelation. His row houses, his cloth cap and stock, Lancashire clogs; the meanness and grime of the coal towns, the pottery towns; the congestion and squalor created by the first great surge of the Industrial Revolution—there it all was on the screen, never to be forgotten. This was a world that the screen, in 1936, had never explored before; it was indeed a powerful image. It was evidence of the condition of man in one particular society; to examine this evidence was almost automatically to take a position, to make a commitment of intellect and conscience.

Lord Ritchie Calder believes that the essential influence of these films of the 1930s was not primarily in terms of a wide public audience, but instead was in terms of a limited, specialized audience of government officers and policy-makers. He felt that the films had dramatized for those officers the true nature, condition, and danger of certain elements in British society. British policy-makers and bureaucrats in the 1930s were not wholly unaware, callous, or cruel, but there were significantly fewer channels of information or representation than there are now.

Grierson's work bore fruit during an eventful decade, 1929–1939. The documentary-film format and viewpoint became recognized.

In the summer of 1939 I came to London, met Grierson, and was instantly recruited for documentary training at Film Centre, supported by a princely stipend from the Imperial Relations Trust of £2/10/0d. per week. I saw many films and met several documentary directors of the early group. But World War II began in September, and government film activity was suspended. After some weeks I returned to Canada, hoping it might be possible to join the film activity that was rumored to be in the planning stages in Ottawa.

In Britain there was a hiatus of several months before the Ministry of Information was formed and all film activities were coordinated for the new emergency. In due course the Crown Film Unit of the British government evolved to produce a voluminous series of wartime films, all at a high level of quality and effectiveness. Grierson's idea that film could bring the real world alive in the consciousness of the ordinary citizen had come a very long way since 1929.

From an unidentified Canadian newspaper, July 1928, in the Archives of Canada:

BRITISH GOVERNMENT TO SHOW
EDUCATIONAL FILMS TO PUPILS

Great Forward Movement Being
Undertaken in Connection
With Teaching

LECTURES ARE FREE

Scheme May Lead to Inter-
change of Films With
the Dominions.

London, July 10. — A great forward movement is about to be made in the use of educational films, the most interesting, but the most neglected aspect of film production.

Conferences have taken place between the Imperial Institute, the

Empire Marketing Board, Imperial Education representatives, and the Royal Colonial Institute, on the one hand, and on the other hand between various Government departments, the London County Council, and British Instructional Films Limited, producers of the wonderful series of films called "Secrets of Nature."

The Imperial Institute will give regular performances of educational films at South Kensington.

These performances will be free to the public and to schoolchildren, and they will be arranged to fit in with the organized visits of parties of schoolchildren to the permanent Empire exhibition. Teachers will accompany each school party, with guide lecturers.

Life in Malaya

Special attention will be given to films showing the industries and activities of the various components of the Empire.

Dominion governments, most of whom have film departments, will cooperate in these performances. It is significant of their interest that the Federated Malay States, for example, should have authorized the production of a film showing the life, scenery, and occupations of the people in British Malaya.

Funds for these film exhibitions will be provided by the Empire Marketing Board. . . .

All these arrangements, interesting though they are, are the prelude to a larger scheme, now under consideration by government departments, which aims at the interchange of educational and imperial films between the different dominions and dependencies, with a view to spreading imperial knowledge and counteracting the influence of the foreign photoplay.

The Future for British Films*

The Imperial Conferences of 1926 and 1930 called easily for "more British films." The amateurs of the breakfast-table have been calling ever since. They either complain wildly of the cheapness and vulgarity of all things American, or they say again, and yet again, that English cinema has only to go to English literature and English scenery to conquer the world. Actually the path of cinematic conquest is a little more difficult. The Americans are entrenched with a production system and a far-flung distribution system which represent the concentrated building of more than a decade. They have already in that time caught the eye and ear of the world. Ordinary sense might warn us that there is a colossal job of work to be done in creation and commerce, if we are to make up the leeway.

I think we rather foolishly underestimate this task when we decry the quality of American films. They represent a command of invention, a mastery of technique and a courage of dramatic effect which our own films only rarely approach. The United States itself, by its very medley of strange races and swift happenings, is almost bound to prosper the more inventive aspect of story-telling. And there has been wealth enough behind the picture business to add almost every possible talent to the team-work of the studios. The larger imaginative qualities have been lacking, but their achievement is nonetheless solid and impressive. Our ostrich game of imagining that we only need "a break" for English films, and the substitution of English films for American by force of law, does not quite take account of this.

Cinema, to be of real influence, must command its audience, and command it on a world-wide scale. It is doubtful if English cinema at its present stage of development can meet the condition.

The real test of our cinema will lie in this question of how good it is. In spite of the American distribution machine, both German and Russian cinema have been able to make a name in the world; and no more than half-a-dozen great films were involved in either case. Their influence has been sufficient to demonstrate that there is a ready-made audience for any creative work which is vital enough.

That we have not yet begun to share even these limited cinematic hon-

* From an article by John Grierson in the *London Spectator*, May 14, 1932, quoted and distributed shortly thereafter in Canada by the Motion Picture Distributors Association, Toronto.

ours is, I think, largely due to the weird parochialism of our production system. We face it with a cinema which is so circumscribed in its material that it cannot even be called a cinema of England. It is London cinema, and West End London at that.

It is not satisfactory to face the world with British films which are, in fact, the provincial charades of one single square mile within the Empire. They neither project England nor project that very much larger world in the Dominions and Colonies. There is an unknown England beyond the West End, one of industry and commerce and the drama of English life within it, which is barely touched.

Alberto Cavalcanti

On a visit to America in 1971, Alberto Cavalcanti also came to the National Film Board of Canada in Montreal. He was our first interview subject, and this took place before Grierson's death. The Grierson film project had been sanctioned for production but work had not yet begun. In his seventies, Cavalcanti speaks with charm but not with fluency in English. As it happened, in the studio where we filmed him was a set for a documentary film then in preparation, on the subject of noise in modern life. This distinctly surrealist set consisted of a number of very large-scale terracotta colored models of the human ear hanging from invisible filaments in a spacious limbo. The largest of the ears was perhaps six feet in height. Suspended in a void, they turned slowly in currents of air. Since Cavalcanti's first contribution to British documentary film-making had been the teaching of sound recording and sound editing, the ears seemed appropriate to the occasion.

The filmed interview, alas, did not appear in the final film. Cavalcanti was one among several non-native English speakers whose slow-paced and tentative delivery finally presented the film editors with a severe problem of length. But his perspective on the British early period is of fundamental importance to the story.

Cavalcanti: I studied architecture at a fine-arts school in Geneva in Switzerland, and about 1926 I came to Paris to be a draftsman with a very big architect there. I used to earn ninety-five cents an hour for my drawing. I was the first draftsman, and I thought I made a bit too little. That's why I moved into cinema, just because I wanted to have a little more money.

I used to see films so often, I believed in films. But we felt that films were not doing what they should do. They were just reproducing plays, and they were not trying to get a proper cinematic expression, so we were dying to study and learn our profession, to try something else. We never were united in any way. Lots of people of our age had this same feeling, but we didn't like each other, we only *knew* each other. In fact, to get truthful, we hated each other. But we had a common interest, and as soon as we could know our métier we started working on our own. I met Grierson much, much later. Because, you see, this period I was talking to you about was the so-called silent period, which is an improper name, because films were never truly silent. In the times of silent film, there was a piano and a violin and later a small orchestra and then a bigger orchestra and organs, and it was very noisy in fact, the silent film. And then sound came, so when sound had arrived and because the producers thought that theatrical people

Alberto Cavalcanti, Brazilian-born avant-garde film-maker, came from Paris in the mid-1930s to work with the young British documentary group and teach them the resources of sound film.

were the thing, and that since the cinema now could talk, these theatrical people should come and make sounds. They didn't go outside at all, they brought us back into the studio.

I did a series in French, Portuguese, and Russian for Paramount, and lots of French comedies for the public, which were very successful. But I was sick and tired. I felt all the time that sound should mean much more than just the way it was used at that time.

I had just signed a contract with a French company to do a picture. But I said I was sick, and I had lots of doctors advise me to just go to London on a vacation, for recovering from that false sickness. And I met Grierson and explained to him how tired I was of doing these bad sound films, and how I believed in a better kind of films. Grierson asked, "Will you come and teach our people about sound?" So that's why I came to London. We agreed on a very small sum—I think it was seven pounds a week. We just meant to work for a few weeks, and then of course I stayed many years, because the group was a very interesting group of young people. Besides, I had experience of art movements, and I quite realized what this was. In fact, the characters were superior, relations between them were much more frank and better than among the French, so it was very happy at the time. That's why I stayed so long, and that's why it was a success.

Question: What was your impression of that group of young English individuals?

Cavalcanti: My impression was excellent. They mostly came from Cambridge, as you know. Grierson perhaps had a little kind of fear of Oxford boys—too talkative, perhaps—and most of the time the boys were Cambridge boys. Of course they were cultured and they all loved the cinema and they were quite prepared to do a lot of work. But I think the most brilliant of them all was Basil Wright, who was not actually in London at the time when I arrived. He was in Ceylon, doing a film that was afterwards finished and cut in London, but actually very early in my stay we had to put the sound on it, and Basil was very happy because he could bring the musicians from Ceylon to come and work on the sound track. And they also had Walter Leigh, a very good musician and a composer to help him in this task.

Question: Do you think that their ideas and ambitions were more cultural, filmic, or political? What kind of aspiration do you think they had as a group?

Cavalcanti: At the time I think they were filmic, actually. They wanted to get the technique, and they wanted to *handle* films, so much so that most of them remained with me after the sound was taught, and learning about sound was finished. And of course they were dedicated, and interested mostly in the social part that cinema could play.

Question: When you were developing, for example, the sound treatment for Night Mail *and* Coal Face, *the ideas used in the sound track—the music and the poetry—did these suggestions come from the group as a whole, or were they your suggestions? Or Grierson's suggestions?*

Cavalcanti: We worked with some ideas on *Song of Ceylon,* which was quite a slow job because it was a complicated job. But meanwhile we were doing other sound experiments. But really *Night Mail* and *Coal Face* didn't come one after the other. *Coal Face* was kind of an exercise for *Night Mail.* Actually, I like *Coal Face* better than *Night Mail* myself, but of course we had a great chance because, besides the boys in the studio, there were three types of people working in this. In those times we had the Grierson boys, and we had the other people from outside who we invited and who came perhaps from my experience in France in which, being the avant-garde, we were very much linked with people of the other arts, like painting, sculpture, literature. And of course we had Auden, Britten, and later many, many people who were interested in what we were doing. We also had some of the young working-class boys that Grierson pushed into being cameramen and technicians, and it became quite a practical school because they were bearing the responsibility of the projection, of the camera, and of the other important kinds of work which the Cambridge boys were not interested in. And of course, apart from those people like Auden coming from outside, we got in Humphrey Jennings. We got in lots of new people of a different generation, as well as the original Cambridge boys that Grierson brought.

Question: So as you recall it—the emphasis was more on practical, technical experiment rather than on any formal theories of film aesthetics?

Cavalcanti: Oh definitely, yes. But do you see, Grierson had a particular genius or—as the French say—élan. For example, any sort of very daring idea was impossible to propose to a committee of the GPO, because it had to be financed by the GPO—all the people who belonged to that committee. If Grierson hadn't been so skillful and so industrious about presenting those projects, they would never have been accepted. Not only did he find the titles for the films, but he also was able to sell the ideas to that committee. The big successes were very few—as soon as the films became too ambitious and too important, they were not so good. *North Sea* was a great commercial success. It was sold also to France, dubbed in French. *Night Mail* was shown in the cinemas in London as an ordinary short picture. But some of the very important pictures in the evolution of the documentary work, like *Coal Face,* I don't think had any commercial distribution at all. But Grierson was very keen about distribution—he had enormous schemes about parish halls and traveling mobile units to show the pictures. But I can't talk to you much about this aspect, because I was mostly interested in making the picture.

Question: How would you describe your actual role? Was it "producer"?

Cavalcanti: No. I was a kind of technician, and I was very lucky because I was well accepted. But I think my best period was with the second generation, Humphrey Jennings and others. The Cambridge boys were quite independent, and they had come out of my hands as full-fledged technicians. But in fact they didn't do many films. We had a very small budget, you know. I believe the sum was ten thousand pounds a year—which is an incredibly small production budget. And we didn't have *any* professional technicians—paid. Well, let's say we had apprentices.

Question: Looking at the GPO work, were the ideas about film technique and wider film possibilities related to other work going on in Europe, or not?

Cavalcanti: To tell the truth, I don't think so, because in those years the communication was not so good. Of course I knew several European directors quite well, but the only reference we had in this English pioneering work was Grierson's. My own work in the avant-garde, which, as you know, preceded Walter Ruttman and Joris Ivens, was practically unknown to people in England. I didn't bother to show it at all. I don't think it would have impressed them in any way.

Question: How would you say that whole experience affected you? What did it leave with you?

Cavalcanti: It's very difficult for me to discuss this point—as a kind of witness of the time—because Grierson always denies his interest in the aesthetic side, but I am not convinced that it was true, because he realized that it was important to establish a sound technique in films. Now he denies it, I believe, but at the time this was not true. He did accept—in fact, he was very keen on this.

Question: Do you think it's possible to make a general statement about the impact or the effect of that whole body of work on later film-making?

Cavalcanti: Definitely! You know I consider that the work done at the GPO and subsequently by Crown Film Unit was responsible for bringing the working classes into films in England, and perhaps into more than films—perhaps onto the stage and into literature, because before those films, ever since Shakespeare, the working class was only considered to be a kind of comic relief. They never had a part in serious discussions, or in films or on the stage or even in literature. So I think that is to me more important than even the experiment with sound and aesthetics. But of course when people say that the film-makers were only preoccupied with the technical side—it's completely untrue, because all of us were quite conscious of this particular duty of cinema.

Question: You recollect the social climate, the temperaments involved, Grierson's own relations with these younger people. What was the feeling among the group at that time?

Cavalcanti: It was perfect! We never had any committee meetings at all.

All our discussions were in the pub—after work! And Grierson didn't come very often to Blackheath Studios. He stayed in Soho Square, and I used to go over to show him the rough-cut pictures. But when he came to the studio he was welcome, and everybody was very pleased to discuss things with him, because I don't think he has ever lost this particular attraction he has for the younger people. All the boys had great respect and affection for him.

Basil Wright

Basil Wright is a senior member of the British documentary film community, as well as an author, lecturer, and classicist. He is well acquainted with the United States and has a special predilection for Greece. We made arrangements to meet him at his home near the village of Frieth in Buckinghamshire. Though it was not far from London, the intricacies of the location and the celebrated English winding roads required an earlier rendezvous at Beaconsfield, in a stylish and agreeable pub. Thence we proceeded to Wright's cottage, Little Adam Farm, tucked away among hedges and roses. His garden contained an opulent display of blooms and the light was fair, but there was a pesky wind to bother the microphone, so the bulk of our talking was done indoors. We filmed him at his ease in his library. Wright was very close to Grierson and maintained contact with him over the years. His discussion ranges widely over Grierson's career.

Wright: I was at Cambridge, you know. I took a degree in classics and economics. It had always been my intention to be the world's greatest poet, playwright, novelist. But while I was there I was suddenly exposed to the cinema. I decided that this was a new art. So I devoted myself to this idea, I got my family all combined together to buy me cinematographic apparatus for my twenty-first birthday, and I started to make experimental films. Grierson went to a festival of amateur films and saw one of mine; he then wrote offering me a job. It was as simple as that. He was then at the Empire Marketing Board; this was November 1929. It was just after the premiere of *Drifters*. And *Drifters* became to me the type of film I really wanted to make. I was hunting about for Grierson to get an introduction to him when he suddenly wrote to me, saying, "Will you come and have a chat with me?" And he gave me a job. Two pounds a week.
Question: What kind of film unit was it then?
Wright: There was a basement in Whitehall and a lot of old nitrate 35mm film shot on the Gold Coast. Grierson told me to make what would now be called a television commercial, which he then called a "poster film." He said, "You have four minutes in which to sell Gold Coast Cocoa. Use trick titles if you can afford it. I will give you seven pounds for the job." In fact the job cost me nine pounds; but Grierson gave me a permanent employment with the EMB unit.

Question: When you made such a poster film, where did it show, how was it used?

Wright: Various ways. A gorgeous technological lunatic called H. D. Waley, the brother of the great translator of all the Chinese poetry, had

Basil Wright, one of the documentary pioneers, at Little Adam Farm.

invented a continuous film projector. This was put up at Paddington Station and Birmingham Railway Station and Manchester Railway Station, and the prints were put on endless bands that went round and round. And having made these poster films, we then had to go every day to the various stations all over the country to check them—they would break down constantly. But the effect was like a small television set set up in the middle of the railway station. This was in January and February 1930.

Question: Were you looking at other films at the EMB with a view to mastering their techniques and so on?

Wright: Oh, yes. If you were working with Grierson, you were always being exposed to that. I mean, he was putting the titles on the English version of Turin's film *Turksib*, and I was there. I used to crank *Turksib* on a hand-cranked 35mm projector in a converted lavatory onto a big piece of blotting paper pinned to the wall. And he designed all the titles, you know. Because *Turksib* had these exploding titles, jumping titles. You would arrive early in the morning and discover that Ermler and Turin were sitting on the steps waiting for somebody to unlock the door into the cutting room. I used to get bawled out by Grierson for arriving late; of course he never turned up until noon anyway in those days because he used to work all night.

Question: Was there a working connection with Soviet film people in those days?

Wright: I don't know. Of course Grierson, with the Empire Marketing Board people, would always show Russian films. Grierson and the rest of us simply had left-wing connections; after all, we were not likely to be conservatives.

At the beginning of the EMB films—I am talking about 1930—we had no money and practically no camera operators. So most of the work was editing, compiling material and waiting to get a chance to shoot. We had little hand cameras called Debries. They used to make a rattling noise and scratch the negative. And we had no tripod. So if we had to shoot something, that was all we had to work with. We had no sound-recording apparatus in those days, nothing. We did have cutting rooms and the chance to experiment in editing. And of course we were very much influenced by the Soviet directors and the whole montage idea—particularly the Eisenstein approach to montage. Grierson of course knew it backwards because of the analysis he had made of *Potemkin* before he did *Drifters*. We were so empirical.

I think he was trying to collect people. You know, this was the time when he was collecting Arthur Elton and Edgar Anstey and that sort, getting them together in a sort of group. He was also getting enough money for us to go out and shoot. Eventually to shoot *silent*, that is—we never shot sound, we were shooting silent on different projects. Arthur was doing agriculture and fisheries in Scotland. I was doing a film about country produce, or else the lambing season in Scotland. Even though there was no apparent plan, I am sure there was one in Grierson's head. I see the plan emerging about the end of 1930, beginning of 1931, which was over eighteen months after he finished *Drifters* and decided to set up a film unit. In other words, this was a period of grabbing everything, trying to make a pattern of it, getting more support and more finance. By 1931 we were able actually to go into production in a more ordered way.

Robert Flaherty rang up from Berlin and said he'd got nothing to do.

Grierson got him over at once, you know, and he shot *Industrial Britain*. I was very much in awe of him. He had made *Nanook* and *Moana*, and he was a great man, and I was a poor little shrimp. And Grierson said to me, "Okay, you are going to direct your first film." It was actually called *The*

Drifters—Grierson's first film led the way towards a new kind of cinema that combined realism and humanism with factual information.

Country Comes to Town, telling how all the people worked in the country and sent their goods to the markets, how people in the towns got the goods, all that. And Grierson said, "I think we'll get Flaherty to come down and spend the first ten days on location with you in Devonshire." So I drove this magnificent chap down to Devonshire—he *was* a magnificent chap and it was a long wearisome journey because we stopped at the pub to have a drink and he discovered shove-ha'penny for the first time, so that took several hours before he had mastered the game. Then passing through Salisbury I had to show him the cathedral. He wasn't very interested in that, but on the way out of Salisbury we passed a cricket match, so we had

Strike—a revolutionary aesthetic in the new Soviet cinema of the 1920s (film by Eisenstein).

to stop again. I had a convertible then; he stood on the seat and watched cricket for a long time. I had to try and explain it to him, you know.

But the great thing was when we got down on location we stayed there for over a week, and he never told me what to do. He would look at what we were shooting and he would say things about the trees, the landscape, the way the animals were standing, and so on. And the cameras, to make the camera an extension of the eye. Then he went off and made *Industrial Britain*. I didn't have any more to do with it except to shoot some extra material at the end, when we had to turn it into a two-reeler. The idea was that he should examine the persistence of individual craftsmanship in the modern engineering type of industry that was developing. In other words, in the world of mass production the craftsman still counted. So that's what he was shooting. But all he shot, as far as *he* was concerned, was some screen tests. By the time he had done that, he had shot more footage than any of us had ever dared to think of, and all the money had run short.

Flaherty had nothing to do with the editing. That was done by Grierson and Edgar Anstey. We shot extra material to build up the film. Because by this time we were selling a series called *The Imperial Six*, made from all our earlier films. We revised them all as two-reelers, which the distributors wanted. Originally we'd made them all as one-reelers, but the distributors wanted two. So we had to enlarge all these films by about 50 percent. Then they were synchronized by the distributors with inappropriate music and commentary, but at least we got them into the theatres, which was very important to us at that time.

Question: What about the Imperial framework as you understood it then? In the Marketing Board was it intended that these pictures would go outside of Britain, or just that other countries would be reflected in the British films?

Wright: As I remember, at the beginning we were supposed to educate the British public about the marvels of the Empire, because we still had an Empire in those days. We were selling New Zealand butter and Ceylon tea and so on to the British public, in a rather imaginative way. And we were also selling the British to themselves: we were selling the British industrial worker and the British agricultural worker to the British nation as a whole, as people who could be treated with respect. You must remember that in those days they *weren't* treated with respect. They were regarded as the

Industrial Britain—in the new
British documentary of the 1930s,

working classes. This was 1930, 1931. Of course Grierson always ha
wider point of view, but he had to play his cards very carefully. It was a
world in which this use of cinema was very new, after all. I'm sure without
Stephen Tallents being sold on these ideas, we would have got nowhere.

*Question: When the Marketing Board ended and the film group went
over to GPO, was there much of a change in goals?*

Wright: There wasn't any change in the purpose of the documentary
group. We had to wear a different hat, but we were still going on with the
same *use* of the film—you know, for sociological purposes. All that happened to us was that instead of selling the Empire, we were now selling
the Post Office.

*Question: How about the group of young people who were there in the
unit? Was all the enthusiasm for film per se, or was it for causes and social
goals, or was it a mixture?*

Wright: It was for *film.* Grierson had to put the brakes on us. What he
was getting was people who wanted to use the film for purposes of aesthetic
experiment, avant-garde and whatnot. And he said, "Okay, I'll let you do
this within a discipline. The discipline is that you are spending public
money and you are working towards a sociological purpose." This was the

a preoccupation with the quality of
human life in a technological age.

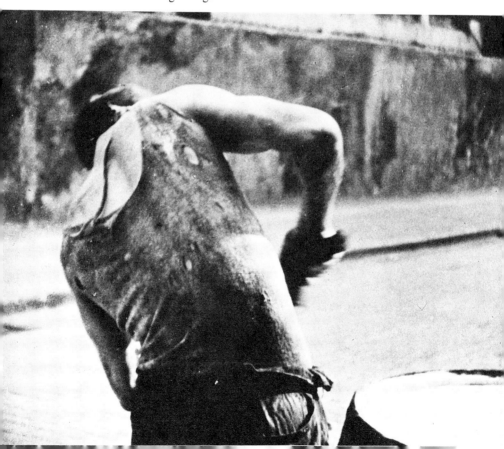

bargain he struck with everybody who went to work with him, and this was the conflict, if you like, he sometimes had with the long-haired young people like myself who were interested in the *motion picture*. In fact we eventually got very interested in the sociological aspect because we could see where the two things came together.

Question: Now, this training, how did it evolve? Were you following your own nose, were you learning on the job, who taught?

Wright: We were all living in a state of confusion, intolerable pressure, with no sleep all the time. It was that sort of setup, but it was marvelous and exciting. There was this dynamic man, everything was happening, every possibility was grabbed, all in the interest of the British civil service, who gave us the chance to learn. Grierson gave Alexeieff and some others enough money to buy food and lodging and an opportunity to make film. But we were the lucky ones. We were the privileged, we were actually being paid every week—bloody little, but we were being paid.

How were we being trained? If Grierson was your producer and you were making a film, you were simply having a tremendous conflict, weren't you. You were trying to make the film, he was pointing out to you how badly you were doing it, urging you on to fresh efforts and extracting from you abilities which you certainly didn't know that you had. When you've got somebody like Cavalcanti, who was a marvelous teacher . . . You've got to remember in 1934 we had many technical problems. It was a fantastic production schedule for people who had never had access to a sound studio before, had never shot in a sound studio. And Cavalcanti was always there. If you think of the fantastic effort and muddle that we lived in at the time, you can't talk about organized training or teaching. It was all from hand to mouth in that first year of sound at Blackheath Studios, 1934. I came back with all this material from Ceylon and we turned it into a sound film. You had *Coal Face, Pett and Pott,* all those fantasies of Cavalcanti's. And one was learning from Cavalcanti by working with him. By osmosis, he could get people to understand how to work the camera, even young kids, Post Office messengers, and so on. By being with Cav and working with him they somehow learned very quickly the *feel* of what they were doing. The technical thing that Cav gave was something that Grierson on the whole didn't give, except in terms of the cutting room.

Question: Let's come to your own work. For example, the Ceylon film, which is very widely known. How did it come about? How did you design it? Did you know precisely, what you were doing?

Wright: I was doing something else, and Grierson said to me one day, "Wright, you're going to Ceylon." I said, "I don't want to go to Ceylon." He said, "Never mind, you're going to Ceylon, so you better do your research." I spent the next two months finding out everything I possibly could about Ceylon. This was being sponsored by the Ceylon Tea Propaganda Board, and was therefore very much tied up with the EMB, for whom we were still working. So with John Taylor as my assistant I went off to Ceylon to get people interested in the idea of the island and therefore inclined to buy tea coming from Ceylon.

I somehow got into a compulsion to shoot more and more material which had nothing whatever to do with four one-reelers about Ceylon. But I simply had to shoot this material, not knowing why until I got back into the cutting room. I came back to England with all this material. I got into the cutting room and the material started to fall into shape, but the shape arose from these inner compulsions that I had in Ceylon. Of course Grierson saw it almost at once, but we pretended for another couple of months that we were still making four one-reelers. Eventually we forgot about all that and the film took its proper shape. As you notice, it is in four parts; you can therefore see how it began as an attempt to make four separate one-reelers, four different subjects, which is a different matter altogether.

You know, this is the one film I made that I still like. Grierson helped me with it in two ways. When I got back, I was absolutely aching to cut the film. He said, "You can't do that now, you've got to become a studio

Song of Ceylon—an aesthetic application of cinema to assist the marketing of tea within the Commonwealth and Empire.

manager for Cavalcanti," who was then starting on *Pett and Pott*. Which was my idea of hell. Yet it was a very good idea on his part, because it gave me an irritant break, you know, like the thing that makes pearls happen in oysters. It upset me, and that was what made me come back to the film in a fresh way. The other way he helped, once I started to cut *Song of Ceylon*, was to support those enormous experiments with sound, with the composer, Walter Leigh, which went on all the time. Walter Leigh practically lived in the cutting room. And every single sound in *Song of Ceylon* was scripted by Walter Leigh. If a dog barked, it was in the orchestral score. While this was happening, Grierson put up a sort of armed guard around me. He knew that this was something which was terribly important to me, and was also important to him and the unit, because they might have a good film coming out of it. I was totally protected until the film was finished—except, of course, from him.

Question: He often anticipated technical things which came much later on—like people speaking to the camera, an approach to "direct cinema" or cinema verité.

Wright: At that time many film people didn't agree with that. Some of the old guard here still don't. Because we were going along very nicely

Housing Problems—people talking to the camera about their problems in 1935, long

making our romantic poesy with *Song of Ceylon* or our dramatic poetics with Auden and Britten in *Coal Face* and *Night Mail*. Then Grierson suddenly said, "*Stop*, this is about as far as we can go along this line. There are four and a half million unemployed in Britain, there are a number of problems on the horizon. There could be a coming world war. Let us stop looking at the beautiful sunsets; let us try and find some beautiful sunrises. And if not, let us just issue a series of warnings. And in order to do this, we must shed our halos and our pretensions, and get down to brass tacks."

This was absolutely fantastic. If you can imagine *Housing Problems*. These were our cinema verité interviews, with people in tiny little slum rooms full of rats, with water running down the wall. But to shoot the film in those days you had to have a sound truck about the size of this house with a crew of twelve, and cumbersome heavy cameras which were always breaking down, that sort of thing. And here you suddenly gave the public a kind of in-depth interview with ordinary people. You had *Housing Problems*, you had a nutrition film called *Enough to Eat*, and so on. Then I did a film called *Children at School*, about the appalling conditions in British education. I was running wild. I had a sound camera, 35mm, which cost a fortune in those days. I used to switch it on and run a thousand feet in the

before magnetic tape or video. "Just shove the camera at them," Grierson said.

classroom with the teachers. Or a thousand feet on the teachers arguing about what to do because the school was falling down. This was unheard of. But it was also, in many people's point of view, brutal. I mean, the old frills and furbelows of film-making had been abandoned for this direct thing. But if you look at it in the perspective of film history, what a tremendous thing to do *at that time*, when we had already established ourselves in poetic films like *Night Mail* and *Song of Ceylon*.

Question: What was the response to the new type of film?

Wright: Oh, sensational. The press picked it up. The films were enormously successful, from an impact point of view. They got a limited theatrical circulation. The sponsors were delighted, because in editorial leaders the *Times* was asking: Why doesn't government make films about these serious national problems? Does it have to be left to industry? and so on. And all these sponsor people were terribly pleased, because they were getting political advantage out of the whole thing. Of course by that time the nontheatrical system of film distribution was functioning well, so these films had a rapidly increasing nontheatrical circulation throughout the country, to clubs and schools and universities.

Question: What kind of job do you think documentary is doing now? Where do you think it's going from this stage?

Wright: You are begging the question because documentary has become in a sense a meaningless sort of word attached to anything that isn't fiction. As soon as television became widespread, documentary passed automatically into television. I am sure if there had been television in 1928, Grierson would have been into television. He wouldn't have touched cinema except as a useful adjunct, recording material for television. So in a way I see documentary as being fully established in the television medium.

But I also see what Grierson saw so clearly in the last years of his life: the whole development of cable TV, videotape, all this sort of thing where the means of production are going to pass into the hands of almost anybody who likes to use them, because they are now easier to use than a typewriter. In countries like India, as Grierson points out, the "peripatetic teachers" can come around with this kind of apparatus and be able to use it with people in remote villages where they have hardly had a film show before. The teachers and villagers could actually make films and videotapes, see what they were making, and so develop their own ideas. This is the next great extension of the whole documentary idea. Look at your programs in Canada, your VTR in Montreal and Newfoundland, all these programs in *Challenge for Change*, local people making their own shows and films.

(The composer Muir Matheson, a neighbor, enters unannounced)

Matheson: Hi there.

Wright: Well met. This is Jim Beveridge and the National Film Board crew from Canada. I'm being interviewed about Grierson. You know that Muir Matheson was a producer at Film Centre in London? He gave up music direction during the war and became a producer of documentary films at Film Centre. And in fact out of that came *Instruments of the Orchestra*, the Benjamin Britten film. After that he went and directed, you see. So it's all part of the pattern.

Matheson: Well, you get back to the store.

Wright: Bless you, see you later. Come back and have a drink.

Forsyth Hardy

Forsyth Hardy is known to many hundreds of film people for his long service to the Edinburgh Film Festival, of which he and Norman Wilson were founders and pioneer members from the late 1940s. He has devoted a lifetime to the pursuit and careful consideration of films and is well-known as the Augustan film critic of the *Edinburgh Scotsman*. Hardy, as he recounts, has known Grierson from the earliest days after the latter's return from Chicago in the 1920s. Their friendship was a lasting one. Hardy's well-known book *Grierson on Documentary* has long been a staple of the essential library on films.

We filmed him in an office of the *Scotsman*. A fanciful intention we tried very hard to carry out convincingly was the effort to track or dolly with the camera along a corridor past rows of somber marble busts glaring down upon the passer-by. These busts were representations of former proprietors of the *Scotsman*. We thought that this progression down the corridor would illustrate that of Grierson himself when he first came to call upon Hardy at the *Scotsman* long ago. However, the intention finally proved to be an artificial rather than an inspirational one, and only the final segment of the scene was used—where Hardy reacts with some surprise and alarm to the bursting open of his office door, which discloses him seated behind his desk, confronting the camera.

Hardy: I first met John Grierson in 1930 not very long after I had been appointed film critic of the *Scotsman*. I had done a review of *Drifters,* which was then going into the cinemas. This review must have come to Grierson's attention because on his very next visit to Edinburgh he made his way fairly quickly to the *Scotsman*'s office down the paneled hallway where the forbidding portraits of former proprietors must have presented rather a strange contrast to the newspaper world of Chicago, which he had known while studying there. And he made his way towards the reporters' room. Suddenly the door burst open and in strode Grierson, a figure of fire and energy, rather frightening. At that time he wore a very long black waterproof and a broad-brimmed black hat. And when he spoke, his voice had all the cutting edge of Chicago. At that time the *Scotsman* reporters' room was a place of cathedral calm, and anyone who raised his voice there was apt to cause a bit of commotion. Grierson spoke to me for a few minutes, I realized that everyone was listening carefully, and eventually I said to him very quietly, "Don't you think we could go out and have a coffee somewhere?" He couldn't see the reason why, but he agreed, so we

Forsyth Hardy, film critic of the *Edinburgh Scotsman*, was an early champion of the documentary movement and its growing importance in the world of cinema.

went out and continued talking, and that is how my friendship with John Grierson began.

I am sure Grierson didn't seek me out because of myself. But because he was always interested in newspapers, he knew the value of the newspapers in making widely known the ideas that he was introducing in the documentary movement. So he looked for newspapers all over the country that would respond to the kind of thing he was talking about. I was one of perhaps six or seven film critics then, and he kept constantly in touch with us throughout the country, so when a new film came along he would let us know about it and we would eventually write about it. And the documentary idea therefore grew not only because of the films themselves, but because the ideas implied in the film were introduced by the press to a wide public throughout the country. Grierson did this both in Britain and then later in other countries, in Canada, in the United States, Australia, and New Zealand. He always seemed to get to know the sympathetic writers. Later on in Europe as well, in France, Poland, Germany, he found people who knew what he was after. So when the new ideas came along, he let the writers know about them, and they in turn wrote about the films, and this in fact became a documentary *movement*, something more than just looking at films.

I never knew him fail to respond to an appeal from Scotland to come and do something here, whether it was opening a school or making a speech on some important occasion. I think that he rendered an important, continuing service to his native country that reflected his own enthusiasm for Scotland, his belief in the value of the quality of life in small countries. He wasn't a narrow nationalist in any sense at all; in fact, he was an internationalist. But he still was always aware of the fact that the roots people have are by their doorstep, and that is where they get their basic inspiration. And the older he grew, the more often he would come to Scotland, to Stirling and even to the very place, Deanston, where he was born.

Norman McLaren

McLaren is very widely known by film people around the world. He has a bountiful talent of a most individual and whimsical kind, combined with a rigorous intelligence firmly in command of the mathematics and the precise calculation and calibration of the effects he devises. His animations "work" by a curious psychological shorthand in which symbols (whether judged in Freudian terms or not), precise timing, the use of sounds and noises (musical, natural, or synthetic), and the utterly free use of line combine to produce an impression of energy, of manic humor, and sometimes of solemn mathematical beauty. There is no doubt that his many innovations in technique (pixillation, drawing directly onto film, hand-drawn synthetic sound, stroboscopic filming) have been widely utilized by other animators.

McLaren is perhaps better known than almost any of the film-makers deriving from the British or Canadian documentary schools because his small experimental films have been circulated widely for nearly forty years among film clubs and film societies all over the world. He is basically a shy and private person who lives and comports himself modestly. He gives one an impression of gentleness, of fragile vulnerability, yet underneath the gentle exterior is an analytical mind of high technical resourcefulness, and a strongly moral feeling concerning social and political matters.

Though McLaren is usually associated with the National Film Board of Canada, what is not so well known is that he developed for the board its initial program and assembled its original staff in animation work, which he established in Canada as a new field. He recruited young art students wholly lacking in previous film experience and molded them into a unit capable of producing speedy and effective animation for many functional purposes, as well as for flights of fancy and imagination. Discipline, dedication, concentration are fundamental to his work. McLaren has often been interviewed and filmed, notably by the BBC in a highly informative one-hour film entitled *The Eye Hears, the Ear Sees*. For some reason difficult to explain, we neglected to film him for the Grierson project. Perhaps we were all too close to each other as colleagues, too familiar, to do it at the right moment. In any case, McLaren, as well as several other Film Board associates, were interviewed on tape shortly after Grierson's death.

McLaren: At the age of twenty I was studying at the Glasgow School of Art; I was in a five-year course, and in my third year I got interested in film

Norman McLaren, film animator and experimenter, with his collaborator Eve Lambart at the National Film Board (1945). McLaren
recruited and trained a staff of animation artists who now comprise
one of the most distinguished creative units to be found anywhere.

to such an extent that I neglected my studies in drawing and painting and
the crafts. I made a number of films in my spare time with one of the
teachers and another student. I had the ideas for these films and I directed
them. Fortunately the year before there had started up a Scottish Amateur
Film Festival, an annual event. Grierson was the adjudicator on my second
year of film-making, about 1933, and I submitted a couple of films. One I
was very proud of—a very elaborate film full of technical tricks. We had a
very fancy camera, and I had used every single possible technical device on
the camera, with multiple superimpositions, animation of various kinds,
direct drawing, and regular photography. It was a kind of documentary of
a Christmas party. I also had another very short film, an abstract film put
to music, which I didn't think much of.

When Grierson came to the final evening of the festival and gave his
assessment of the films, he started with my fancy film and gave it hell. He
said, "Technically it's very competent, but artistically it's nothing but a
jumble and a mess. It's got no sense of form or organization, it's got no
development, and it's totally zero as far as being a work of art." I was

counting on this occasion, so I thought well, there it goes, I had hoped to work in films for the rest of my life and that's it, I've had it. Then he came to my little film and gave it first prize—the little abstract film. He said, "*That* is a work of art." Later on that evening he said, "Come round to my hotel and have a drink." I did. I was very impressed with the man, and I was rather awed and frightened by him too. I'd never seen such a lively person, full of vehement opinions—and then sitting over a drink, he said, "You know you have a very dirty mind, Norman. Yes, that film of yours about the art school ball was full of Freudian and sexual symbolism." I said, "I didn't know that. What scenes?" "Well," he said, "you've got the dancers moving among superimposed impressions of balloons and screw nails," and he mentioned other scenes. And I'd done it in all innocence—maybe subconsciously I had a dirty mind.

Anyway the best thing—and it was much better than the prize I had received—was that he said, "When you're finished your training at the Art School, come down to the GPO in London. You have a job waiting for you, and you can get your training as a professional film-maker." So I accepted right away.

I saw very little of Grierson during the years I spent at the GPO. My first job was cutting-room assistant, an editing assistant to Evelyn Cherry—she was Evelyn Spice at that time. I worked for about four months on a film of hers. Then Cavalcanti was made my producer, and he said, "We want to make a film about the London telephone directory. We'd like you to do it. Take a few weeks for research, a month if you like, and come up with a draft script," which I did. I spent most of my time in the British Museum studying the history of the London directory. Anyway, I produced a draft script about the history, with a lot of little penciled drawings of this scene and the next scene and the next scene. It was very elaborate and very detailed with sketches, which is a thing I'd never done in my own film-making. I'd seldom made sketches as an amateur, I'd just gone ahead and shot. So Cavalcanti took a look at it, immediately tore it up, flung it in the wastepaper basket, and said, "That's not the way to make a film, you shouldn't make sketches ever, because if you have a preconceived idea of what the shot is going to look like you freeze your imagination when you come to shoot. Actual living material in front of you will be much richer than your imagination, and you can make your decision when you are in front of the material with a camera or a viewfinder." Then he said, "Go down into the factory that makes the London telephone directory, and see what you can do there." Well, I went down and spent two days there, came back, and said, "I can make a film of that without a script, just a few notes." So I did this.

Then I was given other films to make, a couple of which pleased me because they gave me some leeway with technical tricks and things that I was fascinated with. Finally I said, "I want to make a film by drawing directly onto the film." I had done a small sample that I showed to Cavalcanti. I think he showed it to Grierson; then they said, "Okay, go ahead, make it, and you're absolutely free to choose anything you want in the sound track," and so I had my first real freedom there.

That was my last film with the GPO. I left Britain in 1939 and emigrated to America, and later to Canada and the National Film Board with Grierson again.

Harry Watt

A robust and picaresque personality among the British film directors of the GPO group was Harry Watt. He was also one of those who at the end of the war period moved from documentary work into the making of feature films. Other interesting aspects of Watt's career are his close relationship with Alberto Cavalcanti and his adherence to the particular viewpoint that Cavalcanti brought to the making of documentary.

We filmed with Harry Watt at a riverside pub in Greenwich, a little downstream from the Observatory and the naval museum. We sat outdoors on a low wall at the edge of the Thames, the chuffing and rattling of the coal docks and passing rivercraft in the background. Strollers and pub regulars were coming and going on the small cobbled street. Watt talked with great vivacity and naturalness, waving his arms about but taking care not to spill his pint of bitter. A light drizzle began, but it didn't interfere with our purposes. Saturday at noon, a peaceful mood, essentially a London atmosphere—all of this felt appropriate to documentary themes.

Watt: I am very proud of the fact that I am one of the few people who came into the film business because I wanted to eat. There was no artist stuff about it. I'd bummed around London during the depression having come back from Canada. In a café in Soho I heard that a Scotsman was forming a film unit. The Scots are rather like the Jews—they have relations in the right place everywhere—so I wrote to Scotland, found that a second cousin of mine had married a third cousin of Grierson's or something like that, and got an introduction. I went along and there was this vital little man sitting in his office. I always remember his eyes, his eyes were the best part of him, you know, tremendously strong eyes. He said, "Tell me what you've been doing." So I told him the rather dreary sequence of lousy jobs I had been doing, and I didn't get to first base—he just wasn't interested, you know. Then I suddenly said, "Well, eighteen months ago I sailed to Newfoundland on a schooner." He suddenly perked up and said, "Oh, tell me about that," so I told him the whole story: how five of us sailed a schooner from Scotland over to St. John's and then went to Canada after that. He said, "You'd better start work Monday." I would never have got the job if I hadn't sailed the schooner, because like me he was mad about the sea. I reported on the Monday to a well-known character called J. D.

Davidson. I stuck my head in and said, "I have to start here," and he said, "Oh, Christ, not another." That was the beginning of my career.

Question: How about Alberto Cavalcanti's contribution to the whole program, his relationship to Grierson—can you say a bit about that?

Harry Watt—a robust humanist of documentary.

Watt: I think the contribution of Cavalcanti was never really appreciated. You see, Cavalcanti was a professional and we were all a lot of bloody amateurs then, trying to learn our job. So was Grierson. Grierson was a wonderful front man, Grierson was a public-relations officer; he was kidding the sponsors, mostly the government, that we were artists. But he could *sell* our rather tatty little amateur films. Then in comes this professional, a sensitive and highly skilled man, and I don't think he ever got the true credit due to him. I would say here and now that anything I know of the film business I learned from Cavalcanti—particularly when sound came in. We didn't know what a piece of sound was, we didn't even know that picture and sound were shot separately. Cavalcanti taught us how to cut sync film, how to keep it in sync; we didn't know that when you took a piece of picture out you had to take out the equivalent piece from your sound track, that kind of stuff. And behind the scenes all the time Cavalcanti was a mentor, quiet and self-effacing. I give him an enormous amount of credit; I think documentary became *professional* because of Cavalcanti.

Question: You said something to the effect that Grierson's relationship to others in the film group was rather austere, a bit puritanical.

Watt: Oh, very puritanical. Of course when we joined first, we sucked his feet, he was a god and he played up to it. He was called "the chief," which I thought was a mistake and I never would do. He rather playacted —kicked doors open and snapped at you and all the rest of it—and we were frightened of him. He paid us bugger-all, as you know—about two pounds ten a week—but we were learning our job. He was frightened of women. Although one or two of us were living with women, he refused us the right to marry, and in point of fact when he got married himself he didn't let us know he was married for about a year, although we knew it. I finally got married, and my wife came on location with me on a picture. She was very useful because we had a very small unit, but he demanded that she leave the unit and we took it. That is the strange thing: we *took* it, we adored him, and we knew that he had the basic idea. He had the idea, started it, and had given us this chance to work on the idea of making a new kind of film. With all the documentaries on television nowadays, this is very hard to understand: that we were putting the British workingman, the backbone of the country, onto the screen. Before that, the workingman was the comic relief in the ghastly British films of those days—ghastly films, they always started with the butler and the maid and then the funny gardener or the funny taxi driver. We knocked all that down, and for that we were looked upon by the establishment as subversive, we were looked upon as dirty little left-wingers. Well, we *were* left-wingers but no more dirty than the modern left-wingers.

Question: Do you think the idea worked successfully at that time? Were there failures?

Watt: Well, of course the main disappointment was the fact that even when we started making good films, like *Night Mail*, we couldn't get them much into the cinema. We were absolutely looked upon as a lot of silly little highbrows by the trade. *Night Mail* is a classic film in its way, but it got only three days' showing in a newsreel cinema, and this frustrated us very much and Grierson particularly. Then Grierson about 1936 had the idea that there are twenty or thirty million people who don't go to the cinema. There are no cinemas for them, so we will bring the films *to* them, the nontheatrical films. This is where the split took place; Grierson left the GPO film unit and took Wright, Elton, John Taylor, and people like that with him. Cavalcanti and I said *no!* We started out to try and influence cinema. Free films at exhibitions, where people go just to rest their feet, will never influence anything; we must try and get into the commercial cinema. So we stayed on, and we made *North Sea*, which did prove our point, because it was sold commercially and it made money. Quite frankly I think Grierson made an enormous mistake in going away from the GPO. Of course he couldn't know that war was going to break out, but the GPO was soon organized as the famous Crown Film Unit and we really took on mature stature because of the war. We were trained, we were ready for it, we were the only such unit in the world practically, apart from the German units that were already making propaganda films.

Question: You went into features and had a considerable career in feature work. Looking back on it, do you have any regrets or second thoughts about this course? What about the relationship between documentaries and features?

Watt: Quite frankly, looking back on it now, I regret that I moved over to features. People don't believe that, because in features you get all the publicity, name in lights and all that crap. But it was inevitable for me, because as I said before, we were looked down upon by the feature people as little amateurs. Then we proved ourselves in the war and astonished the feature people and of course enormously influenced the feature film itself, realist features like *The Cruel Sea* and *For Those in Peril* and other things that came out as a result of the documentary films we had made. Having been poor relations for so long—not necessarily in money terms but creatively—some of us wanted to go into the feature business and show that we could do it, and we did. But it was a mistake. There was an enormous turning point in documentary during the war. That was when the great films were made by the service film units, films like *Desert Victory* and *Burma Victory*; those were shot by tremendously brave fellows in the field. Our reconstructed films became rather out-of-date, you see, as far as documentary was concerned, showing the British under the bombing and so on, because now you actually *saw* the man in the field being killed, and fellows being killed while shooting it. I thought the old type of documentary had become a little out-of-date, so I went to Ealing and made a film called *Nine Men*, which was made as a kind of morale piece for the Army Film Unit. Then I went to Australia to make a film of the Australian war effort in the sky. You had to find a new angle.

Question: In the early days, how did you approach nonactors, people who didn't suspect that they were being used in a film? How did you go about it?

Watt: The interesting point is that I had an enormous advantage being a Scotsman. It's the accent, you see; I wasn't the boss class. Don't forget we are in the 1930s, I didn't have the *pukka* English accent. I could talk with anybody, and he or she would realize I was a Scotsman. I had worked in the depression, too, so I could more or less talk with them familiarly and they wouldn't think I was some snotty-nosed, totty-nosed bloke. This is tremendously important.

As far as film casting is concerned, you always have to find the extrovert. You have to find the dreadful man who is the life and soul of the party; very often he is a good actor. I cast the whole of *North Sea* at the labor exchange in Aberdeen, sitting there as a boss behind the desk. It was during the depression, so there were lots coming in. Somebody would come up and ask, "Any job?" and if the answer was no and he just turned and went away, he was no good. But if the fellow said, "I am the best deckhand in the business, and last time I went out *we* caught more fish. I am a *lucky fellow*." If he talked like that, he was an actor. The pity of it was—though not so much nowadays because of television—that the higher up the social scale you went, the worse actors they became. The simple man is a won-

Harry Watt in a congenial dockland setting.

derful actor, shepherds or fishermen are wonderful actors; a bank clerk is a bloody awful actor because he is afraid he is making a fool of himself. Not so much nowadays, because *everybody* appears on television. You stick out a microphone, people now are all extroverts; it is very different now. But we found in the 1930s that the very simple man was best, like in *Night Mail*, the little man who puts the mailbags out. Generally, of course, you try to get people to do what they normally do, their own job. If you try to take a fisherman and make him into a bank clerk or something like that, that is no good at all. We came an awful gutser at the beginning of the war, with a film called *Men of the Lightship*. We had a director called David MacDonald, who decided to use actors; within three days Cavalcanti had fired the bloody lot. We used the real lightship men, it was a very successful film, and that surprised this professional director from feature films tremendously.

Question: How easy was it in 1933–1934 for people who were quite unaccustomed to be visited by film crews when you "shoved the camera at them," as in Housing Problems?

Watt: Basically it all depended on the director, on his approach. *Housing Problems* was a lovely little film, and I think the credit should go to Ruby Grierson, Grierson's sister who was drowned going across to Canada during the war. She and John Taylor were both simple people. Ruby was a lovely simple girl and John Taylor is a very approachable, warm fellow; they both had the right accents in the sense that they didn't have this "ho-ho" English accent. So the two old trouts in the film, working-class people, just warmed to them, and Ruby and John said, "Go on and tell us about it," and the old trouts just went straight ahead and talked as though they were telling it in the pub. This is so important; if you create any barrier at all between you and the people you're filming, you've had it.

Question: How did it go with the armed services when you and the film units were doing films with them during the war?

Watt: They always wanted to regiment you. When we started in the war the regular army officer was still in command, and we would go down as pretty scruffy civilians—we used to wear flannel bags or dirty old coats with leather. These chinless bloody wonders would say, "Oh, I say, you are the film chaps. Oh, yes, you wear your hats the wrong way around and you do this and that, ha-ha-ha. Well, go round to the sergeant's mess and see if you can get yourselves a beer," and you want to kick them right in the . . . But by the *end* of the war they were saying, "Would you like us to put on a raid for you? Perhaps we could send a squadron up with a camera plane?" They were falling over themselves for publicity.

Question: The film unit people were not made part of the service?

Watt: No. Of course we used to go into the officer's mess with a shirt open or something like that, and they kept saying, "I wish to Christ we could discipline these blokes." So they suggested that we become officers and gentlemen. The funny thing was they wanted to make Cavalcanti, who

John Taylor—apprentice to Flaherty in the early 1930s, a leading film-maker in British documentary from GPO days through Crown Film Unit and thereafter.

was then the head of the unit, into a colonel. That was the biggest bloody joke! He rather liked the idea; he thought about Sam-Browne-belting the bloody lot. But we kept putting our head around the door of his office and saying, "*Monsieur le Colonel*, may we come in?" and pulling his bloody leg. Of course we British knew much better and didn't join the service. Otherwise we'd never have made the films that we made, because then I would have had to go report to the C.O. and I could never have gone and talked to the average workingman, who is usually an AC2 in uniform, while as a civilian I could go and sit with them and talk ordinarily.

Question: What do you consider to be Grierson's major achievements in film?

Watt: His achievements are tremendous. The most important thing was his having the *idea* and forming the unit because he could've battled on himself, you know, after *Drifters*. Quite frankly, I would say—and this is not derogatory—that Grierson was not a film-maker in himself. I don't think he was a film-maker. He was a great front man, a great public-relations man, a wonderful man full of ideas; he could sell films; but actually in terms of practical film-making, I think it was much better for him to get together his extraordinary raggedy-ass crowd and let them learn. They got very little *teaching* until Cavalcanti came along, but Grierson had the theory, the belief, and transmitted to us this faith and this belief that what we were doing was worthwhile.

Irving Jacoby

In the United States, before the expansion of documentary in television, the documentary film has grown in a difficult terrain. Commercial and advertising factors have worked against the flowering of independent, outspoken, critical, or analytical film-making. While certain areas of industry and public relations had provided many sponsors, sponsorship had been rare in public-service and common-cause areas.

Irving Jacoby is a New Yorker, one of the senior members of the American group of documentary film-makers. He knew Grierson and the GPO film group at an early stage, and later came to Canada to assist in the very early phase of production at the National Film Board in Ottawa.

Jacoby is thus an interesting point of contact between the work going on in the United States during the 1930s, and the somewhat parallel work that was being done in Britain in the same period.

He has had firsthand contact with the British, Canadian, and American worlds of film-making during a formative period in the development of each. He remains a talented and dedicated film-maker, subscribing to the classical tenets of documentary method and purpose.

We filmed Mr. Jacoby outside his town house in New York City. Seeking to avoid restricted interior settings as much as possible, we hoped to define an exterior atmosphere typical of the New York scene. Despite this praiseworthy intention, the high surrounding buildings, the restricted light in the interior courtyards, the noise of airplanes and police sirens and the pigeons all cut down on our possibilities. Finally, four crewmen huddled on a narrow fire escape in an unseemly knot at the very feet of Mr. Jacoby, shooting upward from an extreme low angle almost into his nostrils, and so accomplished the main purposes of the interview.

Jacoby: Grierson with his big ears heard that there was an American in London with a pile of records under his arm. (This was the beginning of 1936.) The records included the first recordings ever made by a man named Basie and the first recordings of Benny Goodman's *Return to Jazz*, coming back to jazz in the middle thirties. So I was invited to come with those records to one of Grierson's Friday nights. And if there was any way to intrigue a person interested in the arts, it was Grierson's Friday nights; they were the cultural institution of their time. I came and played my records and I stayed to learn about films from Holland, from Germany, from France, and of course about everything exciting that was going on in England. It turned out that Friday evenings weren't just for films, they were for anything that was stimulating and of interest to film people, no matter what form it was in. And jazz was one of the things Grierson was always interested in. He got interested in America when he was first there. So I came and played and was invited to stay. The great Auden had just left the film unit, and I was first invited to fill the slot that he had as a writer.

Question: Was this the GPO unit?

Jacoby: GPO. I was the only American that ever worked for that British government film office.

Question: What was your impression of the young GPO film group?

Jacoby: Well, let me try to put it in terms of numbers. I had been earning two hundred and fifty dollars a week in New York. Grierson offered me eight pounds a week, which came to something less than forty dollars. It was the salary that all the top creative people were getting then. I can't tell you how delighted I was with the forty dollars in London at that time, as compared to two hundred and fifty dollars in New York. I had been in films then for almost ten years. For the first time in my life I was working with people who were just fun to be with all day. Instead of never having anyone to talk to about my ideas in pictures, there were people who had come up with those ideas before, had gone further, and were willing to let me come along with them. I didn't get a job, I joined a club, a most wonderful exciting club. And as you know, over the years I have remained friends with a lot of the members.

Question: What manner of people were they socially, what kind of group was it?

Jacoby: A funny mixture. The basic group were young men down from the university—I think Grierson was a little snobbish about that. They were mostly upper-middle-class people. None of them were conventional middle class. They were all in rebellion, all looking for some way to change things, to strike back and make something happen in their time. Not full-time revolutionary, but artists in the best sense of the word. The group was sprinkled through with odd characters who came from the arts; William Coldstream, who later became an important member of the Royal Academy, was directing films there. For a while he didn't want to paint because it was too lonely. So he found a more congenial group to work with.

Question: How would you describe the way that Grierson worked with these people? Was he fatherly, bossy, paternalistic?

Jacoby: Years ago in talking about politics on an American newspaper, I said that you didn't have to tell a reporter who got a job on the *Herald*

Tribune that he had to be a Republican. He knew that. And when you went to work for Grierson, Grierson really didn't have to give you the party line day and night. You heard him talk, you knew what it was all about, you osmosed the spirit of the place. These Friday nights that I mentioned had a lot to do with that. Because it was there that he spoke his philosophy in most formal terms. Because the crowd for that was always big. Everybody came to that. Directors, writers, cameramen, secretaries—everybody was welcome. And those nights went on long after the meetings. When the meetings broke up we went to the pubs as long as they were open, and then on to somebody's house to finish the evening.

Question: When you came to the Film Board in Canada in 1940, the Canadian group was just in formation then?

Jacoby: When I came to Ottawa to the Film Board, there was no group. I was the third person hired for the Film Board, on a contract. Grierson was here in New York one weekend, and asked me if I wanted to make a film in Canada.

Question: Did you see a similarity between the Canadian film group taking shape and the one that you had experienced in London?

Jacoby: It took longer in Canada. Younger, less experienced people

Irving Jacoby, a veteran of early documentary in both the U.S.A. and Britain, with crew in New York.

were brought into the Film Board. As you know, Grierson also brought in a few pros, and they had to carry the brunt of the production at first, films had to get out on schedule. From his earliest days there, from when he started, there was already a schedule. It took a while before the same kind of feeling as there had been in England grew up in the Canadian Film Board. It did eventually happen. People shot so many films outside of Ottawa that we never had the opportunity to get together as a group, as we did in the English pubs in London. But you could always find places to go when you wanted to talk film. That was something that never existed in any form in New York that I know of. New York film-makers have always been individuals on their own. They may get together to make a union or association, but that is a different kind of thing altogether. They are talking about what they can get out of film, not what they could put into film. These other sessions in England and Canada were quite different.

Question: What's your opinion about the difference, or the similarity, between documentary work in New York in the thirties and the film activity in Britain when you first went over there?

Jacoby: There was hardly anything going on here in New York. Pare Lorenz was getting ready to get ready; Bob Flaherty was making his kind of films, not in New York exactly, but in and out of New York. Going to London at that time for someone like me was like going to heaven. It was all *happening.* They were interested people. They were going to make the kind of pictures that we had been dreaming about.

Question: How did you feel about Grierson's adaptation to American life? Was he excited by America?

Jacoby: It seemed a little immature, I must say. I was born on Manhattan Island and I've lived here all my life. Grierson came as though it were a great big wonderful hunting ground. Sooner or later I was afraid of what he was going to find. It wasn't really as exciting as he felt it was. It wasn't as easy as he felt it was going to be. He looked at the film industry and felt that he could move right in. But it was a hard, mean world. When I knew him in New York in the thirties, he was still looking in New York for what he had found in Chicago in the twenties. And it really wasn't here in those terms. This is a power town, a tougher town. The energy is more controlled. It is set in little boxes, and he wasn't quite aware of that. He was intrigued by motion-picture business, and that of course he could reach. But there were other sources of power that would take a long time to get to. I think Grierson was very successful with some mass audiences here, some large groups that he spoke to. A few of the New York film groups invited him to talk—even then, the librarians, for instance, had him speak to them. And everybody was delighted with his exciting, block-busting, explosive way of presenting ideas and possibilities. Lots of us sat there and wondered how we could ever make those possibilities into probabilities and realities, but the feeling, the desire to do it, the motivation for it was there after he had spoken.

You see, the business setup in America was so different from any other place he worked. The advertising agency is an old and established barrier between the man spending the money and the great audience waiting to be reached. The agency people feel they know best; they are paid a great deal of money to know what is wanted and what will succeed best for the business. And that made it much less possible for the documentary film-maker to come in with *his* approach, with his attitude toward the material or toward the message.

Question: Do you think that particular sense of documentary has gone into American film-making and into television?

Jacoby: I think it is all lost. It never took firm root. There were only a few people here who were ever inspired by Grierson or his kind of thing. And the success of certain documentaries, which led to a change in attitude in terms of funding, money, and possibilities, never happened here as it had in England.

Question: How about the work today, and also, how about television? What do you think of those two fields in relation to the classic kind of documentary?

Jacoby: I think they are so different now that you can almost not use the same word for them. I find that any arrangement of factual material is called a "documentary" now. That never was the idea of Grierson or of any of the documentary people in England or in Canada later on. The documentary was a film made by a film artist, if I can use the word, although they never used that word about themselves. Things had to have *form*, had to have shape, had to be felt through, had to be going someplace. It was saying something in a medium other than writing. And documentaries don't *say* things any more. Occasionally they reveal little bits and pieces. But very rarely is anybody here permitted to have the right to say anything now. You must have *no* opinion, you must be neutral. Every documentary film must show *both* sides of the coin. And if you really believe something, if you think that something is true, it's very difficult to believe the opposite of that also. Formerly the documentary was not confined to factual material, *data*. It was an emotional experience, both for the film-maker and for his audience. And emotions can't be two-sided and balanced that way. The films are nothing if it's that way. They are dull and dreary, they lack life.

Question: What kind of feeling did Grierson have about news, journalism, in relation to film?

Jacoby: I learned from Grierson what it meant to have a nose for news.

I once saw a fantastic operation carried out in Canada. It was the eve of one of the first commando raids on Europe during World War II. And word had come through in advance that this was a Canadian show, and the Canadians who had waited very patiently for a little news about their boys overseas were aching to hear something, something good about their troops. And so preparations had been made for a tremendous spread in the newspapers. And it was to be filmed, and radio was going to devote a lot of time to it, and so on. And that evening Grierson sat with a little squawk box, a little short-wave radio. It wasn't official equipment, it was a little personal thing he had and he was just playing it, listening to soul singers from Texas, a little jazz from Chicago, switching to Europe. Then suddenly through this short-wave thing came clearly the voice of the German propaganda machine. They were telling about the commando raid, and it was an entirely different story from the one that had come through with the dispatches. And Grierson sat and listened for fifteen minutes to this blatant war propaganda. And he got up from his seat and said, "Do you know what, they are telling the truth. Those fellows are telling the truth." And he had the courage to go to the phone, cancel all the preparations for the big story, and say, "Play it down." And sure enough, by the next morning it turned out to be a terrible tragedy. Most of the young men were killed. This was Dieppe, the Dieppe raid, a tragic heroic action with the Canadians.

In his war films Grierson made use of his profound knowledge about ancient Greeks making war, Germans making war, theories about the migrations and movement of people in the world, about people and space. It turned out these were the same kinds of ideas that had been fed into Hitler's thinking. Through the Germans of course, but way back in the last century it was a Scotsman who made up the word *geopolitics*. And Grierson studied and knew Mackinder by heart.* And he was able to foresee the steps that would be taken in the war, in terms of the European landmass, what Russia must mean to Europe, what England must mean to any real conquest of Europe. And so he was able to foresee military strategy in these areas. And at times he would argue the Axis argument so strongly that we were almost afraid he was on Hitler's side. It was funny, but it was a matter of respecting the enemy and knowing what the enemy knew and understanding which way the enemy would pounce, and then being there

*Sir Halford Mackinder was a British geographer and originator of the "heartland" concept which defines Inner Eurasia as the central heartland of the world, girdled by peripheral maritime lands and continents. This view was embodied in the German theory of *Geopolitik* developed by Haushofer and others, and much regarded by military strategists of the Third Reich.

one step ahead of him, thinking about it and knowing and planning for it. That kind of news and research and reference material went into the war films, and that's what made them so remarkably accurate. You can't *guess* news, not unless you know what the big movements are that are going to happen, and Grierson knew it time and time again.

A Note on Documentary
and Politics

It became evident when we reviewed our film rushes of the interviews with Grierson's former colleagues that we had not questioned them on the matter of a specific relationship between documentary film activity and British politics.

There is no evidence that Grierson had any intention to direct the film programs towards support for socialism as such, or towards support for the Labour Party. That party itself was in considerable disarray during the period of Grierson's early work with documentary, between 1929 and 1934—the period of the Empire Marketing Board programs. During his student days and for some time thereafter, Grierson was in sympathy with the Independent Labour Party, one of the more coherent and purposive factions which had crystallized out of the various doctrinal dissensions which so consistently bedeviled Labour Party policies during the 1930s.

It seems fair to say that Grierson was not oriented towards any outright support of socialist doctrines. In a 1961 term paper for Professor Jack Ellis of Northwestern University, Rex Walford, an English student in the United States, has crisply defined some aspects of Grierson's film work in Britain relative to the political movements and climate of the 1930s. Writing on the subject of "Grierson and the Left," Walford makes the following points:

> Grierson considered the function of the documentary film was one of suggesting broad answers to social problems, but not necessarily of proposing specific solutions to those problems. The final decision as to ways and means should come from the citizen himself, part of his own democratic responsibility and involvement, which he should not abrogate.
>
> Grierson's fundamental socialism came not from the class struggle, but from philosophic premises, from a belief in the dynamic processes of society. He maintained a concept of good and evil in society that made him connect the economic difficulties of society with a failure of moral obligations, rather than of astute or pragmatic politics.
>
> Grierson believed that the function of education was to provide moral imperatives for men.
>
> He believed in the humanism of the Independent Labour Party movement, but not in its single-class identification. He felt that mankind (in Britain, in the

1930s) was entering upon a new kind of society, neither capitalist or socialist, but one in which central planning might be achieved without loss of individual initiative. This would be possible by a process of absorbing initiatives into the function of planning itself.

He was optimistic about the possibility of human beings being able to see and decide what was best for themselves, and the possibility of a form of coopera- tion organized by the state in a pragmatic rather than a doctrinaire manner.

In the event, Grierson obtained more concrete support from the right wing of the political spectrum than from the left. The Labour Party in those years never manifested a specific interest or belief in the creative or the inventive use of mass media. The Conservatives, on the other hand, during the 1930s had utilized the radio effectively as an instrument of national communication, and had paid considerable attention to graphic design in poster advertising and sloganeering on behalf of government programs; in addition to their support of the Empire Marketing Board film activities, actively encouraged by Mr. L. S. Amery of the Colonial Office and Sir Stephen Tallents of the Empire Marketing Board and later the General Post Office.

Moreover, Grierson had been able to promote among certain large industrial and government corporations such as Shell Oil or the Gas Light and Coke administration, lively support for the sponsorship of documentary and educa- tional film materials.

By virtue of the fact that his programs were not allied with the Labour Party nor with doctrinaire socialism, documentary films were not polarized nor asso- ciated specifically in the public mind with left-labour causes. For this reason there was no feeling of political reservation about the expanded use of docu- mentary films at the beginning of the war. Had there been such a feeling, either in Britain or Canada, the great expansion of the documentary medium during wartime would not likely have been possible.

Such factors may account in part for the much greater strength of docu- mentary in present-day British television than on the commercial networks of the United States. The general public in the United States has always to some degree distrusted documentary films, the assumption being that docu- mentary film-making involves special pleading or left-wing propaganda. This has been so from the beginning. In television, the timorous attitudes of networks and advertisers, who shun controversy and try to avoid offending any segment of society, result in the equal-time principle of bland and bloodless information devoid of moral attitudes, much less moral impera- tives. These limitations are notably less evident in Britain, perhaps because the institution of documentary film itself has not been suspect.

Obviously Grierson, though his thinking and tactics might loosely be called "revolutionary," was indeed no revolutionary himself. He worked within the established framework of elected governments; he felt, and en- joined upon his associates, an overriding loyalty to his sponsor, be it government or industry. He would often refer to the obligation incurred when "taking the King's shilling": the element of contract, the duty of delivery according to the bond. His belief was not in revolution but in human rationality and moral law.

American Connections

FROM an early stage in Grierson's career, the United States fascinated him. America was a stimulus, a challenge, a pointer to the future with its dynamic, fluid, technological society.

In America he saw most clearly the possibilities for harnessing and utilizing mass communication in its diverse forms. The energies of American commercial and industrial life, the openness of American society, the pulse of American entertainment—all generated in Grierson a certain impatience with British complacency and conservatism. Yet withal he was a Scot and a European in his inheritance.

During his lifetime Grierson came frequently to the United States, often to New York. Americans in the media and the social sciences came to know him well. American friends in their turn were struck by Grierson's own peculiar energies and acute perceptions. There is no single chapter of American experiences in Grierson's story, but rather a number of sallies into a rich world of opportunities and possibilities, repeated efforts to come up with the magic formula whereby some grand design for fruitful exploitation of the media would become possible. He could never quite come to rest in America or fully harmonize his patterns of thought and method with "the American way." But he did have friends and followers.

Here some of those Americans who had dealings with Grierson during the 1930s and 40s recount their impressions of him.

Lewis Jacobs

Lewis Jacobs is a film historian whose comprehensive work *Rise of the American Film* (1939) was one of the first thoughtful and detailed studies of American film production. We sought him out in New York and arranged to film him at the Americana Hotel on Seventh Avenue. From the Americana, one commands a stunning view of other tall glass towers that characterize the present-day New York skyline. Below us as we talked with Mr. Jacobs was the much more modest structure numbered 1600 Broadway, a nest of cutting rooms and small projection theatres which since the 1930s had been the nexus of independent efforts in documentary film-making in the United States. Lewis Jacobs, whose own career spans the formative years of documentary, compared U.S. and British documentary during the early period before World War II. He continues his writing and is a teacher of film studies in New York and Philadelphia.

Jacobs: I only met him briefly, just in passing. But I know a great deal about him because he had so much influence on the American documentary film-makers—in fact on documentary all over the world. He was a great catalyst. I don't think anybody in film was left uninfluenced, certainly during the thirties and forties, by him. What he did in England was tremendous—to provide and organize and give these young people opportunities to make films for the British government.

Question: Was there any parallel at all between the situation in England and here?

Jacobs: I think the films that we made in the United States came out of another kind of political situation. You know in the thirties we were very much influenced by the depression. And the people who got into the documentary film movement here were in a sense more politically minded. The mode and the objectives of their films were different from Grierson's. Of course both the kind of films Grierson's group made and the kind we made here in America were socially organized, socially oriented.

The films that Grierson made, because they were government-sponsored, were really to dignify British labor, and in a sense to "sell" Britain. There was a certain amount of reform attitude behind it. Ours were individually sponsored—by unions, political groups, even individuals—and they were really kind of antiestablishment. The threat of fascism and economic disaster which loomed over America at that time was a much sharper and much stronger influence in terms of the kind of films that we did here. You see, *we* made films to show up the bad side of the country. *They* made films to show up the good side of the British government. There was a kind of opposition there. But the whole spirit of documentary in terms of activating a social impulse and getting people to make films about society, about your problems, I think largely came out of Grierson's effort in Europe. The opportunity to make documentary almost a commonplace, which became so worldwide in the following years, was greatly due to Grierson's influence.

Question: In your own mind as a film critic, historian, writer, how do you regard the documentary film? What is it?

Jacobs: That's a hard question to answer. The documentary originally started out as a reenactment of a given situation in reality, which was Flaherty's view of the Far North, for example, and which in a sense inspired Grierson. Subsequently it has broadened out to include material which does not have to be reenacted. Even a guy like Vertov in Russia was influenced by Flaherty. Flaherty didn't reenact people, but he took real people out of a real situation and then in the editing room, in the cutting room, he tried to give the film material an objectivity which may or may not have been in the actual situation. And from that we really move along into cinema verité, where reenactment is inadmissible. The cinema verité people want to let the reality of the scene direct the cameraman, and let that emphasis in a sense organize the film. Many of the cinema verité people don't believe in organizing the documentary material that they record outside. So it has gone very far afield. Documentary is going sometimes into a theatrical area, where you are trying to create a situation which isn't even inherent in the original pattern. In a film like *The Married Couple*, you're hoping that something will come out of a relationship if you simply keep the camera on the people for long enough. Or in *Warrendale*, that kind of film. So you have quite a large spread from what Flaherty and Grierson thought to what documentary is today.

Question: Do you think that the original impulse and goals in the early British work, at the very beginning, are still to be found in documentary?

Jacobs: The big industrial corporations have begun to use documentary in a way that was quite parallel to most of what Grierson did. Then you have the other kind of documentary, which is really related to what we were doing here in the thirties. The guerrilla newsreel, the antiestablishment documentary, the antiwar documentary, you have all those things today, going on all the time. And they are all from different points of view. One represents a Grierson point of view, one is individualistic, one is union-organized, one is much more socially conscious, one is much more politically aware. Everybody is using documentary, and one of the reasons for it is because in the war period, in the forties, when the governments took over documentary and mobilized it for the war effort, we became accustomed to what the documentary could do in educational terms. And the

Lewis Jacobs, film historian and scholar, with crew in New York.

word itself became more popular. You take a guy like Pare Lorenz, his films played in 5,000 theatres in America. For the first time documentary film got into theatres, so the average American could see that a documentary could be interesting, could say something about society, could say something about him, and at the same time could have a tremendous social impact. It made us aware of what *could* be done if the government got behind certain social issues that needed to be examined and dealt with. So the documentary got a great impetus in this country, through war and through government sponsorship. And then right after the war, the government abandoned it, and documentary was picked up by individuals, public-relations officers, educational institutions, foundations. These kinds of organizations use it for their own individual needs.

Question: But it never really seemed to find a home in the theatres, in commercial distribution, in either country, did it?

Jacobs: Well, no, except of late. You have a recent documentary by Marcel Ophuls—you know, *The Sorrow and the Pity*—which got tremendous reviews and played in theatres and has roused a great deal of discussion. But now a good documentary—take a documentary which uses the cinema verité technique of Jean Rouch or Alain Resnais or Chris Marker —will play in a number of theatres here; more than that, it will play in many colleges throughout the country. These films have a tremendous impact on the young, on young intellectuals. They also have a great impact on film-makers, other documentary film-makers. But more than that, they are used in colleges in all kinds of social courses and that sort of thing. And they are very individualistic. Sometimes they are almost poetic— documentary in Grierson's day was very seldom that. Although I would say that Basil Wright and Humphrey Jennings were much more individualistic in their treatment of the documentary.

Question: There may be a hopeful sign in the present-day situation where some feature-length documentaries play in theatres.

Jacobs: Yes, that helps a great deal, the fact that they are now sometimes feature-length. They were almost all shorts in the early days, twenty or thirty minutes.

Question: How about television? When you look at the commercial networks and at public broadcasting in America, how much do you see of the original documentary ideas and principles? Do you think that they are found in television at all?

Jacobs: Yes, the original impulse came in the fifties, when television became national. But it was very unimaginative, not inventive. In the sixties with the lightweight film equipment—more portable and mobile cameras and the sound tape machine, that sort of thing—the documentary became very flexible. We then made some very fine, very unusual documentaries for television. As a matter of fact, television simply absorbed the whole documentary movement. Virtually all the documentaries come out of television. But in the last year or so television seems to have turned against the documentary for some reason. They are just going back to talk shows and interviews. I think one of the reasons is that much subject matter is very touchy, you deal with really profound issues, and once you get into the documentary and try to do an honest thing, there may be all kinds of protest by opposition groups. And our television in this country is always trying to take a neutral position. TV people are not strong enough. They don't believe enough in what they are doing, or they get frightened off by crank letters. All these factors affect the kind of documentary that could be made today for television, but that is not being done. Ed Murrow was a documentary man. The McCarthy hearings were very documentary and had a tremendous impact. As a matter of fact, that entire series was bought and subsequently reedited, and played in America with great success.

Another element is the Fred Wiseman documentaries, which have played in a number of theatres. Now they are very strong documentaries. Wisemen is terribly influential because he does films that are really kicking subjects which need to be examined—the performance of certain institutions, high schools, hospitals, even the army in its training centers. He is trying to show honestly what goes on in those places. By simply reproducing the actualities, the real thing is sometimes so startling and surprising that it creates a great deal of discussion and dissension. People have no idea what goes on in many of our institutions. The film can show them.

Question: Do you think that controversy is really implicit in the documentary approach?

Jacobs: If it's a situation which is controversial and if you show it, even if you have no special point of view, if you simply record what takes place as Wiseman is trying to do, it can become tremendously important. Because the film makes us aware of things that we might never have been aware of before.

Question: Going back again to the thirties, you said the American approach to documentaries derives from certain reasons and follows a certain path. Can you say more about that?

Jacobs: We were in a really tough economic depression here. People were still out of work, the banks were closed, and so forth. And the country had never faced a financial development of this kind, not at least in our lifetime. And many people who had been attracted to motion pictures as an art because of the European films moved into the documentary area, because they didn't have to employ actors or anything. And one of the incentives of the whole movement was right down below there in that building, 1600 Broadway, where you might say the documentary-film movement in America began. We all met there, the cutting rooms were there, and we would show films there. The equipment rental places were there. It was a kind of central location for the whole documentary movement. Whenever one wanted to show a film, they would simply rent a projection room there. And we would meet there, we would eat in the cafeteria around the corner, it became the focal point for the whole documentary movement in New York City.

Question: How about funding? In Britain you had an institutional base.

Jacobs: Yes, in England, Germany, France, and Russia documentary film-makers had a government base, they got government finance. In the U.S.A. the government didn't come in until much later, until Lorenz came in the late thirties. But in the early thirties it was all financed by individuals who wanted to make films and were disturbed by social problems. Sometimes the unions or small foundations or educational institutions would pick a subject or would become involved in a subject. Take, for instance, Scottsboro or Harlan County—I don't know if you know anything about the Harlan mines at that time. Dreiser went down there and made documentary films. Several film-makers went down there, and also the Scottsboro boys went down there and made films which were then used to show to the public to raise money to help out in those situations. To publicize the situations, to help the families or the people who were in need.

Question: How about film distribution? How did the documentaries get into circulation?

Jacobs: I would say that most of them were distributed through educational institutions and trade unions. Of course there were real problems in those days—evictions, unemployment, the bonus marches, things of that sort. And all those events were covered in film. And the films were simply distributed among all kinds of labor unions and educational groups. They didn't get into the theatres much, although sometimes an "art theatre" would show foreign films for special occasions and would run some of these documentaries. They felt that the crowd that they attracted in "art theatres," the special kind of audience, might also be interested in the documentary kind of material.

Question: Do you think there was any connection or interaction between the British film work and the American, or did they grow independently?

Jacobs: I think that they grew independently. But don't forget we all read *Sight and Sound,* and we all knew what was going on in British documentary. We would read dispatches or occasionally see films that would come over here. There was some exchange of films. We would see their films, and they had a very big effect on many of us.

Question: How about Grierson's writing? What do you think of his theoretical writing?

Jacobs: You know, you can't put him down. This guy has tremendous influence. And he says right off the bat that he is not interested in film as an art. He says right away that he is interested simply in its social effect. And he is concerned only with the film's social impact on people. That is why his entire efforts were not aesthetic but social. He makes that clear in every one of his pieces. He is not afraid to state that. Guys like Basil Wright or

Humphrey Jennings try to do both. They try to make it social, but they also try to bring into it some creative imagination or some poetry. This takes it out of the polemic sphere and gives it a quality above and beyond it, makes it larger and deeper than simply a social, didactic kind of statement. I understand the necessity of what Grierson did, and I respect it. But it is not enough, it is only a beginning. *Drifters* was very much influenced by Soviet films in technique and composition, even in terms of its editing. And yet he would play this down with the young people that he developed.

Although he was a social scientist in terms of his education, he was also a great salesman. He was a salesman par excellence for the documentary movement. There is absolutely no question about that. For years I argued if we could only get a guy like Grierson here, we could get a lot of films done in this country. A guy like Flaherty, who was a marvelous personality, unfortunately wasn't as good a salesman as Grierson.

Flaherty would have made many more films if he had the opportunity. I knew Flaherty much better than I knew Grierson. He was a marvelous person, but unfortunately he didn't get many films to do. He had a very difficult time making films. I think that Flaherty was a "feeler" rather than someone who really knows what he wants. He had to go out to a place, live there to get the sense of it, and then very slowly articulate a film. He couldn't write a film, then go there and do it. He tried to do that once after *Nanook*, in the South Seas, and it was terrible. He spent a year making his films, which was nothing. But once he got there and absorbed the environment and the kind of culture that people had, then he could work in those terms. And whenever he did that, he came out all right. It was only wrong when he tried to impose a story, tried to do something artificial. There is a curious contradiction, though, between what Flaherty did and the kind of documentary that Grierson did: Grierson always dealt with the present, while Flaherty always dealt with the past. Even though Flaherty himself was living in a particular modern culture, the culture that he was filming was always another kind of culture.

Question: In the early 1930s when the American documentary consciousness was getting stirred up, what films did all of you see at that time?

Jacobs: I can only speak for myself and the individuals that I knew. We were very much impressed by Ruttman's *Berlin*, which was really the first impressionistic film of a city that we had seen. It opened our eyes to the fact that right in our own environment we could make films. Then we saw Joris Ivens's films—I think that Ivens came to America at that time with *Rain* and a couple of his Dutch films. We saw those films, which made a very strong impression on us. Some of these people afterwards went to

Spain—you know, 1936—and made films. Herb Kline went to Spain and made films; Ivens went to China and made *Four Hundred Million*, and he also went to Spain and worked with Hemingway and others. Then he went on to other places and other documentaries. But all these films had a tremendous impact on us in the thirties, because they took us away from the local scene and we began to get interested in the whole international scene. The political scene at that time was becoming very hectic, with fascism in Germany and Italy. Matter of fact, Leni Riefenstahl was making pictures and we also saw those—*Triumph of the Will*, and later *Olympiad*, which had a tremendous impact, both good and bad, on film-makers here.

I have a feelng that the British were a little bit provincial as to the kind of thing that *we* were trying to do at that particular time. They were positive about the British government, while our films were negative. We were in a much more, it seemed to us, critical mood than people were in England. As to the films themselves, ours weren't set up in the same way; we didn't *stage* them as much as the British staged their documentaries. We tried to take more reportage, more *coverage*. We filmed a lot on the bonus marches and all sorts of political demonstrations. There were demonstrations shown in what we now call guerrilla newsreels. Then we made films about evictions and unemployment, and these were all taken from actuality, we didn't stage them. Later we began to form little groups who started to make documentary using some staging and some reality so they could give the material a much more imaginative and much broader treatment. We did some of those films. We also began to make some films to counteract the kind of films that *March of Time* was making in the thirties, because *March of Time* visually took a very conservative position. And our kind of films in America took a much more liberal position. We would treat a subject such as the Black Legion or the problems of eviction or unemployment from one point of view while *The March of Time* might see it from another, different point of view. Nowadays of course the whole field has opened up. Now we can do almost anything technically, because of the portability of equipment. Another aspect—there is more individuality in film-making, because now it is not so group-oriented as it was then, in the depression years.

Richard de Rochemont

A film vehicle that runs parallel to the early development of British documentary in the GPO period is the American-made *March of Time* series. This series of twenty-minute magazine or reportage films, made during the period 1936–40, brought to the commercial movie screen for the first time a sense of film used vividly and seriously to report and interpret broad developments in national (U.S.) and international news. The films were strongly structured, dramatized, and pointed for effective presentation. Technical production quality was high, as distinct from that of the regular theatre newsreels with their scanty, superficial coverage of spot-news events. The writing and voicing of commentary was carefully styled and calculated for dramatic effect.

Louis de Rochemont was the prime mover in the development of *The March of Time* series. Later he made some efforts in feature-film production employing documentary techniques and striving for a close approximation to realism in his production style (*House on 92nd Street, Luther*).

Louis's brother, Richard de Rochemont, had much to do with the European operations of *The March of Time*. Here he describes his contacts with Grierson and the British documentary group in the late 1930s. We set out to interview Mr. de Rochemont in his midtown New York apartment. Things proceeded smoothly until we began to pick up in the sound recorder an inexplicable but all too audible signal from a New York City radio station. In some utterly mysterious fashion this signal intruded into our recording operations within the large apartment building, tincturing the words of Richard de Rochemont with commercials for beer and soap and brief bursts of rock music. We therefore beat a collective retreat, mumbling to ourselves, and repaired to a stately uptown apartment on Central Park West, one better insulated from the overburdened airwaves of Manhattan.

De Rochemont: My brother Louis and I both had a background in newsreel work. He had been in newsreels from his late teens, and after I left college I got into the field through him. I'd done newspaper work, but I was drawn back to the newsreels and Movietone News. Louis was already working there, but he went off to Malaysia to make a series of travel films—adventure films is probably more like it—called *The Magic Carpet of Movietone*. Well, he broke away from Movietone. I had come there as foreign editor, which meant putting out some twenty versions of Movietone News going to various parts of the world. Movietone sent me to Paris to put out their French edition. While I was there, Louis and Roy Larsen got together to begin *March of Time.*

The March of Time—the British edition of this innovative commercial short-subject series brought U.S. and British documentary film-makers into contact in the 1930s.

This was a rather innovative and very advanced step. It went several leaps beyond the newsreel—an attempt to really make a more profound reportage on topics of the day. Of course when Louis became a competitor to Movietone, Movietone naturally fired me, so I came back to New York looking for a job. Then *The March of Time* finally got underway and engaged me to be foreign representative in charge of production abroad.

This took me to France and England. First thing was production, and in France we did a couple of quite interesting stories that made the national U.S. edition of *March of Time*. This gave us the strength to go on abroad, and I went to London to see whether we could arrange a British edition, and also of course to look for stories of *March of Time* caliber, about Britain and the British Empire.

I knew that John Grierson had been aware of the development of *March of Time*, and whether we went looking for him or he came looking for us, I can't quite remember. But it was a natural joining of forces, and as a result I engaged Grierson to be a consultant for the British *March of Time*. His function was to help guide us on subjects from Britain that we should cover, and help us in our official contacts. Also I esteemed him highly for making the British public very conscious of *The March of Time* idea. He didn't try to take it over and say, "This is Documentary," but he pushed it forward and had the people take a look. This was very helpful and gave us some standing that we, as a foreign importation coming into Britain, might not have had.

Grierson was a Scot, and in a way a Scot in England is still a little bit a stranger in a strange land, but Grierson was determined to challenge the British way of thinking—not simply to be a conservative. He encouraged us to take chances, to challenge certain ideas, and I think that this was a very strong point in the character of John Grierson—that he was out for *change*. He wasn't a revolutionary, but he was certainly a man who was moving for change and exploration in this field, communication, and in other fields. I found his presence was very stimulating.

He also gave us a lot of interesting people to work with. This famous crew that he got together for us included Harry Watt, who is known for *Night Mail* and other documentaries made in the Grierson manner, Edgar Anstey, who stayed a long time with *March of Time*, and Humphrey Swingler. Through Grierson we also made the acquaintance of Len Lye. During the war we imported Len Lye from Britain to New York, and he worked as a director for us here for a number of years.

Question: Going back to March of Time *itself, did you plan to develop a documentary film method according to some specific theory, or was it simply a natural outgrowth from the newsreels?*

De Rochemont: Well, I could never claim to be the theorist of *The March of Time*. The method evolved from the work of my brother Louis. He had played with an experimental reel called *March of the Years*, a film which reenacted historic events. It never saw the light of day, but it was an idea, an experiment in dramatizing history and encapsulating events of importance. It didn't succeed, but it did come to the attention of Roy

Larsen of Time Incorporated, the publishers of *Time.* Of course at that time they also had the *March of Time* radio series. The *March of the Years* idea and the *March of Time* radio ideas were fused, by my brother Louis and Roy Larsen and various other people here, into the concept of *The*

Edgar Anstey, a pillar of the documentary movement since 1931, active in retirement as a producer and international film consultant.

March of Time films. I feel this may have had great influence in launching Time Incorporated into pictorial journalism. After that, in 1936 they went into *Life* magazine, and they were in and out of this sort of communication for a long time.

   Question: Looking back to The March of Time, *how do you rate its importance in relation to media development?*

The March of Time—extensive reporting on domestic social issues in
U.S.A., such as racial and economic tensions in the Deep South,
went much beyond the scope of movie newsreels.

De Rochemont: Well, it would not be realistic to say that *The March of Time* was the precursor of television, because I think that Baird in London was doing television well before *The March of Time* got going. In a sense there was a parallel development.

In 1934 the film was dominant, and what Grierson had done in the late twenties was beginning to count. There were other things being done elsewhere in the world: in France there were some films in this area, while Benoit-Levy was at work and so on. I don't see television in that at all; television grew out of radio, later on. About the question of the rather stormy evolution of films and television—the documentary movement, if we take Grierson as a point of departure, was pretty well parallel with the invention and development of television. Baird was doing his television things in London about the time Grierson was there. Then of course there was the commercial, non-government film; *March of Time* was part of the commercial film, in the theatres. Paid for by the exhibitor. The film was pretty strong. But then as television grew, the exhibitor began to object and say, "Why should I be expected to pay for what my patrons are seeing for nothing on television?"

But in my opinion the influence of the documentary and newsreel on television was not as strong as the influence of radio. Television, when it began, was pretty much radio with pictures. It took a long time to get to the true documentary, the important *reportage* approach—and by the time they got it on television, at least here in the United States, they began to be very frightened of it, in case it became too controversial. *March of Time* had been controversial—we had plenty of exhibitors who objected to this —but there were others who liked it, and there was an extremely loyal public. I think that we did as the documentarians generally did, point out that there was an adult audience who wanted to hear the facts of life, at least to a reasonable degree, and we were giving this to them alongside the fantasy world of the commercial movie. Today television has a fantasy world of its own, situation comedies and so forth, and also its own version of the controversial which is building up, not so much in the United States as in other countries where they set a value on freedom of opinion.

No part of this is an isolated phenomenon, because people went back and forth from one type of work to another—radio people into television, film people into television, television people into film. There was a cross-fertilization, which I think was very important, and that was the thing that Grierson always believed in. He was always trying to plant one of his germinal film directors or producers with somebody else in another medium. He didn't care about keeping them working for him exclusively—he was trying to get them working for some other outfit across the street, knowing that in this way he could spread the Grierson doctrine very effectively.

I believe he was one of the great publicists England or Scotland ever produced—if he had gone into public relations purely and simply for commercial enterprises, he could have made a fortune. But he was a teacher, he wanted to teach, he wanted to spread his ideas. He had convictions and he liked nothing better than to make other people believe what John Grierson believed; it wasn't difficult because he was extremely persuasive.

Canada
—the Forties

GRIERSON was given a remarkably unfettered chance to demonstrate the worth of his ideas in Canada. This was due firstly to the fact that legislation and a working plan for films were already prepared before September 1939; and secondly to the fact that the war itself precluded that cautious and suspicious scrutiny of strange new processes and their financing which might otherwise have been expected from the Canadian political and governmental community. Quite simply, there wasn't time to stop and cavil about the new policies for film and public information; the Prime Minister endorsed them, legislation was passed, and the programs quickly began to function.

Canada was a curious kind of political and social community in 1939. Her people numbered something over eleven million. North American, but not American; strongly British-oriented and British-connected, neocolonial in feeling, but not really responsive or acquiescent to British directives; disparate communities isolated within their own great hinterland; a meager, much fragmented cultural tradition; widely divergent pockets of feeling and loyalty, as between English and French-speaking Canadians. The economy was shaky, still semi-paralyzed by the Great Depression of the thirties and its aftermath; the Western provinces in particular had been badly crippled by debt, drought, and crop failure. The mood of the country was diffident, cautious, skeptical—something less than buoyant, less than optimistic.

The change in Canada since 1939 is of course enormous. It continues to be a complex country, but its continuing growth and prosperity are unmistakable. It is rich indeed in crops and strategic resources such as metals, waterpower, oil reserves—in fact, all the undisclosed potential of the Northland. In 1974 the population had passed 22 million. Canada's relationships with Britain, with the United States, and with the world community are greatly changed from those of 1939.

Our concern here will be to suggest what impetus towards these changes can be attributed to a profound shift in attitudes and self-awareness among Canadians during World War II. During those years of involvement with the war, Canadians were furnished with a special kind of network for public information in which films played a significant part. Primarily set up to support the war effort, this network also served another purpose. It worked towards the establishment among Canadians of a concept of Canada not only as an Allied partner in the great conflict, but also as something more—a community with its own special history, attributes, and promise. Up until 1939 this had not been the usual pattern of Canadian thinking and Canadian sentiment. Until this point loyalties and interests had been local and regional rather than national; there had been little sense of a nation in which the citizen might feel positive pride.

During the 1930s a movement towards national self-awareness was beginning to take shape. Grierson had made contact with this movement on previous visits. When he officially began his work in Canada in 1940, it was strongly supported by the nascent nationalist impulse. He looked for "growing points": for young Canadians who might not as yet know more about Canada than about their own particular region, but who still had a sense of the possibility of greater unity, greater promise. Of course in 1939 communication among the regions of Canada was not as easy as it is now.

There were fewer cars, fewer highways, fewer passenger air services, and there was no television. But Canada was a land with a special concern for the principle of communication. This was a natural outcome of the great distances from coast to coast. The national railways in Canada held the country politically together at a time in the nineteenth century when strong American pressures threatened the existence of the feeble young nation. Later on, bush flying—flying freight into the trackless Northland for miners, trappers, and prospectors—evolved as a distinctive mode of Canadian transport. As an instrument of national policy, a unifying link, a contact coast to coast, radio has from its beginning played a critical role in the growth of national sentiment in the Canadian community.

Moreover, films had been used for educational purposes in Canada since a surprisingly early period. The use of short films for educational and promotional purposes was established in Canada long before it was in Britain, as Grierson's statements confirm. These Canadian productions were short silent films produced by the government for such specific purposes as agricultural training. There were promotional films to interest potential American settlers and investors in Canadian agriculture; there were simple educational films to show the processes of primary production in lumbering, fishing, mining; there were touristic films to show the glories of the Rocky Mountains and of the trout streams and waterfalls of forest Canada.

A policy decision to make fuller use of the film medium for purposes of Canadian development was made by the government of Canada in 1938. Grierson was asked to serve as consultant on this policy and to draft legislation for a national Film Act, which he did. He traveled in 1939 to Australia for a similar purpose; after World War II began, while Grierson was returning to Britain via Washington, the Canadian government requested that he come back to Canada to implement the new film legislation by setting up and staffing a new Canadian film program.

This was swiftly done. Grierson, moving briskly, recruited many young Canadians, almost none of whom had previous film experience. The existing government film unit and its equipment was used for the new program of film-making in 1940, then later was absorbed within the newly formed National Film Board. Contact was made with commercial film distributors, who committed themselves to play a series of short films about the national war effort in regular theatre programs. At the same time a network of locally based 16mm film circuits was organized in each of the nine provinces, and the new film program also gained the cooperation of a number of national nongovernment organizations, such as the Canadian Association for Adult Education, the Farm Radio Forum, the Trades and Labour Congress, the extension departments of many universities, and the Canadian Federation of Agriculture. These groups were already involved in the national war effort for increased production and for voluntary wartime organization in many fields. To win their active support for the use of films in all these areas of social action was to help create within Canada the sense of a national community for the first time. National loyalties and a common concept of the national goals and problems were built up over the four-year period of the war.

During the period some hundreds of new films were made; many young film-makers were trained, learning on the job and under pressure; a sense of Canada—its visual images, its special history and tradition (not much studied by earlier generations)—was imparted by the new channels of film distribution; the nationalist sentiment of Canadians (already powerfully stimulated by Canada's role as an Allied partner in the war itself) was strengthened. Schoolchildren in particular now saw the images of their own national community; Canadian films could show them their own spacious country. Previously, the textbooks and other teaching materials used in Canadian schools had reflected very little indeed in the way of Canadian cultural tradition or social or political history.

Grierson's plan for Canadian films therefore powerfully strengthened the new sense of nationalism and common purpose within Canada. After the war was over, the use of film was so firmly established and so identified with national purposes that there was no question of curtailing or canceling the programs. In 1946 retrenchment and postwar economies were in the air in Canada as in every country, but despite minor political criticisms and sniping, no serious attack upon the purposes or performance of the Film Board was made by the political parties. The notion that the government in power would utilize the film medium for partisan political propaganda was never very seriously entertained. Part of this was due to the fact that by now the unofficial network of national voluntary organizations was so closely associated with Film Board activity that this collaboration itself could be translated into real political support through numerous members of Parliament speaking for their constituencies.

During this period of about ten years from 1940 onwards an effective nationwide network of voluntary community support for and participation in the use of films and other media for educational purposes had developed in Canada; and a powerful impetus in bringing about this network was provided by the National Film Board under Grierson and his immediate successor, Ross McLean. The achievement is less a matter of formal government organization than one of sustained promotion among citizens of local communities, members of nongovernment organizations, and community opinion leaders—journalists, university presidents, executives of service clubs, directors of national organizations. This was not a privileged elite, nor was it a formal organization with salaried officers (apart from the Film Board itself). It was simply a bringing together of the active spirits, the leaders, the people who cared about a Canadian future, achieved largely by personal contact and persuasion. It involved the spreading of a sentiment across the country and its scattered communities from Atlantic to Pacific.

After 1950 other new elements entered the national scene and the relatively simple and clear-cut issues of the 1940s were gradually replaced by more complex and less easily resolved issues. As a result of the war Canada itself had become primarily an industrial nation, and a new tide of immigration and increased mobility within the country created conditions of growth quite unlike those of earlier years. In terms of communication, by 1950 national television had entered the scene. The documentary principle entered into television, as it did in many other countries.

During the period from 1940 to 1950 the Canadian documentary film-makers were learning their craft and getting better and better at it. The fast tempo of production and delivery of scheduled programs was a stern discipline. Grierson had imported a few well-trained film-makers from Britain and would bring in an occasional visiting expert from New York or from Europe. The films produced for theatrical release had to meet the requirements of a commercial entertainment situation—that is, they had to have pace, bite, bounce, and "showmanship," a tenuous and mystical quality never defined by Grierson (it is perhaps indefinable) but usually marked by an excited snapping of fingers when it appeared. Skills in camera work, editing, script-writing, sound-track editing and rerecording—all developed as the work went on. There was extensive feedback through the distribution network of the Film Board, abundant critical comment from small communities in the Maritimes or the Western provinces.

Another aspect of the original Film Act and policy requires attention. In 1939 Canada, a country small in many ways other than physical, had little representation abroad to make its individual presence known as distinct from that of Britain, the "Mother Country." Culturally speaking, Canada had as yet little to say or show to the world abroad. In his film legislation, Grierson provided that the medium of film should be utilized not only to make one region of Canada known to another, but also to make Canada itself known to other countries. Indeed, film became the prime medium for cultural contact between Canada and foreign countries during the three decades following World War II. Nor were the films that filled this role custom-made for foreign exhibition. They were those same films made for, and used among, the provinces and communities of Canada. Many were films on specialized subjects in such severely practical fields as child training or mental health, industrial safety or the teaching of biology. In other words, the films might be used abroad because they were useful in a particular field of study, not primarily because they came from Canada.

There was also a whimsical element among these films that went abroad. Among other talented imports, Grierson had brought to Canada the Scottish artist and film animator Norman McLaren. This rarefied spirit among film artists also filled an important practical function of the Film Board. He recruited and trained the nuclear staff of what is now a greatly accomplished animated-film department, one of the most productive to be found in any country.

McLaren designed many short animated film messages for the wartime information campaigns—films about savings, war bonds, official secrets and security, rationing. At the same time he produced his own more personal and individual works based on Canadian folk themes and folk music, often deriving them from French-language sources in Quebec. Throughout the late 1940s and 50s, these sprightly and delightful films by McLaren opened up many distribution territories in foreign countries for Canadian films in general. In Europe, especially in the ciné-clubs of France, Belgium, Holland, and Scandinavia, McLaren's animated films and those of his colleagues paved the way for more substantial film material coming from Canada. McLaren was by no means an extravagance for the state-financed programs of the Film Board; he was, and continues to be, a true innovator, an original spirit whose films create delight wherever they are seen.

The earliest British documentary film-makers often mention the excitement of the first period of their involvement. At Ottawa under Grierson, the feelings were similar. There was idealism, muddle, inexperience, dedication, haste, and true excitement. There was a sense of urgency, an awareness of great events in which the newcomers might take part. Indeed, newcomers felt that their own work in films might have some influence upon the great events by creating public awareness or mobilizing public opinion on particular issues.

Ottawa was a paradoxical city, a seat of government and therefore a nexus of politics, but no metropolis. In 1940 Ottawa was definitely a small town, with a curious muddy backwoods history. Located at the junction of three rivers, two noble and one pastoral—the Ottawa, Gatineau, and Rideau—Ottawa was surrounded by primal North America; immediately at hand were great reaches of forest and an infinite network of clear lakes to the north, west, and east.

The mood was almost bucolic, county if not rural, certainly not that of Montreal, a genuine metropolis two hours distant by train; or Toronto, a hustling commercial city an overnight journey away. Yet Ottawa withal was the capital, the center of policies and decisions, the meeting ground for members of Parliament, delegates, and lobbyists from all across the great distances of Canada. This was where Grierson loved to be. Here contact could be made with ministers, with senior men in public service, with advisers and economists and journalists and generals and seers, young Turks and elder statesmen.

Not only that, the young film-makers themselves could be party to these connections. Ottawa, small as it was, provided a forum, an arena for national discussion, for confrontation, for the meeting and clashing of diverse interests and points of view. At no other point in Canada could one have the sense of the whole country so sharply defined, and of its relationships from day to day with the United States and Britain and the wider world beyond.

For the young film people, all this, in combination with their stimulating work and their discovery of the film medium itself, was heady wine. There were riotous and simple-minded pleasures, with some lurid accents of carnality, roistering, and booze. Day and night, often all night, there was sustained hard work to deliver the product, to meet deadlines, to ship film prints from the laboratory to theatre exchanges in other cities. There was the tension and apprehension of screening with Grierson, showing your handiwork, enduring his laconic displeasure or enjoying his intoxicating praise or (most likely) seeing all your work set at naught in face of a complete revision in the film's message, a complete rethinking of the original plan. But one was exhilarated in any case, sent off tingling and excited if not entirely clear about the next step; one would find the way, do what needed to be done, and deliver. Withal there was a collectivity, a pride in work, a feeling of participation. Indeed, for many people in many different fields the wartime period was a time of heightened feeling and purpose, supercharged. To some degree, the feeling has persisted for long years since. In due time the Film Board became greatly institutionalized and expanded; later it was transported to Montreal, richly equipped, and amply financed—in a word, *established*. Yet it still preserves some sense of this obligation to the national community, to the country at large.

The greatest strain on the Film Board has been the pull of French-speaking Quebec away from the centralist, all-Canadian concept; the outcome of history pure and simple, this is not yet resolved and will perhaps not be resolved for many generations. Mechanisms were established within Quebec to develop film materials and distribution systems equivalent to those which could be formulated in English-speaking Canada. But the real basis of the Quebec situation, the essence of the famous "two solitudes" of Canada, was inaccessible to outside understanding or involvement, no matter how sympathetic or intelligent. Nonetheless, Grierson engaged French-language advisers and lieutenants and thus was able to recruit keen young talents from Quebec to work in French-language film production. For a time, perhaps seven or eight years, a kind of harmony and sympathy between English- and French-speaking personnel prevailed.

In time, however, the French-language group (particularly after the removal of the Film Board from Ottawa to Montreal), strengthened by younger and more militant recruits, veered away into an autonomous and imperious policy of its own, extending into innovative methods of film promotion and distribution in Quebec communities. In the 1960s the intentions of this group became more purely political and militant; the role of film and television in the so-called Quebec Revolution within Canada is of great importance; moreover, the training obtained by many young Quebec film-makers has been utilized to powerful advantage in feature-film activity, which has been a surprising, often impressive aspect of Quebec's creative independence and vitality.

To this day, Grierson's plan for a national film-making agency still stands. Many new factors and problems have arisen; we cannot guess how he would have proposed to meet them. In his last years in Canada, he for the most part kept a canny silence concerning Film Board policy and would not comment much on the work of successive Film Commissioners. It is evident that his original legislation for the use of film has been effective. The use of film in Canada has greatly strengthened the sense of national identity and self-awareness. More than that, a substantial part of the recognition of Canada in foreign countries (including the United States) has been due to extensive showings of Canadian documentary films. Furthermore, the documentary film principle established in Canada during the 1940s and 50s has strongly influenced the direction of television in Canada. Even further, the documentary perceptions and skills developed by the Film Board have now become a basic part of the Canadian film-making tradition; they may be clearly seen in those original Canadian feature films which began in the early 1970s to suggest that Canada at last could muster in its own right the skill and energy to enter successfully into feature-film production, despite all the hazards that attend such an under-taking within the conditions of the Canadian film industry.

These developments can be fairly credited, partially or largely, to Grier-son's groundwork: to his production, promotion, stimulation, exhortation and teaching, his reading of the Canadian future. He loved Canada, for whatever reasons—perhaps the country itself, its climate and light and weather and landscapes; perhaps the grandeur of its spaces and the con-cepts that this grandeur generates; perhaps his friendships with certain kindred spirits in various Canadian cities and towns. He hoped to retire to Canada. He enjoyed his teaching in Canada, locking horns with students whose minds were lively if not rigorously disciplined.

There was in Canada for a time a genuine two-way connection between a national information agency and a broad grouping of liberal-minded elements within the citizenry—a joining for good causes, for high ideals, for public purposes. While it worked, this represented the very antithesis of a fragmented society divided into disparate groups having no contact with or interest in one another. Within the loose framework of a democratic society it seemed to be possible, given leadership and a sufficient supply of the necessary educational materials (mostly films in this case), to over-come sectional and factional interests and make common cause, to hearten and inform the citizen and so help him tackle his problems and work toward his goals.

This was a partnership between the state on one hand and citizen groups on the other, utilizing the assistance of such local institutions as the univer-sities, the public libraries, and some departments of the provincial govern-ments. It was not by any means wholly state-supported, but entailed effort, financing, and participation by the citizens; this was effectively forthcom-ing. It called for good films, responsive to genuine needs and situations, plus effective means of circulating and using those films. The users in their turn passed back to the film-makers information concerning the relevance or usefulness of their product; so a contact was maintained that kept the film-maker firmly in tune with reality, and the film-user in contact with the film-making process to some degree.

The essence of the entire process is communication in the fullest sense—

a two-way exchange between producers and users. Despite the contemporary tendency toward centralism, bigness, and consolidation, it is indeed still possible to decentralize, to establish a local pattern based on local or regional initiatives, on individuals and their needs. Mass communication may work deliberately and profitably against itself, in the sense that "mass" no longer means simple standardization, homogenization, or centralism. The living cell within the large and sprawling body of the "mass" is the community. Functioning independently, yet with common goals and interests, these communities combined to make something other than a monolith; the cellular pattern seemed in essence to be democratic and organic. A new possibility was realized and worked well for a period of years. To a degree it still continues to exist, though much modified by other factors and pressures that have arisen during the past three decades.

By 1945 Grierson had achieved in concrete form in Canada a full expression of his earlier ideas and efforts. It was the good fortune of Canada even more than Britain to provide the ground for his experiments and to profit by the results. Perhaps in future years the awareness of this special history will be more widely understood and acknowledged within the country that made the experiment possible on such a broad scale.

Government Film Activity in Canada (1928)

That Canadian government agencies had film-production programs going at a time much earlier than is generally recognized is noted in the following account by Walter Creighton, deputed in 1928 to carry out a reconnaissance of Canadian film-making by government departments and to report back to the Empire Marketing Board in London. Creighton's report is an indication of British government interest in the Dominions and their continuing allegiance to the Mother Country in the years between the wars. It outlines also the considerable extent of government initiatives in Canada, both in the Province of Ontario and in the Federal Ministry of Trade and Commerce, in using film as a direct means of spreading information and beneficent propaganda. Walter Creighton's letter is provided by courtesy of the Archives of Ontario and the National Archives of Canada (Motion Picture Division).

CONFIDENTIAL.   E.M.B./C/7.
                                                                    (24,1,28.)

EMPIRE MARKETING BOARD
FILM COMMITTEE.
Government Film Activity in Canada.

For some years past the Canadian Government has realised the importance of films for purposes of publicity and education.

In Ottawa there is a Government Motion Picture Bureau working under the direction of the Department of Trade and Commerce and maintained by a Government grant of thirty-five thousand dollars a year. A new Controller, Mr. F. C. Badgley, has just been appointed but had not, when I was in Ottawa in August last, yet got into his stride. He is hoping to develop the quantity and quality of the films produced and feels that the majority of the existing stock of films lack either pattern or human interest. So far they have been turned out chiefly with the object of encouraging tourists to visit the Dominion and up to the present the most successful work has been carried out in the "Seeing Canada" series. These have been made for the most part with the co-operation of the Canadian Pacific and Canadian National Railways, who have enabled these films to be taken with little or no expense.

In addition to these activities the various Federal Government Departments, especially the Department of Agriculture, commission the Motion Picture Bureau to undertake the filming of different subjects which they may wish to have recorded for technical or educational purposes. In such cases the Department concerned is responsible for the expenses of making the film. A catalogue of these Motion Pictures is on sale and comprises a list of some 200 short reels. These pictures are distributed gratis to the Y.M.C.A., the Izaak Walton Corporation of America (to encourge Americans to come and fish in Canada) and the State University Educational Department. They are also sold theatrically on their own merits through the Film Booking Office of London, British Instructional Films Ltd., also of London, the International News Reel in New York and through the Premier National Pictures of Australia. In the latter country their takings have reached an average of ten thousand dollars a year. The revenue for the past three years, as given me confidentially by the Department of Trade and Commerce, is as follows:—

Fiscal year April 1st to March 31st.

1924–25	$27,876.79
1925–26	22,163,50
1926–27	15,129.08

I was told by both Dr. J. H. Grisdale, the Deputy Minister of Agriculture, and Major Parmelee, the Acting Deputy Minister of the Department of Trade and Commerce, that the Government had a great belief in the work of their Motion Picture Bureau and were contemplating the erection of a suitable building for its activities, fitted with offices, a projection room, studio, laboratories, developing and cutting rooms and proper accommodation for the storing of films.

. . .

In Toronto the Ontario Government are tremendously alive to the importance of the film not only from the technical, educational and tourist point of view but also from the entertainment angle for cheering people during the long winter evenings in the solitude of isolated villages and farms. But this Government activity, which is practically that of a Circulating Film Library, was undertaken as a means of inducing people from the farms to attend performances consisting for the main part of educational subjects. The scheme was in the first place originated to introduce better farming methods and special motion pictures of various farm animals, control of insect and bacterial pests and other agricultural activities were made as early as 1917 to encourage agricultural production during the war years. From this beginning the present Ontario Government Motion Bureau has grown into a very flourishing and energetic concern with a vote in 1925–6 of $119,747. In the initial stages, the Government did not make its own pictures but prepared scenarios, and the actual work was entrusted to commercial firms; but in 1923 a film studio and laboratory were purchased at Trenton, and since then all films have been produced under the direct control of the Bureau throughout the whole process. . . .

.   .   .

There seemed to be a very strong feeling amongst all the Provincial Governments in favour of the use of the film for instructing farmers in agricultural methods and experimental work, for inspiring interest in the great mineral resources of the country and for instilling knowledge of the many vast unexplored opportunities throughout the Dominion, as well as for encouraging tourists to make use of the exceptional facilities for big game hunting and fishing which already annually attract so many sportsmen from America and the old country. But it was generally agreed that these films had not improved in selection and photography at the same rate as the entertainment pictures, and that a different attitude towards these moving pictures was most necessary as, owing to the need of short reels for completing the feature picture programmes in the large picture theatres, there was a growing commercial opportunity for beautifully photographed and carefully directed pictures of this type.

It was considered that such pictures could have either a personal or an epic touch that would make them part of some great human and artistic theme. This would in no way interfere with the technical film needed for purely instructional purposes, but on the contrary the two pictures of any given subject should be taken simultaneously with a view to the editing and cutting of the material photographed so as to form both an entertaining as well as a technical film.

Everywhere I found a very active Government interest in the development of the films and a fear of the far-reaching effects of showing American pictures only.

In British Columbia I was told that Canadians were being very perturbed by the effect of the American News Reels. These naturally showed the Americans pre-eminent along all lines and always the winners in Sporting Events, so that Canadian children asked their parents whether these English, from whom they had sprung, ever won anything or always were second to the Americans across the border. Naturally in Canada, with the American influence so close at hand, this is of peculiar importance, but the same thing applies in Australia, New Zealand, South Africa, India and the Colonies where the various Governments are all exploring the possibilities of the Moving Pictures for stimulating interest not only in their problems but in their achievements.

It was therefore felt that if all Government cinema activities throughout the Empire could in some way be organised so that they could keep in touch, the showing of important events, developments and customs in short, dignified, artistic and attractive reels could spread that intimate understanding of each other that alone can bind together such a diversity of lands and peoples as is contained in the Commonwealth of Nations. This might eventually develop into an official Empire News Budget which could be edited so as to form a dignified and accurate history in picture form of the chief events throughout the entire Empire. The realisation of the responsibility of the cinema as a means of spreading the right news and giving the desired impression of various activities seemed so far to be in its infancy.

.   .   .

. . . Already the commercial results in Canada are most encouraging and show that there is a definite market for this type of picture. But they must be a real excellence, the result of enthusiasm and imagination. By means of the existing Government Motion Picture activities throughout the Empire, real progress and worth-while work could be developed along these lines, and a great opportunity for Empire Propaganda by means of methods previously unexplored could be made use of. At any rate in Canada there seemed to be a general feeling that all the various Governments throughout the Empire would welcome a lead and encouragement from the Government at home in the direction of some united policy.

W. R. CREIGHTON
20.1.28.

The Goals in Canada—
A Grierson Overview*

Question: When you came to Canada in 1938, what did you expect to find in terms of film activity, and what did you actually find?

Grierson: First of all, I didn't just come to Canada in 1938. I first came to Canada in 1924. I had been in and out of Canada a great deal before I came over in 1938. I had been all over the country and at one time traveled west to see the dust bowl, to see what life was like in what they call the hungry thirties. I had been routed to speak to the groups in various cities interested with international affairs. I had met people like Dafoe,† and I had been much impressed by the young progressive Canadian point of view, a nationalistic Canadian point of view represented by Frank Scott‡ and his associates in Montreal. Of course, being a Scotsman I had always been very sensitive to the particular movement by which countries rather earnestly seek to find their identity. And the problem of finding an identity was as vivid for the people of Canada in the thirties as it is today. I knew something about Canada from coast to coast. In England I had been very closely associated with the Empire Marketing Board and with what was called the Imperial Relations Trust, closely associated with the consequences of the statute of Westminster under which the Dominions had been allowed, or rather found, a new and separate identity. I had been associated with the different campaigns of information in England which were intended to instruct the British people about these new patterns of relationships they must expect to live with, so far as the Dominions were concerned. That was very much my profession—this question of information within the field of Dominion and home-country relationships.

When I came over in 1938 I was not strange to many of the problems of

* October 18, 1970 interview by James Beveridge with Dr. John Grierson, founder of the National Film Board and first government film commissioner (videotaped at York University, Toronto).

† A long-time Canadian newspaper editor and champion of Canadian autonomy within a modernized commonwealth, Dafoe began with the *Montreal Star* and the *Ottawa Journal* in the last century and then was with the *Winnipeg Free Press* from 1901 to 1944. A most influential editor, Dafoe, in 1935, declined a cabinet post in Mackenzie King's government.

‡ A Canadian poet and essayist, Scott also served as a professor at McGill University. In the 1930s he was associated with the early group of nationalist-minded Canadian intellectuals.

Canada, or to many of the people of Canada. Above all, I had met Dafoe in Winnipeg, George Ferguson* in Winnipeg, and George happened to be a very close friend. Now I must say something further about coming in 1938. I came on the face of it to do a kind of job analysis of the film activities of the Canadian government. But these questions were very familiar to me in '38, because as early as 1930 I had got the British government to send me over to look at the Motion Picture Bureau in Ottawa, and the motion-picture service of the Ontario government. I had made a very close examination of their activities. I had looked at many, many films from Canada. We set up a library of films in England, based on the Canadian material. That was around 1930, 1931—I think in both years I was over in Canada. The results of this observation of the Canadian experiment was the founding of the first big film library for nontheatrical purposes in England. I want to emphasize this, that it was the creation of that library in England that provided a mass of film material on which schools and other nontheatrical groups could draw. At that time there had been no great efforts made to invade this nontheatrical field, which is now of course established throughout the world. I found a situation in England where people wouldn't buy projectors because there weren't films to show. I solved it very simply by getting the films together, publishing a catalogue and distributing it widely. The result was that I had an audience, a nontheatrical audience of one million in the first year, I think three million in the second year; the nontheatrical idea had taken root in England.

· · ·

The example of the Canadian Film Board in governmental film-making is interesting, because when I came over later on—let's say 1938—it was so established in principle that the government should have a film organization, that films had already been of service to the government, that they were concerned with inviting me over to *review* the position of the Motion Picture Bureau and see that it had every opportunity to be as good as any governmental film unit in the world. . . . But by 1938, to be quite frank, we had moved ahead technically and in ambition, moved beyond the early example of the Motion Picture Bureau. This was the feeling in Ottawa expressed through Mike Pearson,† who was the counselor at the High

* A former managing editor of the *Winnipeg Free Press* and editor-in-chief of the *Montreal Star*. Scots-born but educated in Canada, Ferguson and his wife Mary were loyal friends to Grierson from the time of Grierson's early visits to Canada.

† L. B. (Mike) Pearson later served as Canadian Prime Minister (1963–68) and was a Nobel Peace Prize winner in 1957. Formerly he had been secretary of state for external affairs, and from 1935–38 he was a member of the staff of the High Commission for Canada in London.

Commissioner's Office in London. The Canadians felt they had perhaps slipped behind, and wanted to take advantage of the full British technical development. I came over really to put the Motion Picture Bureau back into business as the leader of the pack.

. . .

But also there was in 1938 a feeling that perhaps war was just around the corner. People particularly in my field of communications, governmental communications, national communications, were well aware that if a war came, we should have to depend a great deal on good communications of all kinds. I was supposed to be a specialist in film communications, and it was certainly put before me that I should think about intercommunications, particularly between the Dominions and England, on a film level. So that I had, from the British point of view, the thought of a Film Board or a film organization in Canada, very much in my mind. A film center, and equally in Australia, equally in New Zealand, equally in South Africa. And in fact all these things came to pass. As it happened, we not only set up the Film Board in Canada but I will have you know that I also fulfilled my plan and set up the film unit in Australia, and drew up the plans for the one in New Zealand and later on in South Africa. That was one motivation; although as I said, the chief motivation was this question of observing the film situation in Canada and bringing it back to be the leader of the pack. People like Pearson at that time wanted no less. . . .

Ross McLean

One of the prime movers in the effort to establish a Canadian film program of substance during the 1930s was Ross McLean of Ottawa. While in London as secretary to the High Commissioner for Canada, he made a study of the new British film movement in documentary and urged that John Grierson be brought to Canada to report on film potentialities there. From this effort emerged the National Film Act of 1939 and the subsequent invitation to Grierson to set up a functioning Film Board in Ottawa. McLean served as Assistant Film Commissioner during the Grierson period and thereafter became Commissioner. He inherited a difficult situation: there were strong bureaucratic pressures for retrenchment and reduction of budgets, in combination with the considerable attack upon the Film Board by some political elements as a result of Grierson's being named in the espionage hearings of 1946.

McLean fought manfully to keep staff morale high and his group intact, but finally his feud with the finance authorities became insupportable. He moved to UNESCO in Paris to become head of the Division of Films and Visual Communication. Almost a decade later he returned to Canada and subsequently joined in the first phase of policy-making at the Board of Broadcast Governors (later the Canadian Radio and Television Commission), a regulatory body whose objective was to strengthen Canadian content in all the broadcasting media. A student of international affairs, McLean inclined towards an international point of view in his work with the Film Board. Grierson himself had done so. Similarly, Canadian policy since World War II has increasingly been to strengthen economic and political dealings with the NATO countries, the Far East, Africa, and the so-called Third World; while a fundamental and profound relationship with the United States continues to exist. McLean played an important role in developing an outward-looking viewpoint at the Film Board.

We filmed the interview out-of-doors in fine weather in a park overlooking Parliament Hill in Ottawa.

Question: Around 1936 you were interested in the idea of a Canadian film policy. Why did you feel the need for a film policy? How did it take shape?

McLean: Actually one has to go back even before 1936. During the depression a lot of young people in Ottawa were very active in the arts

while others were concerned about publications, about films—about communications of any sort. And in a way the Film Board was born out of the
depression—and later on became a "war baby." Because it became a war
baby, it also became very much enlarged—different, in other words, from
the original concept. In Canada we needed some form of expression in film,
which at that time was limited to a rather narrow government concept
about trade and travel. There was a Government Motion Picture Bureau,
established a good many years before. We wanted to revitalize it, and for
that reason the National Film Society, as one of the factors in this whole
development, was set up by a group of us in 1934, mainly animated by
Donald Buchanan* and to some extent myself. Among others who were
involved were Charles Cowan of the British American Bank Note Company and a number of Ottawa people who were really interested in awak-
ening the national capital to something significant in terms of expression.
We knew about the documentary movement in Britain when I went over to
England as Vincent Massey's† private secretary in 1935.

On the way over I mentioned to Massey the possibility of revitalizing the
old Motion Picture Bureau, of really creating something new, perhaps after
the image of some of the European countries. Massey then asked me to
look at the documentary movement in Britain. If I did a report for him he
would see that it reached the Prime Minister in Ottawa at once. So between
November 1935 and February 1936 I did this report, and then it went to
Ottawa. Now we have to refer to an important contributor to this whole
process. The Prime Minister, Mackenzie King,‡ was a great film fan. He

---

* A Canadian author, critic, editor, photographer, and gallery director, and one
of the founders of the original Canadian Film Society. In the 1930s Buchanan
worked in several fields of publishing and the arts as one of the central group of
Canadians concerned with establishing Canadian identity and autonomy and with
stimulating development of the arts in Canada. In the media, he worked also as supervisor of talks for the Canadian Broadcasting Corporation, and supervisor of nontheatrical film circuits for the National Film Board. Buchanan's individual contribution to the flowering of the arts in Canada was outstanding.

† A former high commissioner for Canada to the United Kingdom and later the
first native-born governor-general of Canada. Massey was actor Raymond Massey's
brother.

‡ William Lyon Mackenzie King, long-time Liberal Party leader and Prime Minister
of Canada, died in 1950. Mr. King was a grandson of the early Canadian revolutionary
William Lyon Mackenzie, and in his own lifetime he worked assiduously towards
the creation of an autonomous and independent Canada that would still maintain
close and harmonious relations with Britain and with the United States. He directed
the country through the most severe strains and avoided either a breach of faith or an
open break with French-speaking Quebec over the stormy issue of national conscrip-
tion in wartime. Mackenzie King's task was to maintain and strengthen national co-
hesion, yet to honor the special history and rights of French Canada within the
confederation. This was and still is a most difficult task.

William Lyon Mackenzie King, long-time Liberal Prime
Minister of Canada, who sponsored Grierson's design
and subsequent management of a National Film Board
for Canada. Mr. King talks with Lady Hardwicke and Sir
Cedric Hardwicke (partially hidden behind King).

had a passion for the cinema, and in terms of politics he probably more
than anyone else was the main support of the National Film Board
throughout the years. Mackenzie King had a great passion for Greer Gar-
son on the screen, and very often he'd slope out and disappear into a
cinema without telling anybody where he was going, or being recognized.
But he was in fact throughout the war period a tremendous supporter of
the National Film Board. Of course Grierson had impressed him earlier by
his vitality and his imaginative interpretation of Canadian qualities.

*Question: Do you think that Mackenzie King had a clear conception of
what kind of films should be made? Or was it just that he wanted something done?*

McLean: He wanted something done. He wanted a new form of Canadian expression in film, and he was intrigued very much by Grierson's
proposals, in the report which he did as a preliminary to the National Film

Act of 1939. And that was a critical point. The National Film Board that ultimately resulted wasn't really very closely related to some of the terms of the National Film Act at all.

Question: When the act was drafted, was it unique, as far as you know? Was it unique legislation for a film policy in a democratic country?

McLean: Yes, I think it was an original. I don't think there is anything quite comparable to it anywhere else. It was a kind of combination of our National Film Society ideas with that of a public production group—the kind of thing the GPO Film Unit did in Britain. That unit, the GPO unit, was responsible for a great deal of the film work that went on throughout the Commonwealth during the years that Grierson directed it. Grierson collected around him in London a group which was really highly distinguished, and in my judgment he collected around him a very distinguished group in Canada as well.

Question: When the Canadian Film Act was drafted and it was time to make it work, what happened?

McLean: The explosion, so to speak, in terms of the development of the Film Board came of course because it was established just at the outbreak of war, and Mackenzie King as much as anybody—perhaps more—knew it could help significantly with government efforts in the information field. This is why it grew.

Question: The Film Board operations were large. What about the budget factors, Finance and Treasury? How did the board get funds to achieve such a large volume of work in a short time?

McLean: Mainly because all sorts of funds were available for anything connected with the war effort. It was really Wartime Information money that supported the National Film Board for the next five or six years—the greater part of it at least. And that was true until 1945, when Grierson resigned. Afterward, in peacetime, the Deputy Minister of Finance and the Minister of Finance and the rest of them were determined to cut expenses and reduce the funds. By this time I think many of them decided that the film activities were merely frills. The Film Board survived in 1946 because the Canadians had found it an extremely valuable form of national expression. The fact of the matter is, Mackenzie King had no intention of seeing it disappear. Some of the financial group around—ministers like Mr. Howe the Munitions and Supply minister, and Bob Winters felt that it really was too expensive. Clifford Clark, the Deputy Minister of Finance, was a bit leery of the whole operation. And of course they began to cut the budget every year. They told me very soon after the end of the war—by this time Grierson had left and I was Acting Commissioner—that I was expected to reduce the staff of the National Film Board from approximately eight hundred people down to five hundred. I said I didn't think it could be done and still maintain an effective Film Board, but I would try to reduce the budget below the level we had enjoyed during the war. If they were going to insist on continuous cuts, I suggested that the best thing to do would be to abolish it entirely, because they would save more money that way. And unless you maintained a good operation, it was pointless. This was the kind of fight I carried on for the next five years, until I finally parted company with the Minister then responsible, Mr. Winters, and went to Paris to UNESCO.

Question: Do you have the impression there was much personal contact between Mackenzie King and Grierson? Or was it simply an intuitive understanding refreshed by brief contacts?

McLean: I think it was always an intuitive understanding between them. I don't think they met all that frequently. But Mackenzie King was always very much aware of what was going on at the Film Board, and also what was going on with Grierson at the Wartime Information Board too. I think Mackenzie King helped a great deal at a very difficult moment in 1947, when the espionage inquiry commission decided they would like to talk to Grierson, and some of them were deeply hostile to him, which Mackenzie King never was. He, like a good many others of us, was very upset. When one was dealing in the information field, as Grierson was with the Wartime Information Board and the Film Board, and reaching all over the world in many ways, one was bound to get caught up in complicated situations which somebody who wanted to misinterpret could easily do. This is the way the criminal aspect of the whole McCarthy proceedings developed in the United States, and the inheritance was left to us to some extent in Canada. It troubled the National Film Board for years after and had something to do with my decision to leave the Film Board and accept a job at UNESCO for seven years, although I wasn't unhappy to live in Paris for seven years as a consequence.

Question: How did the Film Board as a government agency develop connections with the film industry in the United States?

McLean: Grierson had extremely valuable contacts in the United States. He had been a Rockefeller Fellow in the U.S.A. for some years in the 1920s —and had developed very close links not only with Hollywood groups but with the newsreel companies in New York, and particularly with documentary film producers like Louis de Rochemont and others. From the beginning of the Film Board in Canada, we were in close contact with the newsreel operators.

Incidentally, there was another factor in the story that had a bearing on all this. Grierson was nominated by the British government as its film censor for North America, so from Ottawa we sent Donald Buchanan to Bermuda to receive the film, all the newsreel film from Germany destined specifically for Latin America and the United States, as this was still 1940 —and the British Navy seized everything they could. The films then came directly to Ottawa—in fact, for the first six months or so of the war they came to me—and the people who actually did the work on them were myself and Margaret Grierson. We didn't cut out very much material, and generally we released the cut-out material for counterpropaganda purposes to the newsreels in New York. But we didn't let films go to Latin America unless material was, let's say, properly interpreted. This was German film coming directly from the war fronts.

Question: We often talk about national identity and self-image. Do you think that the Canadian film work, and the wartime information work overall, had something to do with formulating an "image" in the consciousness of Canadian citizens? Or did that come later? Or do you think it came at all? Do you think that the film work had something specifically to do with it?

McLean: I think it had an enormous amount to do with it—not only in Canada, but outside Canada. The Film Board by the end of the war was distributing its products virtually all over the world, sometimes through the help of British channels of course, sometimes through the help of the Mexicans—in Latin America for example; and in the U.S.A., not only 16mm films, but in theatres through United Artists (*World in Action* series was an example of that). Our Spanish-language versions were made in Mexico City. And we had extensive relations also throughout the Commonwealth—for instance with the Malaysian film unit, which is still producing in South Asia certain Asian-language versions of the Film Board productions. The films have been a major factor in establishing a sense of Canadian identity in Canada and in other countries.

The Eyes of Canada[*]

In our complex world you can appreciate that this all-seeing eye of the motion picture is a very prescient power. Here we are all working at our particular jobs in our own local towns and hamlets. Events seem far away. We know they affect us. We know that we and our neighbors are part of the show. But we often feel that our relationship to the show is intangible, and we don't see the wood for the trees. Well, the film can give us a sense of things as a living whole. The film can give us a sense of the communion that exists between people in spite of the apparent distance in our daily lives. By showing the themes of national and community achievement it can conquer the isolation of our personal existence and reveal our reality. It is, and who does not want it, a way of national self-realization.

I have been seeing recently some other very interesting film shots of Canada at war. *The March of Time* people are up here just now. *The March of Time*, as most of you know, is that dashing account of world events which comes out every month. It is very important in the film world, for it shows to eleven thousand theatres and to forty million people across the world. It is one of the great influences from an international point of view, and we are naturally giving *The March of Time* unit every facility and cooperation. It is valuable to a nation to have its story told to the whole world. *March of Time* photographers are being very thorough. They are shooting something like 30,000 feet of film—that is to say, five hours of running time—though the final edited account will run for only 25 minutes. That means that in the final stage they will show only the very quintessence and fiber of Canada's energy today.

I have been watching the rushes—that is what we call the first rough prints—as they come in from the laboratory. I was as surprised as ever at how much the film can bring together. I sat in on the research for the film, and I knew the main line of the script; in fact, I thought I knew a lot about Canada at war. But not really. One knows it in the head, one knows it on paper. But the film brings it to life. I knew about economic mobilization, but here was living traffic at the docks, puffing and steaming and looking like a nation in full power. I knew about the research behind the war, but here was the patience of science working on aircraft, squeezing the last ounce of mechanical safety for the men with wings. And so it went. Soldiers drilling and training. War Supply Board, censor controls, financial

[*] A broadcast talk by John Grierson (January 21, 1940).

controls, Canada's navy headquarters, air force controls, all beginning to pile up into a massive general effect of skill and power and assurance and purpose.

That is the kind of work we are interested in at the National Film Board in Ottawa. The National Film Board was set up last year by an Act of Parliament, as film headquarters for the Dominion government. The act most dully says that its function is to coordinate government film activities. But when that sentence was drafted I remember thinking: why can't we say and be done with it, the National Film Board will be the *eyes of Canada*. It will, through a national use of cinema, see Canada and see it whole—its people and its purposes.

Walter Turnbull

A central problem in the promotion of the documentary film idea is the inescapable relationship between film people and senior civil servants. Grierson's entire concept of developing the use of the film medium as a broadly informative and educational vehicle was pegged upon the government's support and financing of film work. The measure of Grierson's skill was that both in Britain and especially in Canada he was able to advance the film idea and its potential persuasively but diplomatically to the public service. This is a demanding kind of diplomacy. In it, the film-makers must comport themselves in a discreet and responsible manner, and must deliver according to the bond, while the civil servants must try to meet the film people halfway in understanding what the medium can do to bring alive those aspects of the story which concern them. Some civil servants in Britain and Canada have made an essential contribution to this development of documentary film as a contemporary means of communication. Both their financial support and their willingness to cooperate in exploiting the possibilities of film for public purposes have made the documentary development possible.

Among these civil servants is Walter Turnbull, formerly principal private secretary to Mackenzie King, former Canadian Prime Minister. Turnbull dealt with Grierson in Canada throughout the war period, while the National Film Board was achieving its sudden creative flowering. Turnbull in effect represents the community of top-level functionaries, at Deputy Minister level, with whom any film-maker must ultimately deal if he seeks to work with government funds or on a government account. Turnbull helped facilitate the growth of the Film Board and establish the *bona fides* of the film-makers and their efforts within the public-service community in Canada.

We filmed Mr. Turnbull in brilliant spring sunshine amid the natural boskage and artificial Gothic ruins of the late Prime Minister's estate. Mackenzie King had the fancy of collecting picturesque ruins amid garden landscapes. Against one of these clusters of crumbling stone carefully sited in a romantic grove, we photographed our subject in his shirt-sleeves. Though retired, Mr. Turnbull is nimble, has a puckish wit, and lent himself readily to the situation. His good humor was indeed a blessing, since on this location he and the film crew were beset by the native Canadian mosquito, one of the largest and most malicious of man's natural enemies. These insects settled in a loose cloud on any member of the group who stood still for more than three consecutive seconds, not only torturing their victim but constituting a visible darkling nimbus in the camera's view. Only an intermittent brisk breeze dislodging the mosquitoes from their prey saved the day and enabled filming to proceed.

Question: How did Grierson come to your attention? When did you meet?

Turnbull: Well, John got around. He felt that if he was going to do a job he had to move around and meet people in the government. He came to see me, it was as simple as that. There was no formal meeting. He came to me once with a problem. One of the ministers was doing a little bit of interfering—he was blocking progress shall we say—and I reported this to the Prime Minister for Grierson. This happened only once or twice.

Question: Do you have the impression that the Film Board would have had a very lean time of it if it hadn't been for the war? Wasn't the rapid growth of the Film Board somewhat remarkable in a government context?

Turnbull: I think that was practically the whole *raison d'être*. If it had not been for the needs of the war, the Film Board might never have come into being.

Question: During the war, what contact did the Prime Minister have with information matters?

Turnbull: He was very conscious of information matters. He realized that speeches by the Prime Minister were pretty dull stuff. In any case, they were quite a heavy strain on him; he felt it was not the way to do it. His attitude was quite a simple one. Politicians are not the people to sell the war effort to the public. You do your own job, get on with the work, but the selling of the war effort, that is different. For instance, in the various war-bond drives, they created a lot of hoopla bringing in Hollywood actors and so on. There was a lot of money put into that. And you may be sure the cabinet was aware of spending that money. Mr. King at least had no objection to it. When you come to war bonds, that was in the hands of the Department of Finance, they had a budget for it. And they turned it over to the information people, to spend that particular budget as they saw fit.

Question: How were the different media coordinated? How did the government make sure that everything was tied together?

Turnbull: Of course they had the Wartime Information Board. They had a Minister in charge of Public Information. He wasn't very good, but they had one. And I presume that if he had any new projects that seemed dubious, he would bring them to the cabinet. The cabinet at that time, even though it was wartime, went into a lot more detail than a cabinet would go into now.

Question: Early in the story, The March of Time *made a film about the Canadian war effort, and it had a curious history. What was your experience of this?*

Turnbull: When *The March of Time* made a film in Canada in 1940, they did one of their usual excellent efforts, but they made the Canadian war effort look a little too good. And Mitch Hepburn, then Premier of Ontario, was feuding with Mr. King, the Prime Minister, and decided he didn't want him and his government to get all this glory. So he persuaded (I am assuming this, the evidence isn't clear that he did) Famous Players, who were distributing the film, not to show it. So when *The March of Time* said the picture was ready for release, and days and weeks went by and nothing happened, we began to delve into it and found out that the distributor, Famous Players, was not releasing it, but was using a variety of excuses. I then decided to play a little politics. Famous Players had a representative in Ottawa, on the Information Board. John Grierson was in Australia at that time, and this representative was actually in command of the Information Bureau. So I called him up and said, "It seems that Famous Players, the distributors, are becoming a cat's-paw for Mitch Hepburn. What I am saying now to you of course will never happen, but in order to put this situation into perspective, how would you feel if none of your Hollywood feature films got through Canadian customs because of certain technicalities, the same kind of delays that you are putting on this *March of Time* film? I don't think you would like it." Actually, I don't think he really believed that we would not do such a thing. So he got right on the telephone with his people in Toronto. Mitch Hepburn was told about this, and he instructed his board of censors, who were simply tools in his hand, to censor the thing. They refused to allow the film in. On what grounds, I'm not sure. I think in a vague way, he said the film was some kind of a lie that the public shouldn't be exposed to, but he didn't use those actual words. So then it became a *cause célèbre,* this *March of Time* film banned by Hepburn, the Premier of Ontario. Then we got on the telephone and interviewed Louis de Rochemont, the producer. And he said only once before in history had a *March of Time* picture been banned, and that was by Hitler, the man we were now fighting. This was a very good interview. We then arranged for the picture to be shown in Quebec and Manitoba, and the theatres would publicize the picture, saying, "See the picture banned in Ontario." Great Stuff. We were just a few years ahead of our time. Anyhow, this created a furor with Mitch Hepburn's cabinet. So they said, "Mitch, we can't stand this," and finally he released the film.

Question: What do you think of Grierson's performance as a public servant? He was working with creative media and with artists; how do you think he handled the duties and obligations of a public servant?

Turnbull: I think that Grierson represented a happy combination of idealism and a practical approach, with his eye on the main objective—to serve a purpose. He got good men. He had a great knack for picking talent. And he held on to that talent by giving them a reasonably free hand and full credit for what they did. If anything went wrong, he didn't rush around saying that idiot of a director did this or that, but would defend them. In his dealing with them, he would keep pointing out that they were there to do a job for the country, not there to do a job for themselves. They were not there to inflate their own egos, they were there to serve.

Question: How did he fare in the community of senior public servants? Did he fit into the landscape well?

Turnbull: Grierson kept his cool so well he could fit into any scene. He never became an integral part of the establishment, yet nobody had any impression that he was an outsider. Grierson was a real internationalist, and I don't think that anybody at any time felt: Here is a fellow who doesn't know us. I think the question might be what Grierson thought about the people, rather than what they thought about him. I think in the main he liked them. But I think there also were some who were phony, puffed up by their own conceit, and I don't think that kind of conceit ever impressed Grierson. That was just padding that he thought should be stripped away. But *he* didn't do it. He fitted in immediately.

Question: As a man in public service, do you yourself feel there is anything basically odd or inconsistent about having a structure within government that deals with the creative arts?

Turnbull: I don't know how you can have creativity aided with taxpayers' money without subjecting it to some type of structure; the problem develops if the administrators start fancying that *they* are the creators and want to take over the role of the creators, and I used the word "creators" in its largest sense. Administrators tend to think that they are superior beings, and they usually *are* paid higher. Years later I startled some people in the postal service when I suggested that there should be men employed who should in some cases get more than the Deputy Minister. This was heresy. I felt the same way about creative artists. Administrators should not take over the creative part of it and in many instances shouldn't necessarily be as well paid.

Question: Looking at the Film Board work, do you feel that by the standards of government performance and the public service, the work has been well and coherently done?

Turnbull: I don't see how you can in effect do it any other way. You can have an independent board, but an independent board is also made up of men and women and they too are going to bring in their prejudices or their own views. I don't see any difference between a board that is part of a government structure and a board that is independent of the government structure. They all have to work within a budget; presumably they all have to prove that they are doing a good job. If the job is good it stands on its own. For instance, I never felt that I was restricted by having to go through a certain amount of government red tape. Irritated, yes, occasionally infuriated, but I didn't think that I should be just that free to do anything I liked. . . .

Question: What about the use of federal money, government money, for what amounts to an effort of self-advertisement? Is there anything wrong with this kind of expenditure of public money, and what sort of ground rules should govern the spending of it?

Turnbull: Of course that's a broad question. . . . I think the rules are fairly simple. You make sure that you are not advertising a *government*. You are advertising—and I am using the word in a broad sense—a *country*. For instance, you are talking about the work of the National Capital Commission. If you extol one particular program, it looks as if you are praising the government that set up that particular thing. Instead you want to say that *successive* governments have supported the idea of beautifying the national capital. That takes the political element out of it. But if you play up politics, and say in the last two or three years the NCC has been given expanded funds and has gone ahead with a great vast program, people will say, "*Aha* . . . so the Trudeau government, or whatever government, is trying to pretend it's doing more than the other governments did." I think it is a matter of good sense and integrity rather than trying to set down rigid rules. I am against rigid rules, because then you start defining things. The more you define things, the more you limit them, and the less chance there is of accomplishing something.

The Film at War*

So there you have it. There are two sides to propaganda, and two sides to the film at war. We shall go on mobilizing the film to give the news and the story of a great historical event. In that sense we shall use it for all its worth to secure the present. But we shall also, I hope and trust, use the film more and more to secure the future and serve the still wider needs of the people of Canada.

War films, yes, but more films too, about the everyday things of life, the values, the ideals which make life worth living. We shall use the film, I hope, to give visual significance to the words of Mr. King when he said that the spirit of mutual tolerance and the respect for fundamental human rights are the foundations of the national unity of Canada.

In that way we may rescue, from these barren days of trouble, something we can hand on to the future.

* Statement by John Grierson (1940). Quoted from the National Film Board of Canada, *The War Years*, which is a collection of articles from the war era and a selected index of production. Edited by Peter Morris, *The War Years* was published in 1965 by the Canadian Film Institute as No. 3 in the Canadian Filmography Series.

Reaching the Audience*

About three hundred of the points served by the rural (film) circuits consist of farming areas populated by Canadian citizens of foreign origin. Here the real test of the documentary movie comes. Will these people respond to its stimulus? They turn out in crowds for the showings, but at first they seem to be merely passive spectators. A new movie technique, however, is proving effective in encouraging these and other audiences to come forth with their own opinions. This technique consists briefly in the presentation of a three-minute "discussion movie" in which four people appear on the screen in an informal argument centering on some topical theme. The National Film Board has now made "trailers" of this nature to follow the movies *Battle of the Harvests, Forward Commandos, Inside Fighting Russia*, and *Battle Is Their Birthright*. The last one has been particularly effective and has called forth much debate on the place of youth in modern society.

In such ways the motion picture with its visual impact becomes a gadfly to social discussion. It can relate one part of the nation to the other, as in *Coal Face Canada*; it can make local problems fit into the scheme of world events, as in *Battle of the Harvests*; it can serve as a spur to group activity, as in *The Peoples's Bank*.

That is how the value of the Canadian documentary movie appears, not as an entity in itself, but as part of a larger entity. Those who direct, photograph, edit, and prepare a film for 16mm distribution, are only the first participants in its creation as a living object. The men and women who finally bring it to life and useful activity are those who project that particular movie; in some small hall, some factory or club room, and so relate its values to local needs and aspiration.

* From an article entitled "The Projection of Canada," by Donald W. Buchanan, published in the University of Toronto Quarterly, April 1944.

On the Projection of Canada[*]

*Question: What do you consider to be first priorities in a national infor-
mation program?*
   Grierson: For me the departmental needs of Ottawa are the most important of the Film Board's duties. Ottawa has the key to the kingdom. It is in
the departments of Ottawa that the great frontiers of this country are
managed. I'm not thinking of it as one would of a socialist country, but
nonetheless the frontiers of management in agriculture, fisheries, mining
resources, and so forth all belong to Ottawa. The Film Board is required
not just to make films for the departments but to see that they, the whole
film industry, does its duty by the nation. . . .
   The Film Board of course has done tremendous things in creating an
image of Canada abroad. Let me say quite blatantly that in some countries
the only damn thing they know about Canada culturally is through the
National Film Board. So far as a cultural image is concerned, Canada's
only gift to the world has been the Film Board. And some people say that
in the Film Board, the only gift really is Norman MacLaren, who incidentally comes from my home village in Scotland (I once promised his mother
that I would look after him). The Film Board achievements have certainly
become known throughout the world. . . . It has become known in the
cultural fields, in the film festivals, by other people throughout the world.
   There are some films that really reflect the spirit and the tribal memory,
call it the tribal memory of Canada. But I think it is disappointing that they
have sought for the idiotic empty places of show business. I think that their
triviality in the pursuit of feature films is not to be recommended. I think
they wasted both their time and their money on many of these occasions. I
can't think that I want the boys at the Film Board to introduce me to (shall
we say) the nudities celebrated by the Swedish cinema. I don't want the
boys at the Film Board really to introduce anybody to nudities, because it
seems to me beside the point for an organ of government with so many
very serious, splendid things to do. . . .
   The Film Act can be a very important thing. And it may be, if you don't
mind my saying so, that the greatest export of the Film Board has been the
Film Act itself. It's been translated into many languages, it has become the
model of serious intention by the cinema in the service of government, all
over the world. You will find it translated in Chinese, you'll find it in all

* From an interview videotaped at York University, Toronto, 1970.

developing countries in Africa—they know the Film Act, whatever else they know. I was in Algeria last year talking to ministers there, and the one thing they knew was the Film Act. So when you talk about what is good or what is disappointing, I say that what is good has been the Film Board's service to the government with its initial intention of reflecting the country, Canada, to itself and to the world. The success of the Film Board has been in helping the External Affairs department to present the Canadian capabilities. The Film Board has been important in saying to countries of very different kinds, all over the world, that *the film is an instrument of great importance in establishing the patterns of national imagination.*

Question: We seem to worry a lot in Canada about our national identity, the Canadian character, this sort of thing. Have you any comments on what film itself has done in speeding up the process of creating an identity? Has film delayed the process because of the diffusion on our own screen, due to films from Hollywood?

Grierson: Like some other countries, you live under the shadow of a great and mighty neighbor. Your lines of communication, many of them, run from north to south, not from east to west. The sheer weight of American publication must affect the Canadian educational process, not only on the television level, the film level, but of course on the school level and from schoolbooks. I suspect in some of your schools you are teaching American history, not Canadian history. You have a problem because your results are limited compared to those of the great neighbor to the south.

There are other countries in that position. I grew up in a country in that position; Scotland had to be very emphatic about its identities in the presence of the great and mighty neighbor that was England. What we did in Scotland or what we tried to do in the old days—and I don't know if we do it today—was to *declare education a priority.* Wherever you've got a problem of identity like that, then you need to reestablish or reaffirm your own identity. Education becomes a priority; it is how you make the most of your people if you have limited resources. Nothing can compete with you if you're *educationally* in advance. By education I mean not only the education of the normal academic sort, whether at the university level, high school level or elementary school level. I think of education as a *process* which appears at many levels indeed. I think of education as very important at the university level, but I also think it is very important at the luncheons of the Rotary Club. I think of education not only as a matter of training people to have a professional craft of one kind or another, but also as a matter of having an imaginative front—it is on the imaginative front that people's affections and loyalties are created, and people's willpower is reaffirmed or established.

I think that America has made a great job of establishing an American identity. You may laugh a little at its overdoing of the Stars and Stripes, you may find them a little extravagant in their need to pronounce themselves 100 percent hygienically pure Americans, but damn it, it really is, I think, *that way*. Here in Canada you have the job of using every means possible to create an imaginative front for yourselves. You need to use education for your own present good and future welfare. It means of course that you've got to use the imaginative media, like television or radio or films, to the hilt. . . .

What about the Canadian himself? Have our films created a stereotype in the minds of people around the world? Have they established a kind of Canadian identity abroad? I doubt it. I mean, one doesn't take the claims of small countries very seriously. But do we really have to concern ourselves greatly abroad, with the description of smaller people? The Scotsman wears a kilt—well, that is not important. A Scotsman because he produces songs, yes—the Scotsman because he produced, as some people say, the best love songs, because they are translated into most languages. So the Scotsman has got an identity although he comes from a small country, because of his association with Robbie Burns. And he also has a certain identity because he is associated with first-class football, which is now an international game. Canada has an identity abroad with ice hockey. But I would doubt if the Canadian is easily separable from the American in the minds of most countries.

I would think that to solve this problem, one would have to follow Mackenzie King. One day Mackenzie King asked me if I realized that Canada was only a stretch of habitation to the north of our good neighbor to the south. And I said I understood that. And he said, "Wouldn't it be a great pity if we lost our sense of independence, if we freed ourselves from a sense of spiritual dependence on the motherland only to find ourselves fall into a state of spiritual dependence on our good neighbor to the south?" And I said, "Yes, sir." And then he asked, "Well, what do you propose to do about it?" And I replied, "I suppose the only answer is to look to the *North*." We conceived the idea to look to the North as a basic part of our policy in information. It was then that we began to conceive of the Pole as the center of the world, because it made Canada so much more important to be on the projection of the Pole. And of course the whole history of air development has helped this idea all along. But I would like to see Canada even more developed, the Canadian image even more associated with this conquest of the North. Command of the North represented by your very great achievements in air travel, your mastery of Northern climates, your capacity to build great hydroelectric construction in very severe weather, the building of dams in Abitibi and Kitimat. These are very great achievements. But you are not as much identified with the winter as the Russian is. It's the *Russian* with snow on his great boots, not the Canadian. That seems to be a mistake. I think that I would have had the snow on *my* boots if I was really concerned about being a Canadian. You asked me a question: how do you make the Canadian a different person from the American? I say by identifying a Canadian with what he has uniquely and differently from the American to the south. So this is a deliberate policy, and if people object to it, I think they are foolish, because the whole thing about Canada is that not only does it have a North, but this is a *part* of the Canadian's life. Canada can be many things, but what a Canadian is separately and distinctively is a child of the winter. He is not scared by twenty below, and you must try to think in between the simple publicity in which you want to emphasize summer, and the very propagandas which must see far beyond simple publicity, and think of the *identity* of nations, the *identity* of Canadians.

Sydney Newman (1)

One of the initial group of would-be Canadian film-makers recruited to the Film Board on its inception was Sydney Newman of Toronto. Newman, who was not blessed by a wealthy family or a classical education, had instead considerable talent as a painter, leftist political sympathies, a strong sense of the vernacular, unlimited self-assurance, and the divinely given quality of showmanship. These qualities made him ideal for film work, which he learned quickly and naturally. When television first got its start in North America at the end of the 1940s, he cleverly joined the Canadian Broadcasting Corporation at a very early stage of TV development in Canada. Here his native sense of dramatic and filmic possibilities soon flowered. He went to Britain in 1954 and entered upon an extremely successful and influential career in television drama, being at one stage director of Drama for the BBC, with the governance of almost one-quarter of that body's majestic annual budget. In 1968, Newman returned to Canada to become Film Commissioner and chairman of the National Film Board, the first alumnus of the organization to become its executive director.

In Ottawa during the early Film Board period, in Britain during the 1950s, and again in Canada after his return in 1968, Newman had frequent close contact with Grierson. Not many of Grierson's colleagues have had such sustained connection over the years in the varied areas of Grierson's activity.

We interviewed Sydney Newman in his office at the National Film Board of Canada. His office overlooks an awesome, turgid flow of heavy traffic grinding along the Boulevard Métropolitain, an axial highway cutting through industrial Montreal. The Film Board is itself virtually a large industrial plant, with laboratories, sound studios, theatres, machine shops, a commissary, distribution and production offices—all the panoply of an integrated film studio. Considered as a single entity, it is likely the largest government film organization among the nations of the Western or (as we say) peace-loving world.

Newman: Well, I was seventeen in 1939, and I went to a theatre, a movie house in Toronto, and they had a film in a series called *Canada Carries On*. There was the name of John Grierson as the producer, and I couldn't believe that it was made in Canada. I got in touch with Graham

McInnes, who was a writer and art critic; I was a painter, and he had written about my work. I wrote him, asking: is there a Film Board in Canada and is there a man Grierson in charge? He said yes. And I said, "Can I get work? I want to make films." He said, "Why don't you come up and get yourself into it and see what happens." I came to Ottawa, but Grierson wasn't there, he was off on one of his junkets in the United States. Ross McLean interviewed me; then a day later Grierson turned up and interviewed me. I had under my arm a great packet of my still photography and some films which he at that time couldn't bother to see. He looks at my paintings, my still photography, and he rejects 90 percent of it as being too arty. I'll never forget him turning the pages over, saying, "Too arty, too arty, very interesting but arty"; then he said, "Well, there might be work for you later on." . . .

And then of course I saw him over a period of four or five years from 1941 to 1945 in Ottawa in that old sawmill, the sawdust falling out of the cracks in the building. He dominated us entirely. I mean this was an incredible person who was so bloody certain of every damn thing he ever did, he never indicated that there was ever any doubt in his mind. Mind you, for myself, I always rather questioned the adoration that a lot of my mates here used to display, very subserviently going along with whatever he said. I was one of the kids around; I was a native-born kid. Some of his colleagues were pretty arrogantly English and they used to make us remember that we were sort of colonial kids who didn't know a sprocket hole from the proverbial hole in the ground. But Grierson had an incredible faculty of bringing out in us deep wells of understanding and responsibility.

He was insulting—I mean he used every possible technique to evoke a response. He quite often used to say to me, "Newman, you've got a B-picture mentality." Interestingly enough, I learned later he meant this as a bit of a compliment, because having a B-picture mentality meant having the common touch, and he attributed this to me; I was one of the more vulgar ones in those days.

Question: What about his social relationships among the staff? Did you meet with Grierson often?

Newman: His house was more or less open on Saturdays and Sundays, and some of us who were bolder and not afraid of his vigor used to turn up on Saturday afternoon. His marvelous wife, Margaret, somehow always managed to produce a ham and there was always whiskey and drink, and the odd cabinet minister of the Canadian government would turn up. There were we, young kids of twenty-three and twenty-four hobnobbing with senior civil servants or ministers of forty and forty-five, who were running the country in the middle of wartime, and he allowed us in fact to mix in with these decision-making people. This was tremendous for us. It opened vistas of a world that existed far beyond our own pitiful little concerns about montage and joining two pieces of film together.

As far as I could see at my level, he was arrogant, bold, and vigorous. He felt he knew what was right; these were the war years and he felt he knew about winning the war. I'll never forget that he chuckled with glee when Russia entered the war and Churchill declared he was going to fly to Moscow; I don't think Grierson ever liked Churchill—in fact I am positive he disliked him intensely. He chuckled with glee and danced that little prancing goose step of Hitler; and he said, "I can't wait to see Churchill going to Moscow and meeting Joe Stalin for the first time." Three days earlier Churchill, in print, had referred to Stalin as "that guttersnipe," and Grierson said, "I would love to see how Churchill is going to meet him and say: 'How do you do, Comrade Stalin.'"

.   .   .

It was always mysterious to me how his own wife Margaret could in fact bear him, because he was so obsessed by his work. At these soirees that took place endlessly at his house, his wife was always loyally there, feeding out the drink, the food, aiding and abetting the conversation, always being sympathetic. Whenever any of us would be extraordinarily angry at some rash decision that Grierson would hand down, she would always smile in a beautiful Mona Lisa–like fashion and say, "Yes, well, you know, you must understand, John is under pressure. I am sure that he means well and you mustn't take it unkindly," and so on.

. . . I remember one time where I was asked to make a three-minute little film about encouraging women to come into industry, to work in factories, on assembly lines and so on, because Canada had a terrific manpower shortage with a big war effort on. I made this film and I was following the edicts of the Department of Manpower; my commentary said: "Women, you owe it to your men on the front to work in the war plants; get out of the homes, do this, do that." Grierson was around on one of his rare occasions. He came down to the theatre and I screened the thing. It was only three minutes long, but before one minute was up he had leaped to his feet, run up to the front of the darkened theatre, pointed at the screen, and said: "Who are you to tell the Canadians what to do? Are you a fascist or something?" He began to berate me thoroughly, so for the whole course of this magnificent three-minute film with me pouring my heart out, he was berating me. Then the lights came on, and he was white-faced, livid with anger. I said, "I don't understand," and he said, "How dare you! You must never *tell* people what to do. You must say, 'Intelligent Canadians, intelligent Canadian women are today leaving their homes, going into the factories, and doing this and doing that.' Don't tell them what they *ought* to do. Cite examples, what they *are* doing." And I agreed with him. Then he said, "Give them a reason, *why* they are doing it, on their own impulse, and then they will understand it. Tell them they are doing it because they *are* intelligent and they realize that their husbands and their sons are knocking themselves out risking their lives at the front. *That* is the reason why people act in the way they should act, but don't *tell* them, because you demean them, you insult their intelligence." And it was a great lesson to me. At the end of that session while we were leaving the screening, he put his arm around me and said, "Don't take it too hard, I wouldn't talk to you this way if I didn't think you were worth it." Before I heard that, I was dying of shame and embarrassment. This was the way I think he handled all of us ignorant kids, told us how to go about life.

What I think excites me is the fact that England to him from 1927 up to the war was a kind of dummy run; it was in Canada where there was a kind of general innocence; here he was able to use all his experience in the real tough growing-up fights with the Treasury in England, with the various sorts of crown corporations, and all that he had learned there. He was able in our rather naive—and I use the word advisedly—*colonial* setup to be the kind of man he really wanted to be. He had the courage and the prestige, since he was so close to the Prime Minister in Canada, to be able to carry the weight, and he communicated this to all of us.

.   .   .

Believe it or not, I last saw him five days before he left Canada for the last time. I had just received from the Secretary of State in Canada the concept of a new film policy which involved certain radical changes in the role of the Film Board, in the role that was the direct heritage of Grierson. So I phoned him in this modest little hotel here in Montreal where he lived, and I said, "John, I have a piece of paper here, and I am trying to write a long reply. Would you, could you give yourself to me and help me hammer out a reply?" He said, "Great," and I said, "I'll come to you or you come to me"; he said, "Oh, I want to get out of this room." In twenty minutes he had reached my house by cab; he read the long document from cabinet on this particular suggested change in the Film Board. He and I sat there for four hours and argued about how I was to answer this piece of paper, and here he was now seventy-two. It turned out it was just five days before he flew back to England; he died six or seven weeks later. And he regarded the problems of the Film Board in the most realistic terms within the context of Canada today. He wasn't relating to the Canada of twenty or twenty-five years ago that he knew then. He queried me thoroughly; we had a terrible row; I didn't take a lot of his advice but in the process—and that is why he was such a marvelous, what is now called, social *"animateur"*—in the process of his querying me and arguing with me a marvelous kind of concept evolved as to how I was to counter and bring some wisdom to the secretary of state, and this was Grierson still in there punching with everything he had for the bloody Film Board that he helped create, because he wanted it to go on and he believed in it.

Education and the New Order

The essence and meaning of education is a recurring theme in Grierson's writing. We must understand where we are, what is happening, what is needed, what is required of us, says Grierson. Education is the process whereby these things are made known to us. It is a process that extends far beyond the schools and all formal institutions.

The following piece, written in 1941, reveals Grierson's philosophy of education—or better, his passion concerning education—with a rare eloquence and power. Thirty-five years have passed since he wrote it, at a time when World War II had just begun. It is a statement that arises from that apocalyptic struggle, and yet looks clearly ahead to a time after the war, when we would have to take stock and reconsider our human condition. The essay, given originally as a public speech in Winnipeg in 1941, is quoted by Mr. Forsyth Hardy in his book *Grierson on Documentary*. Perhaps no other statement by John Grierson conveys so lucidly and powerfully the substance of his belief, a striving for the rational and humane future of mankind.

Education is activist or it is nothing.

There is nothing I can think of so cynical today as to teach a boy that the world is his personal oyster for the opening, or talk as Lord Birkenhead did of the glittering prizes that fall to a flashing sword.

There is, and of course must be, a place for individual talents, but it becomes ever clearer that the heart of the matter today lies in teamwork and in unity. Individualism, that dream of so many centuries, has given us one of the golden ages. But what was so great a force in a simple world has been a nuisance in one more complicated. By its own bright energies, individualism has in fact created its Frankenstein. It has loosed energies and forces which it is, of all philosophies, least fitted to coordinate and control. We have arrived at an ironical situation. The spirit of competition which was so great a breeder of initiative yesterday has become only a disturber of the peace today. Rugged individualism, so honorable yesterday, is only rugged irresponsibility today. A philosophy in which nobody is his brother's keeper has become impossible when a decision by a board of directors hundreds of miles away will wipe out a town overnight and doom the inhabitants of a rich country to desolation and despair for years. We have seen just that, no less, in Scotland, Wales, and Northern England, time and again. I need not emphasize how, in international affairs, the philosophy of irresponsible competition, governmental *laissez-faire, laissez-aller*, and failure to plan has landed not towns but nations and continents in the deepest disaster in the history of mankind.

I know this may seem an exhausting analysis. It is a job that I do not relish doing, for when you deal with alterations that challenge the accepted and honored attitudes of society, the path is always dangerous. I am not going to pretend that I do not realize how totalitarian some of my conclusions seem. But I beg you to remember you can be totalitarian for evil and you can be totalitarian for good and totalitarian for the sake of humanity, if humanity is to be served. Some of us came out of a highly disciplined religion and see no reason to fear discipline and self-denial. Some of us learned in a school of philosophy which taught that all was for the common good and nothing for oneself and have never, in any case, regarded the pursuit of happiness as anything other than an aberration of the human spirit. We were taught, for example, that he who would gain his life must lose it. Even Rousseau talked of transporting *le moi dans l'unité commune*, and Calvin of establishing the holy communion of the citizens. So the kind of totalitarianism I speak of, while it may apply to the new conditions of society, has as deep a root as any in human tradition. I would call the philosophy of individualism Romantic and say we have been on a spectacular romantic spree for four hundred years. I would maintain that this other, totalitarian viewpoint is classical.

In our generation men's needs were never hard to see. They have to do with such simple matters as food and shelter and the good life for everyone and, more particularly, as a *sine qua non*, they have to do with the mobilization of men's will to these essential ends without any deviation whatsoever. These ends may have been forgotten in sectional selfishness and private privilege; and the privileged ones may have allowed every kind of complacent, urbane, cynical, and indifferent attitude to hide from them the primitive fact that their neighbors, national and international, have been starving and dying in their midst. Or it may be that the leadership has been depressed by the progressive difficulties of a complex world, has lost its willpower, and has wearily given up the task of leadership without abandoning its privilege.

Whatever the analysis, if education is to find its moral imperative, it must get back to the forgotten fundamentals of men's need and take upon itself the courage and the will to realize them. It will have to clear itself, in the process, of a lot of bric-a-brac so often called culture. For example, it will hardly get away with anything so easy as telling people that they are fighting for the old way of life, even if people are reminded of its unquestionable beauties and benefits. Education will not get away with it, because too many people believe in their hearts that the old way of life is the mother of chaos; and they will settle for something short of its beauties and benefits. We will have to give a plain demonstration that we have willed a new way of life and mean it. The details, even the plan, will not matter so long as the will is patent and the demonstration real; for of all men's needs, the first and most principal is hope, and it is of the essence of belief that the fact must follow.

The solution is straight and simple; and in an educational world which has come perversely to worship indecision and feel honored in unbelief, I hope I shall be forgiven my certainty. I suggest simply this, and it is the moral imperative for education as I see it.

Go out and ask men to mobilize themselves for the destruction of greed and selfishness. And mean it. Ask them to forget their personal dreams and pleasures and deny themselves for the obliteration of economic anarchy and disorder all over the world. And mean it. Mean it so much that men will know that no power on earth will stop you in your tracks. Tell them that in desperate unity and before God they will give the world a greater leadership—a more humanitarian new order—than the thwarted and vengeful people of Germany can be capable of. Say with the Prime Minister of Canada that "never again in our own land or in any other land will the gods of material power, of worldly possession and of special privilege be permitted to exercise their sway." Mean it, and mean it so much that the people will know that, as far as human fallibility allows, the age of selfish interest is over and done with. Say it and mean it and think it and act on it. Make it your religion; which is to say, make it your bond with the people. I haven't a doubt that they will accept the new loyalties and the new attitudes of sacrifice and effort without a qualm or a question. And I haven't a doubt whatever that they will march with you till the skies open and the future is born.

Ralph Foster

Newspapers and newspaper people played a large part in Grierson's world. His first studies concerning public opinion and public information were based upon the press and its workings. The press's inability to encompass all the complex aspects of contemporary events drove Grierson on to examine the potentialities of the film medium.

Many young newspapermen and women came to join the new film movement. Journalism is implicit in documentary. Research, the digging out of factual backgrounds, putting events in perspective, the evaluative methods of "news in depth"—all these are involved in the production of the factual film.

Visual impact, however, is not exclusive to cinema. The poster, the billboard, the logo, the symbol, the slogan in its visual layout—all these elements in the graphic arts can, like cinema, speak sharply and instantly to the passer-by. Grierson sought to utilize these elements directly in films (use of specially designed film titles, animated or graphic sequences, maps drawn according to a special perspective). Throughout his lifetime in film, Grierson was as concerned with exploiting the artistic effectiveness of these materials as he was with the principles of good journalism.

Ralph Foster, a journalist from the *Toronto Star*, was similarly preoccupied with graphic art and design and their uses. During the war years Foster and some others at the early Film Board—Robinson MacLean, Dan Wallace, Allan Field—brought in the sense of day-to-day journalism, the news events taking place in Canada in a period of explosive growth and change. These men also made contact with the established U.S. newsreel organizations in New York to ensure the placement of Canadian news stories in the U.S. national reels, which also (in the manner of *Time* magazine) entered Canada in the demure guise of a Canadian edition.

Ralph Foster is a very tall, big-built, quizzical man with piercing blue eyes and a hearty sense of humor, two attributes which he shared with Grierson. When the two walked together down a long corridor, each with his highly characteristic gait, one a rapid pattering step and one a leisurely long-ranging lope, the spectacle was very diverting to their colleagues. Foster is now retired, living in Toronto and Florida, and paints for his own enjoyment. We filmed him in his studio in Toronto, working on a large canvas in incandescent yellows: the theme of the painting was blinding sunshine reflected off still water, with motionless fishermen under their straw hats numbed by the glowing light surrounding them.

Foster: Most of the newspaper people developed an immediate affection for Grierson when they met him. He was really such a natural man in every sense, and they discovered surprising things about him. If they were interested in sports, they discovered that, curiously enough, Grierson the scholar was also aware of every prizefight in England, Europe, and the United States—for the previous twenty-five or thirty years. He knew who held what titles, and at which weight. He knew who fought on such and such a date, and who had won. And all this vast store of inconsequentia was all part of his bag of tricks. He knew it, and he used it.

One of the interesting people that Grierson was involved with was Arthur Gottlieb, who ran a motion-picture laboratory in Toronto, and built a considerable studio as well—which, come to think of it, had a steam bath in it. Arthur very often entertained visitors in the steam bath—three or four men sitting around, with beer or a whiskey and no clothes on, the sweat pouring off them. It was really quite a comfortable spectacle. Arthur was one of the people with whom Grierson talked about prizefights. Arthur had a rather special interest in prizefights because he had worked in a laboratory in New York during the gangster-ridden period, when in order to protect your franchise in the fight-film field, you damn well had to grab the film right from the cameraman, run it to the curb with a bodyguard on either side of you, and put it in an automobile full of armed men, who took it to the lab, processed it, and got it out to the theatres, since of course there was no television in those days. Arthur was the man who climbed the ladder, took the film from the cameraman, climbed down, and was ushered out by the bodyguards. But he was the last person in the world you would expect the academician John Grierson to associate with. They had great affection for each other. And they had a wonderful time together; I shared it occasionally, so I know.

But there's no doubt in my mind that Grierson was profoundly intuitive, socially and politically and in every other way. It's really the only way you can explain the fact that Grierson originated the idea to apply motion pictures to social problems. He was so intuitive in that regard that today it seems every university is training students in motion-picture production, high schools are assigning motion-picture projects instead of essays, and that sort of thing—all this Grierson anticipated—because film is being used today in exactly the way that he preached as a pioneer so many years ago.

Grierson with Ralph Foster (1944), Head of Graphics
for the National Film Board in Ottawa. Graphic design
in poster publicity and informational material has been an
important element at the Film Board from the start.

As for his sense of politics—no question about that. Grierson always said that the position of the public servant is one inch to the left of the party in power. To me, "one inch to the left" is a pretty clear description of the function of the public servant. It means that he has to be out in front in terms of progress, but not too far out in front. Not so far out in front that he attracts attention to the radical values in his ideas. . . .

Stanley Jackson

While journalism constitutes one important element of the documentary pattern, another of equal significance is teaching. The teacher is the channel through whom knowledge is imparted to the group, the community. One of the teachers who came directly from the classroom into films was Stanley Jackson of Winnipeg. He was an early arrival at the Film Board; the circumstances of his entry were quixotic, as he recounts. His adaptation to film has been an interesting one. From early efforts as a director, for which role he had a natural feeling and sensitivity, Jackson moved into writing, researching, advising, consulting, voicing, and (to use a loathsome contemporary term) conceptualizing film treatments and scripts. Like a true teacher, he has the gift of clarifying and simplifying his material; his films and commentaries are lucid and sharply defined. He has an archetypal Canadian voice—unforced, unaccented, somewhat wry, and with a natural "neighborly" sound—which can be heard on scores of Film Board documentaries and has been popular for some fifteen years. His voice is the opposite of rhetorical or theatrical, the opposite of the voice of the commercial radio announcer or the pitchman. Its acceptability in film reflects the swing in feeling away from the exhortation and emotion common during the war and the immediate postwar period, towards a more thoughtful, low-key kind of communication.

Stanley Jackson was recorded for the Grierson project at the Film Board in Montreal in 1972.

Jackson: I was a scholar at St. John's College, Winnipeg, teaching mainly high school history and English—that would be 1940–1941. And there was a phone call: I was to go to the Fort Garry Hotel. I was to spend the evening with a man who announced himself as "John Grierson," whom I had never heard of. I did not know anything about the documentary film movement. Anyway, down to the Fort Garry Hotel, where there was this extraordinary man who said he wanted to talk to me. And at this point George Ferguson—the editor of the *Winnipeg Free Press*, and later the *Montreal Star*—was there and two or three others. Let us say the most influential citizens of Winnipeg were present, all of them great talkers and all of them much older than me. I just sat by and had a very enjoyable evening indeed—a very stimulating evening. And all the while they talked about Canada and everything under the sun. So, the end of the evening—

and that was that. Whatever this man wanted to talk about, he never got around to it.

A few months later, exactly the same thing. I had moved to Toronto to teach at Upper Canada College, and again a phone call from the man Grierson, about whom I had now heard a great deal, to come down to the King Edward Hotel, as I recall. He wanted to talk to me. This was a precise repeat of the previous encounter. I remember the novelist Morley Callaghan and some other high-powered minds and some very great talkers were present, the Scotch flowed freely. And again, it was a highly interesting—oh, a fascinating!—evening, but I obviously had nothing to say. I was simply listening, of course! And then, perhaps a month later, there was *another* summons. I think this was probably to the same hotel. I've forgotten who was present at that encounter, but it was exactly the same performance as before. All I got to say was "Thank you very much." And that was it! About the middle of that school year there another phone call— Grierson phoned me at my school—from Ottawa. And he said, "I want you in Ottawa on Monday morning."

Question: There'd been no discussion?

Jackson: No discussion of anything! Of course I knew by now that there was a Film Board. A couple of friends of mine were at the Film Board. Anyway Grierson said I was to be in Ottawa on the Monday morning. This was absolutely, totally absurd. I was in the middle of the school year. I obviously couldn't do anything about it, so I called him back to say that— you know—I had my responsibilities and I couldn't consider dropping them to arrive at Ottawa Monday morning, but if he was still interested in me for the Film Board, that I would *like* to come and see what it was all about at the end of the school year, in June. So he said something typically Griersonian like "Oh, if you think it's more important wiping little boys' noses than saving the world . . . All right! Come and see me at the end of June." And so, indeed, at the end of June I went to Ottawa to see what it was all about. At this point Grierson was not in evidence.

That spring he had been told that if he didn't get completely away and *rest* for six months, that he would be dead. Anyway Grierson was away, I don't know where, I think Florida or Mexico. He was simply doing what the doctors said—it was absolutely essential if he was going to remain. So he did that and did not arrive back in Ottawa until the autumn. Meanwhile I had come to Ottawa and was given a job. This was purely for the summer holidays, a job doing film research, what amounted to economic research and so on. Ross McLean was the acting commissioner; he hired me and within two or three weeks I was out as a grip with a camera crew, and so on. I just got caught up in the machinery and I never got away!

And now Grierson was away and I didn't see him until he arrived at the Film Board and raced around the building. I thought, The man is crazy! The way he hires people. He shook my hand and said, "How are you getting along? What are you doing?" and then he said, "You have a great distinction in my eyes. You're the only person in my life that I've hired without hearing him say anything." It was obviously in his mind that he wanted to sound me out and almost certainly to indoctrinate me. We hadn't got around to that! He did realize the appointment that we should have had, had never really taken place—all I'd done was enjoy his booze.

Anyway, the Film Board at that point was a small, chaotic, struggling, very hard-working place, turning out a lot of film, but with Grierson into *every*thing, every detail. One got to know him—there were parties and so on. He was very close to his people. And very close to things that were being done. And of course working extremely hard. Oh—an extraordinary man!

Marjorie McKay

In the area of pure administration, Grierson himself made no claims. He launched the enterprise, collected the right talents and personnel, then infused them with his own brand of energy and vision, and thus, by a particular chemistry, formulated a team, a company of like-minded and complementary talents that would bring dedication and intelligence to their collective work.

Marjorie McKay, a woman of remarkable good sense and resourcefulness with an innate gift for management, was recruited to the Film Board in 1943 and rose to unexpected heights of responsibility, as she here recounts. Her tact and skill in restoring the respectability and good repute of the Film Board with that most awesome of all agencies, the Treasury Board of the Government of Canada, was outstanding. She describes something of the process.

I'm probably the only person who ever came to the Film Board by accident. I wrote a civil service examination for economists in Vancouver, passed it, came back to Ottawa, reported to the civil service commission and was sent down to the Film Board. And the Film Board said, "We don't know anything about all this. We don't need any economists. But look, civil service is paying your salary, so stick around."

So for the first two weeks I typed addresses on letters and stuffed envelopes. Then I got promoted to the filing department and worked there for a bit. This was July 1942, and on July 30, the controller, A. G. McLean, called me in and said, "Have you ever done a payroll?" and I said, "Yes," and he said, "I find we haven't anybody doing payroll, and nobody's going to get paid the end of the month." And he said, "I have to have it by tomorrow morning." (It was 1:00 p.m. at the time.)

Well, there was one list of the civil service people. My name was on that, thank God. And there was another typed list. And there was a stack of little pieces of paper, backs of envelopes, torn bits of scratch paper, with things on them like "Lou A. 65 per." Lou A. happened to be Lou Applebaum, the music director, and his salary was supposed to be sixty-five dollars a week. But I thought he was the office boy and I put him on at sixty-five dollars a month. He was very gracious about it.

I did that for about two months, I think, and then one day I got called into Grierson's office and he said, "You're running the stock-shot house library. Get down there." I didn't even know where the house library was, but I found out and went down, and Betty Brunke introduced me pretty well to the house library. The only difficulty was that Grierson was head of the Film Board but A. G. McLean was head of Administration, and A. G. McLean had never admitted that I was working for Grierson. (A little difference of opinion there.) So there I was doing cost accounting for A. G. McLean, and also running the house library for Grierson. But it was fascinating. Here was A. G. McLean—with Legg and Spottiswoode; they wanted to know what every film cost. At that time, there were no costs accumulated by film. There were just a few—about 5 percent of the cost. The rest was overhead. So you had 5 percent direct cost and 95 percent overhead and it became a question of getting that set up, working out time sheets, lab costing, optical costing, and so on.

This went on for a bit and then suddenly Grierson called me again and said, "You've left the house library. You're doing production management." Then Legg called me in and told me what he meant by production management (which was quite different from what Grierson had said, and quite different again from what A. G. McLean had said). But I started in on that anyway, and I stayed there about three months.

Then I had a fight with Grierson. I can't remember what I fought with him about, but I had a fight with him and said, "To hell with Grierson. To hell with the National Film Board." I went back to Vancouver and started trade-union-contract research. Well, I was enjoying that very much when I got a wire from Jim Beveridge and then a wire from Stuart Legg, followed up by one from Grierson saying, "Come back. We're sinking." So I thought, Well, hell, I can't even remember now what I was fighting about so I might as well go back. So I went back.

I thought I was going to get into production where I wanted to be, but instead I was called in and Wesley Green, who was Head of Distribution at that time, told me I was now Administration Manager for Distribution.

Then after Wesley left, Grierson said, "You know, we're in a bind. The labs in New York have been terrific to us, and the labs in Canada, they've pulled us through. They've printed masses of material for us. But now they won't print anything. They won't do anything for us. When I ask them they either hang up on me or they say, 'You don't pay your bills.'" So I started checking into it and it took a considerable amount of detective work, but I finally found, in the Distribution department, a filing cabinet stuffed with invoices. The whole bloody filing cabinet. The girl who was in that job didn't know what an invoice was, and all these months she hadn't known what to do with them, so she'd filed them. Fortunately she'd filed them by company, which was nice. It speeded the whole thing up. So that was done.

By that time I was really getting interested in Distribution; it was fascinating. At that time the rural circuits were active, and we were providing many film prints for national defense circuits. I was all enthused. But then the phone rang and Grierson said, "Get a taxi and come right over." So I got a taxi and got right over.

Meanwhile, A. G. McLean had left and had been replaced by Collins, who had just resigned that day. He'd cleared his desk out, and when I got there Grierson said, "You're supervisor of Business Management right now. Your office is down the hall. Take over." That included purchasing, stores, shipping, all the accounting, preparation of estimates, and everything else. No preparation. Just take it over. At that stage I really got introduced to estimates and preparing them.

But preparing estimates wasn't so bad. The hard thing was to calculate, to imagine ahead of time what possible questions Grierson was going to be asked on the floor of the House of Commons and to get the answers ready. And the thing that made it a little more difficult was the position of women in those days. Women did not go down and sit with the Commissioner on the floor of the House. Some man who didn't know any of the answers went down and sat there. So I had to sit up in the gallery with a messenger, and when a question was asked that I knew Grierson didn't have the answer for, I had to scribble the answer on a piece of paper and give it to the messenger; the messenger gave it to the page; the page had to go and give it to the man who was sitting with Grierson, who then gave it to Grierson.

From then on, I stayed in that position, although I managed to get a stretch down at Paramount Pictures to see how they did their cost accounting, in order to set up a cost accounting system here at the board so we would know at any time not just how much money had been spent on a film, but how much money had been committed for the film.

All this time I was still hoping to get into production. But I seemed to be getting further and further away from it.

Then about 1947 I took another year away from the board, this time with Stuart Legg in England on production, and came back again on a written promise that I'd go into production in Canada. I got back and two days later they announced the Parliamentary Commission on the Film Board, and less than a month later, Ross McLean, who was then Commissioner, was replaced by another commissioner, and there was just no hope. I was stuck. And I was stuck in business administration for another two years, including the writing of a new Film Act.

Then finally I got into what was called Production Research, which was absolutely fascinating. At that time, it involved surveying any given field of subject matter, and deciding what was of interest in that field for Canada.

For instance, *The World of Work* series was one, and what I did there was to read anything about it I wanted, get any books I wanted, and find out what subject areas were of particular interest and importance to Canada, and then decide what possible film could come from that, and prepare a very rough treatment for each film.

I stayed with that until we were no longer making films of that kind. About that time my health packed up anyway and I left the Film Board.

Boris Kaufman

Some film-makers have gone from documentary into feature film. Some who work on the technical side of films have done likewise—cameramen, sound recordists, designers, optical- and special-effects men. The skills are common to both fields of film.

Boris Kaufman's career is of unusual interest in this sense. He is one of the great film cameramen. He comes from a family now established in film history. His own work has moved from the avant-garde, to the independent (prewar) French feature film, to documentaries in Canada and United States, to New York-based feature films characterized by their authentic and strongly atmospheric locations. Hollywood alone he has avoided. Kaufman is well known in the United States for his close collaboration with Elia Kazan on many films. We filmed him in a series of "walk-shots" on a wooden pier stretching into New York's East River, in view of the Brooklyn Navy Yard and the passing tugs and tankers. Tied alongside were aged ferryboats, lightships, and schooners, elements of a new maritime museum being completed for the city of New York.

Here again there were practical problems. In speech, Kaufman is diffident, tentative, and slow-spoken. He still has a strong Russian accent, with French overtones. The background noises of our riverside setting added to the difficulties of sound recording. The problems of selection and continuity which the film rushes presented to the editors proved insurmountable. The length of footage required to include a fully rounded statement, free from any technical fault in picture or sound, was too great to be accommodated in the final cutting copy. This interview therefore does not appear in the film.

Kaufman: My brother is Dziga Vertov. I think enough is known about him as an early pioneer of a certain way of film-making in the Soviet Union. As you know, he rejected the help of other media like theatre, and maintained that cinema is a new, self-sufficient medium with its own vocabulary. His approach was that you shouldn't ask people to *act* but to be themselves, and as a matter of principle *capture* the event unawares. The same kind of principle applied for me in *A Propos de Nice.** We stopped shooting as soon as people became aware of being shot. In some cases we

---

* A film made in 1929 by the youthful Jean Vigo, French avant-gardist of cinema, in collaboration with Kaufman. It represents an early effort of cinema verité documentation, plus a satiric and ultimately moral intention.

were hiding the camera, and in some cases the camera could be visible, but people were unaware of it.

I left my family early and wound up in Paris, where I spent my adolescent years. I started to work in the film medium in Paris. Both my brothers remained in Moscow and are in the film world, quite important in the development of film history.

In 1941 I arrived in New York. When I came over to America I didn't know if there was any film production in New York, and I was without work. At that time Grierson found out that I am in New York and invited me to Canada. So I arrived in Canada in 1942, the spring of '42. Grierson told me that he knew my work in Europe and this was the reason that he called me. I felt flattered. He explained what this Canadian Film Board was about and introduced me to the early nucleus of young people. They had assembled from all over Canada, and they were all more or less inexperienced. It took me a little time to get familiar with the program, and my English was very weak. But it was exciting to discover a new country and it wasn't doing the same thing that I had always done before. What I found was documentary style film-making. Grierson trusted his young people, including myself, without interfering and just relying on their own ability to handle graphically the subject matter, whatever it was. This made it easier. They were enthusiastic, which compensated for their lack of experience. I was supposed to be teaching at the same time as shooting films, and this may be the best way to learn. I didn't even realize that I was teaching, but I was given credit for having done some experimental work when I was young. I myself started in the French avant-garde and learned the craft first by just experimenting with the camera. Just walking around Paris, I learned how to capture the essence of things, to translate them into cinematic language. My first picture in Paris was called *Twenty-four Hours in Thirty Minutes*. I did it with Jean Lodz; he had never made a picture before, and I had never made one. So we were lucky that our picture held the screen in an art theatre for six months, and we got financial credit, which allowed us to continue. Then several others were made the same way. We made a picture about a long-distance runner. And we treated it visually in a certain way, trying to make visually plausible the inward effort of the runner, an effort to surpass himself. And I remember my idea to do it with the camera, to suggest his own body leading him. I also used a lot of slow motion to show the mechanics of his legwork. Later I got a letter from Jean Vigo. He wrote and asked me to show my work, and when I did, he invited me to consider making a satire on a town where wealthy people, becoming fat, were walking about and lying in the sun. This was *A Propos de Nice*. It was a documentary. In the pure sense, right.

Question: When in Canada during the war, what did you think about the Canadian theory of making documentary film? Did it seem workable to you? Were you conscious of the particular style they were trying to follow in the Film Board work?

Kaufman: The best I could do on many of these assignments was just to capture the event on film. It was mainly journalistic work because we ourselves had no control over how it would be edited later on. Therefore it was documentary material, to be shaped later on by others into the series called *Canada Carries On.*

Question: I don't suppose you had any idea that you were also training cameramen who would in turn train other cameramen, and that in fact you were establishing a kind of school?

Kaufman: This I didn't anticipate, I just did my best and I was taken up by the work. I was discovering new things myself, for you always learn. As a matter of fact, it proved to be useful later on for me when I had to face similar working situations here in this country, when I made my first feature in New York, *On the Waterfront,* one of the first major pictures shot entirely on actual locations, not in the studio. I tried there to make use of some of the documentary methods and possibilities we had used in Canada.

I was really surprised to see how Grierson managed to bring so many talented people together in a country where cinema practically didn't exist before. They all had the desire, enthusiasm, and potential. They were all potential film-makers. Probably, indirectly, I taught some of them technical skills; otherwise I was taken into the Film Board to shoot documentary films with very young Canadian directors. The difference between the French documentary pictures and this specific war propaganda film work that I was doing in Canada was that the Canadian films had a purpose to *inform* the public of Canada and also the people of other countries. This is also the difference between the Film Board and the U.S. Office of War Information, where I started to work after I left Canada. That very valuable documentary work done in the U.S.A. was not available to the American audience for some reason—some idea about misuse of taxpayers' money. Those U.S. films were destined to be shown only abroad.

Question: Have you seen The Sorrow and the Pity *recently?*

Kaufman: Yes, it was done by the son of Max Ophuls. I knew his father. It's a sad picture, I think it is very true. Collaboration is sad. But then the self-sacrifice by the people, trying to save other people, was also represented. We too retreated in France and I saw on the roads ten-ton trucks abandoned and baby carriages and stranded automobiles and all this. But I never returned to Paris. I went south and lived in Antibes near Nice. I was hoping to find some work but it was nonexistent.

Question: What was your contact with Grierson and the British film group?

Kaufman: I knew about the British film group in the 1930s, as a matter of fact I was in London at one time. I don't remember if I met Grierson, but I met Cavalcanti, who was part of it. And he showed me samples of the work of the British film-makers. This was my early contact, so when Grierson invited me to Canada later on I wasn't completely unaware of why he did it. I suppose he did it simply because he saw something in my own previous work that made him think I would be valuable for the film work in Canada. *A Propos de Nice* Vigo and I did together, shot it together and edited it together. But the later picture, *Zéro de Conduite*, was entirely Jean Vigo's idea and my function was simply that of the closest collaborator and cinematographer.

Question: Do you think the documentary idea is an English kind of expression? Does it lend itself to French styles and approaches to work? Or do you think now it is simply international?

Kaufman: I think that cinema is an international medium and there is no basic difference between documentary film-making in France and in England. The only difference, as I mentioned before, is making a complete documentary where the subject matter is a complete entity. It was different from the fragmentary shooting in Canada, during wartime, which was shaped later by other people into the final film.

A Note on the Aesthetic Aspect

1

I have been correctly associated with the Message rather than the Medium. There have been moments when I've said the Hell with the Message and had rather an affection for the Medium, but I was always scared that I might be found out, so I was careful to say the Hell with Art. The more I pursued it, the more I was careful to denounce my own pursuit of it.

JOHN GRIERSON

2*

The penalty of realism is that it is about reality and has to bother for ever not about being "beautiful" but about being right. It means a stalwart effort these days: one has to chill the mind to so many emotional defences of the decadent and so many smooth rationalisations of the ineffective. One has even to chill the mind to what, in the vacuum of daydreams, one might normally admire. In our world, it is specially necessary these days to guard against the aesthetic argument. It is plausible and apt to get under the defences of any maker in any medium. But, of course, it is the dear bright-eyed old enemy and by this time we know it very well. Documentary was from the beginning—when we first separated our public purpose theories from those of Flaherty—an anti-aesthetic movement.

What confuses the history is that we had always the good sense to use the aesthetes. We did so because we liked them and because we needed them. It was, paradoxically, with the first-rate aesthetic help of people like Flaherty and Cavalcanti that we mastered the techniques necessary for our quite unaesthetic purpose. That purpose was plain and was written about often enough. Rotha spent a lot of time on it. *We were concerned not with the category of "purposiveness without purpose" but with that other category beyond, which used to be called teleological. We were reformers open and avowed: concerned—to use the old jargon—with "bringing alive the new materials of citizenship," "crystallising sentiments" and creating those "new loyalties from which a progressive civic will might derive."*

. . .

I look back on Munich as representing a milestone in my own outlook on documentary. From that time the social work in which we had been

---

* Excerpt from an article by John Grierson in *Documentary News Letter.*

engaged seemed to me relatively beside the point. Munich was the last necessary evidence of how utterly out-of-category our English political thinking was and how literally most of our political leaders did not know what it was all about. From that point it seemed clear that we had, willy-nilly, to relate the interests of the English people to new world forces of the most dynamic sort—physical, economic and ideological.

I am one who believes in personal creative talent and in the obligation of society to employ it and develop it, but under conditions. I place against the right of the "person" the duty of the person to serve men's needs, which must always appear in the guise of living reality. I allow, however, that the priority of need can always be argued and that the deeper needs of mankind will not always be the apparent ones. For example, it is possible to maintain that the disintegration of the image in Cézanne and the abandonment of perspective in abstract painting represent an important directive to modern thought and appreciation. It is also possible to maintain that the nobility of line and the harmony of masses in Cézanne and Picasso overrule all question of representation—non-perspective or otherwise. Yet neither was at first allowed by the current aesthetic. Such manifestations I account as representing the creative leadership of the new forces of thought and appreciation which attend changes in technological pattern and therefore of the pattern of human relationship in society.

But this difference from the current aesthetic which is "ahead of its time" is not in any wise a justification for the "personal right" of the artist to express himself as he pleases. If the "personal inspiration" or "personal right" represents a nostalgic return to human relationships and evaluations which are not longer possible within the technological economy, they represent, for all their attraction, a subversive element in society which is the antithesis of creative leadership.

It is obviously not sufficient to "look in one's heart and write." The principal law governing the development of art in our time is that art, however it may look in its heart—and who can avoid it?—must find there what men in reality live by. They surely live in and by the creation of tomorrow.

Stuart Legg

Of the group of Englishmen whom Grierson brought to Canada to help produce the first films of the new National Film Board, probably Stuart Legg and Stanley Hawes were most influential. Of the others, J. D. Davidson, an experienced London cameraman, served not only as a functioning cinematographer, but set up and taught the initial group of young Canadians new to film and with little previous experience in camera work. Raymond Spottiswoode, author of the well-known *Grammar of the Film* (1936), came up to Ottawa from California and assisted in an all-round capacity as a technical planning officer, supervisor, and film producer. In addition to making a large number of films, Hawes and Legg personally schooled many young Canadian recruits in the essentials of scripting, shooting, and editing.

Hawes and Legg brought to their own film work and to their teaching a distinctively British sense of workmanship, emphasizing careful attention to detail in every department of film production. Young film people today display an almost innate understanding of film principles, due largely to their immersion from childhood in the TV medium, but in the early 1940s there was no television. Film construction and film theory were still a kind of mystical knowledge, secret skills to be learned at the feet of a master on an apprenticeship basis. Many of the film people who worked under Hawes and Legg in the early days of the Film Board have become extremely able and assured film craftsmen in their own right.

Legg's emphasis was chiefly on film editing, the reduction and shaping of film material into an organic unity. He had a tremendous sense of the individual film image, its dynamic and compositional aspects, its visual and psychological impacts, its immediacy and power. This derived partly from his understanding of the dynamics of Russian film-making during the great period of Eisenstein and Pudovkin, and partly from a rigorous intellectual discipline of his own which he enforced upon himself and his coworkers. Legg generated a great deal of tension when plunged into the periods of maximum creative intensity in film work. One such period was the final sound-recording session. In the 1940s the recording process was infinitely less controllable and flexible than it is now, and consequently fraught with anxiety. The atmosphere at this recording session could be described as combining the solemnity of a religious initiation and the anxiety of a difficult childbirth.

Legg's consistent discipline and care, his awareness of the film image

Stuart Legg, one of the early group of British documentary
film-makers, came to Canada to assist the setting-up and
training process at the new Film Board in 1940.

and of an essential pattern and progression in the arrangement of the film
sequences, have been implanted in a number of Canadian film-makers
and have come to characterize the continuing work of the National Film
Board over the past thirty years.

We filmed Stuart Legg amid the stone monoliths and green burial
mounds of Avebury in Wiltshire. We felt that no other landscape could be
more anciently or authentically British in nature. Legg lives a few miles
away in a country cottage of great charm in the village of All-Cannings,
near Devizes. Retired from film, he writes occasional works on historical
themes (the Mongol invasions, the Battle of Trafalgar) and pursues his
interest in history in a gentlemanly fashion.

*Question: In that GPO period, the 1930s, what was the mood of the
time?*

Legg: Left. Young people were left in those days, probably more
orthodoxly so than now. That's all there is to say about it.

Question: How did you feel as a group about future prospects, about the state of the nation, about the international position?

Legg: Well, of course there really wasn't any international position in those days. I mean as far as documentary was concerned, it was national, it was local to the country. It was a complicated situation moving into a possibly revolutionary situation. There was the depression, there was enormous unemployment, with the whole economy rather undermined, and so on.

Question: But in terms of today and the mood of students today, would you describe your group at that time as a kind of revolutionary group? Or was it more within the established framework?

Legg: It was within a framework, but in some senses it was a movement of protest. But it was a movement of protest with a constructive approach, seeking solutions.

I think that very much of what we were aiming at and preaching and prophesying and so on has since become a matter of legislation, which was perhaps a very difficult thing to have happened. Because there is nothing like winning elections to take the wind out of a minority movement.

Question: During the war years in Canada, you produced the film series which was, I think, almost the first one to receive a really extensive theatrical distribution for a substantial length of time. How did it start? How did you achieve distribution in theatres?

Legg: World in Action grew out of a smaller, local monthly series in Canada. I think one of the principal factors was that United Artists, who were the distributors, happened at that time (in 1941) to be short of product. And they were quite glad to take a series of two-reel short films and to be able to rely on them. I think in a way that was the piece of good luck that launched the whole thing. And obviously Grierson was a key factor in it, in that he promoted it by his knowledge of the American industry. Of course the action was based in Canada and the films were primarily addressed to Canadian cinemas, about seven or eight hundred Canadian cinemas, which was most of the cinemas in the country. But it went very much beyond that; I doubt if it would have been justifiable to make these particular films unless they had a wider field to speak to.

Question: These films were commercial products—that is, they paid their way?

Legg: Yes, I suppose they did, they probably just about met their costs or a little more. They had about six thousand cinemas in the United States and a certain number in other countries, in other parts of the commonwealth. We were very much feeling our way because it was the first real theatrical enterprise that Grierson had embarked on. There was a *World in*

Action unit in the National Film Board with two editors, Tom Daly and Gordon Weisenborn, and Margaret Ann Adamson researching and collecting film material, a very vital process. At that time during the war there was an enormous availability of film material, of actual film material shot by Allied cameramen on all the war fronts.

Question: How did the small production unit keep up with the delivery schedule?

Legg: Oh, in a general state of chaos. We were all learning as we went along. There we were trying to make a monthly series of two-reelers to feed into about seven or eight thousand cinemas on really very small resources and very small budgets. The easy thing was the film material, because at that time there were vast resources of film being shot all over the world, by the U.S. Signal Corps, by the British Ministry of Information, by the Free French Newsreel, and by others. There was all the captured material from Germany and Italy, and then later from Japan; there was also Russian material; it was an absolutely Tolstoyan panorama of the world in conflict; one would just sit and screen twenty, thirty, forty thousand feet at a time and then begin to whittle it down, narrow it, and see what you could use to express certain aspects of your theme. It is all a question of imagery, you see. We shot practically nothing ourselves. As to the style that evolved, I never concealed my admiration for *The March of Time*. I had indeed worked a little with them, and I always thought they had hit on a way of presenting important things that was quite new. This was in their first ten years or so.

Then I think another considerable influence was the distributors. The man in charge of it at United Artists was a chap called Dave Coplan, who used to come up to Ottawa to see the film rough cuts. He was tough; he was simply concerned with distribution and whether it would work in box-office terms or not. And we would see a rough cut and there would then be a long silence, during which Grierson and I sat waiting, and then he would say, "Do you think I can *sell* that?" And back we would go into the cutting room with about twenty-four hours to spare and try to produce something that Dave Coplan could sell. That meant an element of drama, of conflict, and all the rest of it. A very considerable influence also, though he probably didn't know it, was James Reston of the *New York Times*, whom I consulted whenever I was in a state of mental muddle. He always came out with words of wisdom. I remember one particularly difficult passage, how to bring some item of international politics onto the screen, and Reston said, "Always remember that there is a *reason* in history for everything." Of course then you began to dig back a bit and to look up certain events, and it all comes to life in a magical sort of way. These were all elements in

Tom Daly, former apprentice to Stuart Legg, has in turn trained many film-makers in a thoughtful and analytical approach to film-making.

working out a style that we developed as we went along, on a purely ad hoc and improvised basis. But it came out of the framework of what we had to deliver. We had two reels, twenty minutes each month, to put on the screen—an editorial. These things weren't *films*, they were screen editorials on some aspects of international strategy or international politics—the background, the *pattern* of events rather than the event itself, how the events related together, and twenty minutes to do it in. This meant that every shot you put on the screen had to *tell*. We tried to discipline ourselves never to use a shot unless it had about three degrees of revelation in it. This was simply for the sake of saving time on the screen. Then we had to reason that nobody was going to sit and watch these things—and Dave Coplan assured us of that—unless there was a degree of *tension* in them. And so one found oneself faced with the question of making tension, providing tension, all the way through.

As I said, the cutting was always tense and was always compressed, as much as one could make it, simply for reasons of the twenty-minute length.

Then one tried to get another dimension into that compression and tension, in the writing. No words were ever wasted, if one could help it. Every word had to tell, and every word was part of the film. The words were not a sort of dissertation, divorced from what was happening on the screen. They were closely connected, every word where possible falling on a cut between scenes, to add to the impact and the force of presentation. I think this is largely from Eisenstein. You know the conflict, the impact of two shots juxtaposing, exploding into a third entity.

Then we had to record in a certain very primitive way, because there weren't the technical resources to do otherwise. We never had more than two sound-track dubbers. There was a sound-effects track, usually put together by Gordon Weisenborn in the dead of the night. There was a music track, provided by the very fertile musical mind of Lucio Agostini in Montreal. Then Lorne Greene came up from Toronto to add his impressive voice on top of the whole thing. And we recorded it spontaneously, a thousand-foot ten-minute take complete, right through. You couldn't patch it at all. I think this itself created another element of tension, because everybody was on their toes.

Question: What about the choice of themes, the topics? You worked with Grierson and collaborated and discussed—how did it go, what was the process?

Legg: It depended what was going on in the world at that time, and what appeared to be in the process of becoming the most important stages in the war, important areas geographically and so on. This could be either military or political. The overall idea was to see world events through Canadian eyes, to interpret them from a Canadian viewpoint—and so help to secure for Canada her due place as a power of rising importance.

We were asked on occasion to make films by the External Affairs Department and other departments who were concerned. I think Grierson contributed enormously to the shaping of the films. As I say, he did a wonderful job on promotion, but he also contributed in the sense of *speculation.* He was enormously interested in the possibilities of related events, events at that time, and what would come out of them. And he would speculate and speculate, and we would sit together over endless bottles of rye at 30 Cooper Street in Ottawa and I would try to take out of the speculations some ideas that appeared to be more possible or likely than the others. It would all come together in that sort of way.

Question: This was for theatre audiences, and they were quite tough. You were providing very concentrated information. Did you aim the film at a certain level? What determined the way you addressed the films?

Legg: We were *informing,* but as dramatically and as interestingly as possible, for the theatrical audience. And that meant doing it within the limits of what the box office would take. I think one had audiences in mind all the time, from start to finish. It was never a question of looking into one's own introspective mind, that kind of thing. It was highly extroverted.

Stuart Legg played a major part in building the production team at the National Film Board, while delivering a steady flow of incisive editorial films for commercial distribution.

Question: Did you sometimes see the films in theatres and get a sense of the audience response?

Legg: Yes, yes. And one would be quite often guided by that sort of thing. Like silences that would fall in the wrong place, or sometimes silences when you could hear a pin drop. The two films that I found most interesting were first of all *Geopolitik*, which as far as I know is the only time that the geopolitical theory of the Germans was put on the screen. As you remember, it was elaborated by Haushofer and in turn derived to some extent from ideas of Sir Halford Mackinder. And the other film was *Global Air Routes* [1944], which was particularly interesting from the Canadian viewpoint because it dealt very largely with the aerobilities, so to speak, of the Arctic. And I think the film reasonably accurately foresaw the shape of the postwar airlines, and particularly the commercial flying across the Arctic.

Question: How did you work with the film material captured from the Germans?

Legg: As far as the German film material was concerned, it just walked away. You couldn't fool around with it, it was majestic. There were exceptional films, *Triumph of the Will* and some of the other big Nazi films, and they kept their own shape and being, always.

Question: So how would you define the way you made use of such film material? For example, in your film The War for Men's Minds?

Legg: The objective was to describe the propaganda machines of the world as they then existed, and then try to transcend them, and point out that this was a war that was also going on in people's minds, and what people expected as a result of their participation in the war. There was a four-reel version of the film which was very editorial and went a good deal into the failure of certain of the propaganda machines. The British Ministry of Information came in for considerable castigation. The four-reel version was a sort of almost private, satiric performance, but it was then theatricalized into a two-reel version which Dave Coplan bought.

Question: This is an interesting exercise for an information machine itself to be doing.

Legg: I suppose it was, and again I suppose it was one of the very few efforts to do that on the screen.

O Canada! We Stand on Guard for Thee

During the war years and in the early postwar period, the association between British and Canadian film-makers of the respective government units, the Crown Film Unit and National Film Board of Canada, was essentially one of comradeship and solidarity, but it was not wholly free of rivalry or rancor. A number of British film-makers, directors, and cameramen made brief expeditions to Canada, usually for wartime filming purposes. Grierson's sister Ruby, accompanying and filming a group of children being evacuated to Canada for safety in 1942, was lost at sea when the liner *City of Benares* was torpedoed.

The Canadians received the new British films and studied them respectfully, for the volume of British production was large and the documentary medium itself was gaining in professional technique. British production was more polished and refined than the Canadian at this period, since the Canadian units were relatively new and had to compensate with vitality and innovation for what they lacked in experience.

Grierson stoutly championed the Canadian efforts and did not hesitate to utilize—some would even say pirate—film material from the British productions, incorporating such material into the wartime Canadian films without acknowledgment. The British film-makers were, understandably, frequently outraged by this piecemeal exploitation of their own considerable creative efforts. In terms of usefulness the British material had great value on Canadian and U.S. screens, yet in their original format the British films were often not wholly suitable for North America. The reportage aspect of Britain at war, the human and emotional value of the film material, was important, and to take the most advantage of it in North America it was necessary (according to Grierson) to reshape it and reissue it in the format of Canadian or North American films.

There was therefore some small residual rancor on the part of the British film community as far as the upstart efforts of the Canadians were concerned, and perhaps a degree of condescension; certainly not hostility, for there were many personal and professional friendships spanning the ocean. In any case, at one stage in 1948 the British *Documentary Film News* carried a somewhat lofty review of a number of recent Canadian documentaries that had been screened in London. The review panel was a group of seven, and in his rebuttal Grierson jumped upon their collective judgment with happy ferocity. His letter was written after his departure from Canada, but his defense of the Canadian work and its purposes reveals his own attitudes concerning the public role of documentary and the practical requirements that films must meet in order to be distributed effectively among wide audiences in commercial cinemas.

To the Seven-Headed Board of Review of DFN*

SIRS: When you set up that Reviewing Panel, I had my doubts as to how you would fare if some of your less composite selves got the gang into a judgment that was seriously challenged. This, so to speak, is it. If you tell me your composite self has no body to be burned, and no soul to be damned, you had better listen a moment, for I am going to have a shot at both. I am concerned, if you please, with the page of criticism on recent Canadian films in your January issue. I am concerned for two reasons. The first is that I was once associated with the National Film Board in a local, more or less Red Indian capacity, and have a regard for the people who work there, and I could not believe on the face of it that they were as bad as you compositely, or uncompositely, said they were.

The second reason is that I went to see four of the seven films you reviewed and now say quite simply, for what it is worth, that your criticism was thoughtless, and from any serious point of view, either in documentary leadership or documentary criticism, inadequate.

.   .   .

I have in my time kicked some films around, but I doubt that I ever was totally sore about seven in a row and when I see seven good men and true being sore about seven in a row, I find it quite a phenomenon. I even doubt if it is possible, either in good criticism or good manners.

Good manners we shall leave aside, except to say that the Canadian boys can be articulate too, and it does nobody any good to be superior, and start a slanging match over each other's films which no one can win. Who, for example, is anyone in documentary to talk about a 'mere programme filler' when so many of the damn things don't even manage to hit a theatre programme? Whatever their virtues or failings, the Canadian films referred to did manage to do just that.

.   .   .

Tomorrow's Citizens is another, more serious matter altogether. The task was to produce a serious film editorial for theatres on a world subject;

---

* Article, "O Canada! We Stand on Guard for Thee," by John Grierson published in *Documentary Film News*, March 1948.

in ten-minute length. To my knowledge, it had never been done before and represented an experiment which was important to all of us. I have, myself, been so technically interested in the problem that I must have seen the film seven or eight times. Your review does not seem to be even conscious that in seeing a ten-minute theatre discussion of educational principle and ideology, it was seeing a very rare bird indeed, not to mention a very literate account of the ever-recurring gap between technological progress and educational substance.

There could be a deal of argument about the formula used. My own complaint is that the film proceeds too much by assertion and too little by easy illumination; but I'm damned if I can see at this stage how a one-reel editorial form can do otherwise, any more than the shortened editorial forms of, say, the *New York Daily News*.

The tabloid shape tends to a propaganda shape and it is true that *Tomorrow's Citizens* hits you on the head and is done with it. But when your review talks of 'biting off more than it can chew' and being 'slick, shallow and smug' this, too, is proceeding by assertion and with a vengeance. In my view, it is not 'shallow' because in fact it does raise what has been one of the profoundest problems before education since Marx first posed it in *Poverty and Philosophy* a hundred years ago. Nor is a film 'slick and smug' which goes to the pains of putting the subject within a world framework which includes Fundamental Education, and does the courtesy of including an almost incredible variety of international illustration.

I would have thought, among other things, that a film which attempted to describe the British documentary school's theory of 'bringing the world alive to the citizen' was worthy of greater consideration. That apart, I would certainly have expected a professional journal to take note of the superb use of sound to pace and punctuate the narration, the extraordinary economy and integration achieved by the development of the visual metaphor, and the deft editorial violence of, say, cutting 'the proper study of mankind is man' into the baby chittering to death after Hiroshima.

However these one-reel editorials develop—and we shall hit the theatres everywhere if we can develop them simply, clearly and dramatically—here, I suggest, is an object lesson in what a pioneer effort involves in the matter of technique. It should not have been missed as such, if only to develop the appropriate argument and clear the ground for further effort.

. . .

What all this amounts to is not that everything from Canada is good. I love Canada dearly, but in some respects, it is not good at all. I say this just to demonstrate that I can be as stuffy a character as your composite self in certain matters Canadian.

I have the impression, for instance, that Canada is not very knowledge-able about political philosophy or the law, especially in the higher branches of these disciplines, though on the other hand it is enormously good at economics. It is somewhat crude in parliamentary debate and there are more cockerels growing on local editorial dunghills than you could con-ceive outside Lilliput, but on the other hand, it has a remarkable Institute of International Affairs and solid groups of political study in every town in the country.

Its public life lacks courage and Canada is the village that voted the earth was flat, in the denial of its size and destiny. Yet its carelessness of distance is fantastic and its individual adventures into the Arctic, epic. Its educational standards are in many quarters grotesque, and in some quar-ters, subject to a sort of provincial fascism which is both ignorant and vicious. Yet the library work, the adult educational developments and the extension services of the voluntary associations are heartening and good. Canada, especially, can be a great bore when it tries to match its sophisti-cation with the larger and deeper versions thereof. 'Sunset, and evening star and one clear call for Bill the lone fisherman.' But over and under these variations and anomalies, there is a profound element of common sense and good taste about Canada and Canadian life which is a precious thing to know.

.   .   .

If you think that, out of personal affection and regard, I am prejudiced, be sure that I am. But if you want to make anything of it, at least you won't find me a composite individual to go after. I am at your service.

Lorne Greene

Endowed with a rich and resonant voice, Lorne Greene has become variously a radio announcer, an actor in legitimate theatre in New York and London, and in the 1960s a universal father figure, Ben Cartwright of the celebrated television series "Bonanza." Early in his career as a young radio announcer with the Canadian Broadcasting Corporation, Greene was approached by the National Film Board to voice the commentaries for some of the new wartime documentary films; thus his voice was eventually heard by audiences in movie theatres all over Canada and subsequently the United States. Indeed, in Canada he became virtually the tribal voice of the nation, familiarly known as the "Voice of Doom." Greene was thus concerned with the final stage in the making of films rather than with the planning or production work itself. Nonetheless, his voice gave the films that final sincerity and authority which commended them strongly to the movie audience.

There is a distinct resemblance between the Lorne Greene voice style of the wartime documentaries and the older *March of Time* voice narration of Westbrook Van Voorhis in the late 1930s. The camera work, editing, and writing on *The March of Time* were more stylized, and this stylization extended to the voicing of the final films. *The March of Time* voice was truly sonorous, authoritative, and full of doom, but it lacked the personal shading that Greene imparted to his commentaries.

We filmed Lorne Greene in Hollywood on the broad deck of his canyon home, perched high on a wooded hillside above the highway. The Canadian film crew and Greene himself had a good time reviewing things Canadian, hometown events and personalities of thirty years before. Almost fifty years before, we reflected, Grierson had been here in Hollywood visiting the magic world of movies, assessing the powerful pull of movies upon the growing mass audience, conjecturing that the movie medium might be harnessed for purposes other than simply fantasy and entertainment.

Greene: I was doing the news for the CBC at the time; it was in April 1940 and I had a call from Montreal. A very light British voice said, "My name is Stuart Legg. I'm with the Film Board here, and we're just completing a film for a new series dealing with the war. This is the first of them and I'd like you to do the commentary." I said, "I've never done that." He said, "Well, this is the first one we've done here, so you'll learn with us, and would you be interested in doing this?" I said "Yes, I would." So I went to Ottawa where I met Stuart Legg, this tall, lanky gentleman. We talked about the making of films, what the films were about, the Canadian war effort.

Lorne Greene, actor, in Hollywood—the wartime "Voice of Doom."

I remember the first three words of that very first documentary I made—"The vast Atlantic." I remember them very well because some months later I went to the movies one Saturday night, and I was sitting there with a huge crowd when one of the short subjects came up. Suddenly I heard the words "The vast Atlantic," and it scared me. I said, "Oh, my God, it sounds terrible! I have friends in the theatre here and I've got to get out," but I didn't because I was trapped there and I saw the film and sort of got acclimated to my voice. But it was a tortuous experience to hear my voice

coming out of the motion-picture screen for the first time in my life.
*Question: Did you have any feelings of heavy conscience or obligation
about being both The Voice on the national radio network news, as well as
The Voice on the national screen?*

Greene: At that time I'd just begun my career as a news broadcaster for
the CBC and I didn't know if this was going to continue or not. Certainly
there's a responsibility that you have in whatever you do, to do it to the
best of your talent. I finally wound up making what I'd guess was hundreds
of documentaries for the National Film Board. I think it was after the third
film they asked me to become the official voice of the *Canada Carries On*
series and later on the *World in Action* series as well.

During the making of the third film I met John Grierson. The circumstances were strange and very vivid in my mind. This was in 1940. Stuart
Legg did the first two films and Stanley Hawes—who was later Film Commissioner in Australia, I believe—was producing and directing the third
one, which dealt with the work of the merchant marine during the war and
the hazards of the whole experience. It was a very tough and strong film
and the commentary was beautifully written. That was one of the things I
remember so clearly about all the films I did with the Film Board: the
choice, the selection of words was extremely careful, very precise; the exact
word was used. This commentary dealt with the *Manchester Progress*,
which was the name of the merchant vessel. One of the lines said, "Come
to your haven, *Manchester Progress*, and rest after your hazardous journey," things like that which seemed beautiful. There was a portion of the
mariner's prayer in this commentary. We were recording the film in Ottawa. There was a very tiny little booth for the man who was speaking; you
could put out your hands and touch either wall. I was going over the
commentary, listening to the sound to make sure everything was round and
florid and proper with plenty of authority. I was going through the lines
reading the mariner's prayer when suddenly through the soundproof walls I
heard an anguished scream. I said, "Oh, my goodness, somebody has had a
heart attack." It seemed like that. Suddenly the door to this little booth was
flung open and there was a man standing there. His blue eyes were just
impaling me against the wall; he looked at me with burning hatred, and I
thought for a moment he was going to kill me. I *knew* he was going to hit
me, and I sort of shrugged back. He said, "Who told you to read that?" I
said, "Well, I was just—" He said, "Get up out of there." This was my first
introduction to John Grierson—we hadn't been introduced yet. He said,
"Get outside and listen." So I slunk out of there, went into the theatre, and
sat down. Then I heard *him* read the mariner's prayer over the loud-
speaker. He didn't read it just one time; he read it twenty-seven times in

twenty-seven different ways, and I said to myself oh, my, am I an idiot, here I am an actor and that man who is not an actor is teaching me my craft, because there are an infinite number of ways to read any line and I had only been concentrating on getting the best possible *sound* and had forgotten everything else. Of course he was reading it with his gut, with his heart, with his fantastic intellect, with his perception, with his feelings for the sea, because he loved the sea. Then he said, "Get in here," so I went back to the booth. He opened the door and just looked at me and said, "If Bill Auden was here he could do it." I went in again and sat down, because of course I knew the great W. H. Auden had done commentaries for him in England. For the first time I began to really work with the commentary. It taught me a great lesson which I've never forgotten.

Question: You hadn't seen films of this sort before. Did you think of them as propaganda?

Greene: No, only as very exciting film. The war was a horrible thing and yet there was a certain excitement; everybody was girding up together and getting together because the odds were against the Allies. There was a visible archenemy in Adolf Hitler, and we knew he had the upper hand, but there was an excitement about it, everybody really pulling together. Today, I don't know, wars don't have the same visible villains. I looked at the film subjects as very exciting *film*. I was astounded by many of the shots that had been taken. About the fourth or fifth film I suddenly began to realize the complete concept of using motion picture in this way, to bring focus to a common purpose, to illuminate it. I think that the Film Board then probably did among the best films in the world.

Question: When Grierson was talking about the aesthetics of these short films, he used a term which I had never heard. He said, "We tried to get an action beat in the films, which is essentially an American phenomenon or an American concept." He said the French, for example, could never put an action beat into films, and they could never find an ending. There were certain cadences and modulations in the Canadian short films, the way they were edited and phrased . . . and the voice had so much to do with the lacing together, emphasizing the rhythms in those films.

Greene: Very much so. The voice helped to put in the action beat, blending together the different film shots, one piece of film taken from here and one taken from there, bringing them together to create a common idea. My part in that was to lace them together, and to do it as authoritatively as possible. I remember that in those days we didn't use recording tape, so we'd work from nine in the morning until sometimes ten-thirty at night, because my train back to Toronto from Ottawa left at eleven o'clock, and there were no planes then flying at night. I had to be back in Toronto for an early broadcast in the morning, so we'd work all day with half an hour for lunch. They put the music track on one dubber, they had the sound effects on another, and they put the voice, live, on a third channel, there were only three channels. So it had to be mixed, at a certain time certain sound effects had to come in at a precise moment on the film, and the poor sound man, sometimes he missed his cue, I'd be talking my gut out and suddenly they'd say *cut* and we'll have to do it again; sometimes we would do as many as twenty-five or thirty go-throughs on a single ten-minute reel.

Question: How did your particular voice style evolve? We used to call it the "Voice of Doom."

Greene: I tried to make the best possible use of my voice. People say that I have a very deep voice, but I really don't: I have the chest tones which give it a certain depth. They made use of that at the Film Board, because that gave it the authority, the feeling of strength and durability, which they wanted for the films.

The mood of the picture was set by the film image itself, the tone of it. It was my job as well as the job of the producer to see that my mood emphasized the mood of the film. Some films were more lighthearted—not as many as I would have liked, but then, it was not a lighthearted time. It was a time of emergency. Most of the films were hard-hitting, tough, strong, and their purpose was to create a feeling of great strength in the country—a strength that was indomitable and unflappable, and had to be victorious.

Question: It used to be kind of a joke about Grierson, "accentuate the positive"—no thought might be thought nor sentence written unless it was upbeat and positive.

Greene: No, there was absolutely no equivocation about that, it was upbeat, it was positive—*we are going to win*, this is the way we're going to do it. Of course he was a great philosopher of the "win" policy. Remember, *Churchill's Island* won a Hollywood Oscar in 1942. That was by the National Film Board; it was named the best short subject made that year.

Question: It was as close as the short film could come to real topicality in the days before television.

Greene: Yes, that's right, the documentary is extremely immediate. Even though it might be ten years old, there's still an immediacy about it because it deals with the actuality, the actual things, so it always has that immediate feeling.

A Note on the Royal Commission on Espionage (1946)

In Ottawa in 1946 the Soviet cipher clerk Igor Gouzenko disclosed the existence of a small network of Canadian agents in regular communication with Russian operatives in Canada, based in the Soviet embassy. Among the names noted in Lieutenant-Colonel Motinov's small notebook was that of Freda Linton, at one point Grierson's secretary at the Film Board. Freda Linton had not been recruited for her job with Grierson but had been allocated from a wartime typing pool. The cryptic entry in the colonel's book read: "Linton to Professor through Grierson" (at that point her employer). . . . The significance of the notation was that Linton, as an actual or potential agent, would be of more value to the network if she could be placed with or near Professor Raymond Boyer of the National Research Council, later sentenced on espionage charges. At the time of these disclosures, Linton had vanished from sight. Much later she appeared before the authorities and demanded to be cleared of any and all charges. No evidence of any concrete kind was found against her, and her case was dismissed. Because Grierson's name had appeared in the colonel's notebook, he was asked to appear before the Royal Commission on Espionage in Ottawa. There was no evidence that he had ever made contact with or offered his services to the Russians. His being called before and questioned by the commission of course exposed him to future suspicion and attack in the United States, at that point entering the period of the cold war and the House Un-American Activities Committee. There were in Ottawa people resentful and jealous of Grierson's achievement in Canada and of his end-run methods in consolidating facilities for the furtherance of the Film Board program. Some distorted and malicious notions were communicated to the American authorities and to elements of the U.S. press. The outcome was that Grierson, already in the United States after his earlier resignation from the Film Board (some time previous to the Gouzenko affair), was harassed and in effect blacklisted in the United States.

These developments of course did serious damage to the promotional and production plans which Grierson and his colleagues were formulating in New York. In a situation already problematical, in view of the weaker tradition of documentary film work in the U.S.A. and a general sentiment against government-produced information, the Grierson group had sufficiently weighty obstacles to overcome. With Grierson's name and reputation suspect, the chances for building a successful New York–based independent documentary film venture gradually dissipated over the following two years.

In an effort to help Grierson clear his name, Grierson's friend George Ferguson, then editor of the *Montreal Star*, spoke with the Canadian Justice Minister, Mr. Louis St. Laurent, late in 1946. Mr. St. Laurent (later Prime Minister) wrote the following letter:

MINISTER OF JUSTICE AND ATTORNEY GENERAL OF CANADA

Ottawa
November 14, 1946

G. F. Ferguson, Esq.
Editor
"MONTREAL STAR"
Montreal, P. Q.

Dear Mr. Ferguson:

I refer to our conversation in New York on the subject of John Grierson and your letter of November 5.

I am at a loss to understand the report which you state is now current in certain newspaper circles in the United States to the effect that Mr. Grierson was a leader of the spy ring now before our courts.

It appears to me that Mr. Grierson's name can have become linked with the espionage case only because of the fact that he was called as a witness before the Royal Commission. I am informed that his presence and testimony were required there because his name appeared in some of the Russian documents produced as exhibits. There was also the fact a secretary of his, one Freda Linton, was investigated by the Royal Commission and later charged before the courts. The charges against her have not been proceeded with, as to date it has been impossible to locate and apprehend her.

I sincerely deplore the loose and ill-founded conclusions pointing to Mr. Grierson as "head of the spy ring" or as consciously connected with it in any way. I can only suggest that certain persons have been too ready to make false capital of the fact that he was called before the Royal Commission for the reasons outlined.

Yours very truly,

Louis St. Laurent

This letter was of some assistance in forestalling publication in a major U.S. weekly of a malicious article concerning Grierson. The unpublished article was based upon wholly incorrect information confusing Grierson's name and his activities with those of another person. In any case Grierson's visa was withdrawn by the U.S. State Department. He left New York to take up a role as adviser on mass media development at UNESCO in Paris, before the first general conference of that body in 1946. Julian Huxley was then Director General of UNESCO, and Grierson worked as adviser directly to him.

This chapter of Grierson's professional life was no doubt a painful one. He had completed a major achievement in Canada; he was embarking upon a very challenging but by no means implausible undertaking in New York; and his gifts for promotion and persuasion were at their peak. But even the slightest taint of suspicion in connection with the espionage affair did him major damage. It was the beginning of a bad time in the United States, a time marked by much persecution, cowardice, and fear. Nor did the Canadians behave much better: Grierson's accomplishment in Canada, his large contribution to the creation of opportunities for native talent and expression, went almost totally uncredited and unacknowledged. Nonetheless, George Ferguson remarks of Grierson that throughout the following years and in the face of numerous ailments, slights, and disappointments, Grierson "never indicated bitterness."

The events of 1946 and '47 happily did not conclude Grierson's connection with Canada. He returned on several occasions, and more than twenty years later taught at McGill University in Montreal. Indeed, he hoped, to retire to Canada with his wife, Margaret. Both of them had greatly enjoyed the stimulus and friendships of the wartime years in Ottawa. But when in 1947 he returned to Europe from Ottawa and New York, he might well have felt legitimate cause for bitterness.

A Note from
Martin Quigley, Jr.*

Grierson had tremendous influence on young British and Canadian film-makers. In the United States the trade generally ignored the documentary film movement, believing that it was inconsistent with the prime entertainment objective of film production. However, the work of Grierson, his peers such as Paul Rotha, and their followers had significant effect on *The March of Time* film project and a whole host of features that came during and immediately after World War II. Moreover, the yearnings of film-makers of recent years, and at present, to be realistic and "show it like it is," are definitely in the "documentary" film spirit.

This writer's last meeting with Grierson was at the Airlie House Conference on films held by the U.S. Information Agency in 1966. Each of us was speaking on the uses of films to influence men's minds and actions. In private conversation Grierson told me that it was Martin Quigley, my father, who was then editor and publisher of the *Exhibitors-Herald*, predecessor of *Motion Picture Herald*, who was the first to encourage him in his approach to films and who first published his film opinions. That was in the mid-1920s, years before the writings assembled by Forsyth Hardy in the book *Grierson on Documentary* (U.S. edition, 1947).

During this same conversation, Grierson told me something that, so far as I know, has never been published. His real mission when named Government Film Commissioner and executive head of the National Film Board in October 1939 was to help bring the United States into the war which had started the preceding month. His nominal job was done with great success. The Canadian Film Board has grown from the initial one-man operation to a large organization with a fine record in film-making. It is not likely that Grierson's work as a propagandist for the British Government can ever be documented or fully appreciated. In 1939—in fact all the way up to Pearl Harbor Day—there was great sympathy for Britain and her Allies but a strong isolation spirit in this country, especially in "Middle America." Grierson traveled far and wide in the United States on

---

* From a column by Martin Quigley, Jr., *Quigley Comment*, in the *Motion Picture Daily*, February 23, 1972, entitled "John Grierson."

his mission. He had films to show and knew how they could influence opinions.

Every time a film or television producer tries to put over a message of some kind he is in John Grierson's debt. For Grierson pioneered in both understanding and applying the basic techniques of message pictures.

A Note on Security
and Hyperbole

The matter of the Royal Commission on Espionage raises the question of Grierson's political beliefs and affiliations. His statements to Bosley Crowther and Martin Quigley, Jr., quoted in these pages also raise the question of what affiliation, if any, he may have had either formally or informally with intelligence agencies of the British government. There is a quixotic quality to these statements, a mild mystery, an ambiguity that might be seen as troubling or droll depending on the bias of the researcher. Those who know Grierson intimately feel that there is an element of hyperbole in his accounts of involvement with intelligence services, either as an active element on the British side, or as a victim on the American. There is no doubt that Grierson was really harassed and pressured by American agencies as a result of his connection with the espionage hearings in Ottawa, and that some Canadian public figures also joined in such harassment. Virtually no public figure in Canada at the time specifically defended him or rebutted the imprecise charges against him.

His claim to have carried out a function on behalf of British intelligence agencies, is another matter. Being party to privileged information, being widely known as a skilled psychologist, being a specialist in matters of public opinion, Grierson was indeed in a position of power to implant or modify opinion, to boost morale, according to the needs and strategies of the war. But every kind of evidence indicates that he was not concerned with the manipulation of power and influence but with the rights, responsibilities, and capacities of the citizen, of mankind. His whole work is constructive. If he affected a touch of the cloak and dagger, this must be seen in the context of a person who used theatrical effects and heightenings and foreshortenings of fact or interpretation as tools of his trade.

Moreover, Grierson was a humorist, a spellbinder who delighted in the telling of tales. He was not without vanity, not without a full awareness of the central role which he had to play in influencing public attitudes and understanding. He was party to the councils of government leaders and policy-makers, and his own keen intellect was usually fully equal to that of such leaders. Some civil servants of substantial intellect and experience mistrusted Grierson because of his evident brilliance.

His appearance before the espionage tribunal was damaging to his own interests. As an old friend commented, "He couldn't have been a worse witness." Grierson was outraged and furious at what he regarded as the presumption of the tribunal in casting doubt upon his integrity as a public servant. In the overheated atmosphere of these events, each side felt a woeful lack of confidence in the other.

The final record is surely in his work, his writings, his teaching, the programs and agencies and courses of study that he generated during a lifetime. It is all constructive, all for the common weal. Surely such a man may be forgiven his peccadilloes of pride, vanity, and hyperbole.

Paul Theriault

The existence and claims of French-speaking Canada have been somewhat dramatically projected both within and outside the country in recent years. In Canada, use of the French language is not limited to Quebec, but Quebec is by far the largest and most cohesive French-speaking community, the settlement of the area and its cultural development reaching back to the seventeenth century.

In the 1960s the Quebec community entered into a stage of activist and often militant self-assertion. The balance between English- and French-speaking Canada has considerably shifted. Much more recognition and deference is now accorded the rights and feelings of the French-speaking community. The desire for political separation still exists; indeed, in various quarters there is a distinct militancy of feeling, as evidenced in the victory of Le Parti Quebecois in the Quebec provincial elections of 1976.

During Grierson's time in Ottawa, French-speaking Canada had not yet begun to assert itself. In fact, the old established order of a rather parochial and culturally defensive community still prevailed throughout Quebec and other French-speaking areas. Only in the 1950s and thereafter did increasing militancy in the trade-union movement and in political life following the collapse of the Union Nationale party (under the autocratic rule of the late Premier Maurice DuPlessis) pave the way for a strong separatist movement that flared into disturbing violence during the late 1960s.

Nonetheless, during the Grierson period at the Film Board, the bilingual, bicultural situation within the Canadian federal framework was there to be faced. Grierson had a distinct feeling for the French-speaking community. As a consultant providing insights into the attitudes of the Quebec community and indeed of French-speaking Canadians in all the provinces (then nine in number), Paul Theriault found himself in the classical position of the native *Quebecois* exiled in Ottawa, the federal capital, among uncaring Anglo-Canadians. He refers to the early efforts at the Film Board, made under the aegis of Grierson and Ross McLean, to effect some kind of working partnership between English- and French-language elements. But the thinking and planning went much beyond the short-term war emergency. The Film Board, as Theriault comments, was one of very few agencies that made genuine efforts to achieve a working partnership between the English- and French-speaking communities.

We interviewed Paul Theriault on a park bench in front of the Parliamentary Library on Parliament Hill in Ottawa. Mr. Theriault speaks in a majestic and extremely literate English. In interviews produced for television, time is of the essence, and a very deliberate speaker presents the producer and editors with the problem of length—how much footage, how much time is consumed. Therefore, while Mr. Theriault is an important spokesman in the French-language film on Grierson, he regrettably does not appear in the English film. This omission constitutes a shortcoming in the film. Grierson's relation to French-speaking Canada, his concept of a national dialogue between English-speaking and French-speaking peoples, were fundamental elements of his policy during his years with the Film Board in Ottawa. This aspect is discussed in the French-language film on Grierson and neglected in the English-language film. An error of omission in terms of overall balance and representation was therefore regrettably committed.

Theriault: He understood that creation cannot really perpetuate itself in the conformity of a totally stable and comfortable situation. The creative mind requires crisis, turmoil, and the challenge of difficulty to maximize its own potential, and therefore like a seabird in the storm, I think it is probably true to say that there was an affinity between Grierson and trouble.

Question: In terms of the relationship between French and English Canada, at the time when you knew him, what do you think of his effort? How do you rate it?

Theriault: I would say that right in my first meeting with Grierson, he gave me the complete outline of how he visualized the future of French Canada in this country. In retrospect there's absolutely no doubt about it: he had somehow managed prophetically to anticipate and grasp the ultimate result of a great number of parallel, simultaneous processes that were taking place obscurely at that particular time in French Canada.

In terms of the activities of the Film Board, he told me he was profoundly disturbed that after four years, except for marginal creative activity in film production, the bulk of the French-Canadian contribution was simply to dub the French versions of the numerous English films produced by the board. This he felt was intolerable. He was very preoccupied that the French Canadians should contribute very extensively to the whole creative field of the National Film Board.

Another thing which concerned him was the fact that in the 16mm distribution of the Film Board films, practically the only French-language circuits were those to be found in the Province of Quebec. He felt that somehow the distribution in French, as in English, should encompass *all* of the nine Canadian provinces at that time. There is some suggestion that he realized the difficulty of organizing French-language circuits in Alberta, or British Columbia, but I think he wanted to achieve precisely this objective. He dismantled the French-language unit within six months following my arrival. We then rebuilt it, but this time he put an *Anglophone* producer to head it and attached a good number of young aspiring film-makers to the operation. He made it practically a dogma that any creative young French Canadian coming to the area of film production would at the outset learn the ABCs of his art within an English-speaking unit. The other extraordinary thing he asked was that each senior producer would be responsible totally for a quota of documentaries produced in English-speaking Canada, as well as a quota in French-speaking Canada. This naturally forced all the producers, whether French or English, to learn very quickly if they wanted to survive.

If you look at what has happened in Canada since 1964, you will find that on an enlarged basis the Canadian government is now endeavoring to do across Canada exactly what Grierson in 1945 wished to do in the context of the National Film Board. For this, I think that my generation, the young French Canadians—and there were indeed a very large number of them who came to the Film Board at that time, with enthusiasm and sometimes with great candor and naiveté—all of us I believe owe an eternal debt of gratitude to Grierson. Because it was really the first time for most of us that we came fundamentally to grips with "the other solitude" in this country, and "the other solitude" was as great for us as it is for many English-speaking Canadians of goodwill.

Question: Do you think that he had an accurate grasp, psychologically and otherwise, of the French-Canadian community?

Theriault: I think basically what attracted Grierson to French Canadians and vice versa was the question of temperament. To some extent, there's a capacity in French Canada traditionally to give a free rein to *la feuille de logie*, which I believe you would translate in English, "to tolerate bats in the belfry." Grierson had very great sympathy for this trait of the French Canadians. Also, because basically he was a Scotsman, he was the pure product of an extraordinarily strong minority who had been tried in history very severely, and he had somehow succeeded in safeguarding his own identity, and what is even more important, his original pride.

Because of this, he had an understanding of the really pretty desperate odds the French Canadian faced on the whole North American continent. Yet they had somewhat magically survived, at least until now, though cut off long ago from the mother culture. I think he also realized that the French Canadian, maybe at that time alone in Canada, had developed a culture as totally naked as the Yankee culture in New England. It was somewhat a shadow of the old culture, but it operated on an entirely new dimension of value and a new flow of energy. Then his amazing grasp of the mechanics and the impact of the social and cultural environment suggested to him that a cultural revolution had already started, at least in his mind, and that sooner or later the French Canadians would try very desperately to assert their own identity. That meant internally putting their own house in order, and it was clear that this process had started at least in Quebec, in the trade-union movement all through the late thirties. It had continued at an accelerated clip during the war years, and he probably also assumed that the very substantial number of French Canadians who had served overseas in the armed forces would come back with a great determination to make the world much better for their children, much less precarious than the one in which they had grown up. Which of all these factors was the dominant one in the mind of Grierson, I'm afraid he's carried the secret with him. What is certain is that neither I nor any other French Canadian I've known who has known Grierson and worked with him has anything on balance but a rather warm, fraternal, and deep feeling of friendship for him. This is perhaps the greatest compliment that I as a French Canadian can pay to this very remarkable man.

Question: In his approach to Quebec, who were the elements that he sought out, what particular groups or communities? Were they clerics, intellectuals, or politicians? Where did he find his support in French Canada?

Theriault: In my opinion, because of the problems of time, commitment, and so on his contacts with French Canada were reasonably restricted to the intellectual community in the broader sense of the word—scholars, artists, journalists, anyone who creatively has a hand in molding the milieu. He had very little time and actually spent very little time with other elements in the province.

Also let me say he had a particular affection for the *maverick* that French Canada produces in every generation in large numbers—the strong individualist not gifted for anything functional who takes life as a vagabond poet and spends, if you want, most of his energy in the pursuit of a happy life, but one that isn't chained to the collective process. These types had an infinite attraction for Grierson, and whenever these contacts occurred, a very strange phenomenon occurred in his behavior pattern. He instantly stopped, if you want, his *Napoleonic* approach. He changed his behavior pattern very drastically, and the only description that I can make is that suddenly he was seized with a kind of delight, like a child watching the fall of a clown at the circus. He was deeply amused and deeply in empathy with the clown, he was *un compagnon de la liberté*, a companion of the heart. This is another dimension of this very, very strange and complex man.

Question: Do you think that the Film Board worked fairly well as a bicultural institution, because that's what it set out to be in Canada? Thinking back, how effective do you think it was in that role, working both in English and French Canada?

Theriault: I think that it really was the mother lode of any organized process of communication between the main cultures of Canada. It effectively developed most of the methods to make the other cultural value known to each of the two cultures. This was forced mainly by the determination of Grierson and his successor, Ross McLean, to continually examine the evolving processes of one culture, and to translate and explain and expose them to the understanding of the other. The men who went through this process could legitimately claim to be well ahead of their time.

In this very essential problem of Canadian identity and life, as far as I'm concerned, I don't think that anything that has happened in my life since I left the Film Board has demanded an effort even remotely connected with the intense passion of those years. All of us who were concerned with what should be, with the future of the entire Canadian community, we shared in the same common dream, the same common aspiration, the same desire to make it *work* one way or another. This is, if you want, the gift that we always have from Grierson. I hope it doesn't sound like a fable, but that is true.

Evelyn Spice Cherry

Evelyn Cherry is the sole Canadian who took part in the initial work of the documentary film group in London, and thereafter she played an important role in the Canadian production program of the National Film Board in Ottawa. She comes from Scottish stock and from the wheat country of Saskatchewan. This Western province of Canada has a distinct tradition of outspoken liberal and radical thought, and also of active, energetic, independent women. Something of the pioneer experience of the West, of the hardships of drought and depression, of the suffering brought down by banks and creditors on the defenseless prairie farmers, has entered into the outspoken Western tradition.

As Evelyn Spice, an independent young woman with a strong social conscience, she fell in quite naturally with the young British group who gravitated towards documentary film as a means of focusing attention on social issues. In England she married a compatriot, Lawrence Cherry, also a film-maker. After their return to Canada they met again with Grierson and soon joined the National Film Board as producers of films designed especially to speak to a rural audience. The Cherrys' work in Canada was intimately connected with the development of mobile 16mm film circuits, which were organized during the war and brought to small rural communities a regular flow of information films related to social and technical farm matters and to the wider aspects of national production in wartime. This program of producing and distributing films especially for rural people provided a major strength for the Film Board in terms of broad-based public support after the end of the war in 1945.

Evelyn Cherry is again in Saskatchewan and continues in local film production. We did not succeed in making arrangements to film her, but asked her to tape or write for us as informally as possible her feelings regarding Grierson and her own experience in the documentary world.

In comparison with the early work in Britain, there was the same spirit, same philosophy, same rundown kind of equipment, same work under difficulties, same government-persuaded-to-act situation, same freedom for the individual, and also the same trust. The tempo was the same, in spite of different locations; but a much larger thing in Canada, on account of the war.

The Film Act permitted a much larger field of operation in Canada. In

Britain the prewar movement was tied to just one government department, however wide its field of operation. In Canada the Film Act governed the placing of film work for all government departments and gave NFB powers to act in this regard. At the time the act was written of course, television was not on the books.

In Britain, Grierson and Tallents stretched to the widest limit the interpretation of the GPO function so that film could blossom as much as possible. In Canada, given a war situation, this was more easily done. It was significant, however, that this was Grierson's way of looking at an act—to give it the widest possible interpretation, whatever.

Today we see how limited thinking can hinder the development of film in changing situations. It takes a lot of fire and energy, and creative excitement, to stir up this other sense of wide possibilities.

Perhaps it is true that when he went to the United States in 1945, this stirring up was no longer possible. Perhaps even in a different time it would not have been possible, for the background conditions were not right. I expect we must admit that before the war, when Grierson came along with

Lawrence and Evelyn Cherry of the National Film Board (1945). Both the Cherrys had worked in film during the 1930s in Britain; Evelyn was an early recruit to the GPO Film Unit led by Grierson in London. Later they returned to Canada and did important work in the development of the new Canadian documentary movement.

his ideas to Canada, we were still to a great extent thinking *colonial*—it was all an extension of things British, and that helped to get the film development off the ground. After the war, the situation changed, as we know.

It seems that a proper understanding must take note of international changes; how in Canada after the war we stepped into a new era of the cold war. From the Fulton speech in Missouri, times changed very quickly—and how vulnerable was Grierson, and all the film-makers who work in the public services, in information, in film anywhere—as was shown in the Hollywood situation. We know how disastrous were the effects of all this period on film-makers—not only the ones who suffered deprivation of income and opportunity but those who had to forgo expression of their true thought and hopes, and do only what they were told to do.

The times were right, we say, when Grierson set up the British thing in the 1930s, and he had a splendid sponsor in Sir Stephen Tallents. The times were right once again when he set up the Canadian Film Board on the eve of war, with a sponsor no less than the Prime Minister, The Right Honorable Mackenzie King.

But after the war, the cold war began, with the Fulton speech or even before; in Canada, Mr. King resigned and Mr. St. Laurent took his place; in Canada, the Igor Gouzenko affair; in the U.S.A., the Rosenbergs, in '49, I think; then the rise to prominence and great power of Senator McCarthy in the 1950s; then the Korean War, '52 to '54.

The role of Canada changed. From support of a just war, it was now a matter of preparing public thinking for a third world war. Also the role of Canada had changed in another sense, swung away from a type of British dependency to a kind of extension of the United States.

If we put the Film Board in context, we can see how the total change in the situation of our country in relation to other nations, with Canada becoming more and more tied to U.S. policy, how this made it next to impossible for a man who stood for social justice and freedom through democracy, and the special kind of education that would bring this about; he would never stand a chance unless he had tremendous support from the people, from the rank and file. Only those people who fell in line had a chance—and those like J.G. were not given a chance to decide whether or not to fall in line.

Perhaps the moral nastiness of this was the worst—the dreadful spectacle of people bound in fear, afraid to speak a good word for a friend. I think that in fairness to Grierson, we must think and speak of these events —or not speak at all. . . .

As to the film work in Canada, there was a great rapport between the rural areas and the film-makers, and perhaps this was strongest in relation to the agricultural film unit—for the rural film circuits were primarily aimed at the farm audience outside the radius of commercial houses—as the Film Act laid down. The field men brought to us comments, criticism, and suggestions, and I think that we tried our best to listen and act on them. At any rate we appreciated the effort to communicate, and found excitement and inspiration in it. I do not believe anything like this exists today.

I think that the overall program in the large sense was right on for the times—but the distribution of films except for the rural circuits, was a different matter. It was restricted—and for the most part outside Grierson's control. His good sense prompted him to make use of the act as best he could in establishing the rural circuits. But for the rest, when it came to cinema houses, it was a different story. There the art of persuasion, and the fact of war, caused some small concessions, but they were simply concessions, as witness what happened when the war ended. I have always thought that if the audience had been more sophisticated and therefore able to be better informed, they might possibly have become more aware, and Grierson might have had some protection in his hour of real need. But we must remember that we lived at that time in a very unsophisticated country on the whole, when unawareness of things international was the mark of our thinking. And so perhaps we just had to grow up. Cinema could help us do this; and there is no doubt that the documentary did help, and is still doing so, even today's documentary—expensive bastard stuff mostly; pretentious, ashamed of its own tradition, even its name; hiding behind polish and presentation and gimmicks instead of story; seeking international applause instead of genuine appreciation from the Canadian people at home.

Today we seem to be a country a little ashamed of our *being*—always seeking reassurance from those outside. When we make another film like *Paperback Hero,** we do nothing to change this.

Canada's position changed after the war; our status changed in the world of nations. The Film Board could have given leadership in the visual field, instead of struggling just to stay alive and struggling with television, jockeying for place amidst the total cinema situation. Rather it should be using its powers from government to strive for first place as an institution and to

---

* A Canadian feature film produced by John Bassett, Jr., in 1973 and financed partly by the Canadian Film Finance Corporation. It is a mordant story about a loutish small-town Westerner and the sterile community he lives in. He aspires to big-time, U.S. media-patterned success and so comes to a tragic end. The film achieved some commercial success, but encountered criticism as an unworthy model of Canadian creative expression.

assist individual film-makers. I believe strongly that a great opportunity was missed—and that it still could be taken today. To find this right path for Canada, with the Film Board giving some leadership and helping toward unity; to draw together the skills and strength of Canadian cinema generally, into a force that will grow progressively stronger; growing into a film industry in the broadest sense of the word, with funds from the box office flowing back into the home industry, which is making use of international expertise and trends, instead of just being subservient to them. Whatever is unique about Canada, whatever makes it worth preserving as a country, its people, feelings, traditions, and history, would go into visual, for the world to see what we are.

As to Grierson and his mistakes—no man can be all things to all people, no one can do everything even if he sees why and how to do it. I think his main mistake was in protecting us all too well. He was the front man, he made arrangements, opened new fields, took up the ball and carried it when we went to him with ideas, found the means and money. All we did was make the films, in great freedom. When bad times came he was the most vulnerable. And we acted like lost sheep running for the fold, with no shepherd to guide us. We bleated around in a strange, lost manner, rushed for individual cover, sold out our friends for personal gain—in all, acted as if we should never have been worthy of hire to serve our country.

That Grierson came to grief implies perhaps a good deal of mistake on his part. Whereas the forces of change in the country were so great after 1945 that no man alone could stand against them, however strong. Perhaps if there was a mistake, it was in going to the United States, where there was no tradition of documentary and therefore a limited understanding of his work, with a corresponding lack of support. Perhaps.

We failed him at the NFB. He found no support there among his people. The bitter travesty of that NFB twenty-fifth anniversary party bears witness to that. It wasn't done for Grierson, but for the film-makers, to help find a forgiveness that cannot be granted them. I shall always feel bitterly ashamed of my country, for there was no voice raised in his defense, no one among those in high command in this country spoke for him or publicly recognized his great contribution at that time. If there was, I did not hear it; and I am sure the Canadian people did not.

Future generations will inherit this shame, along with the documentary idea that has so much influenced all the arts—from drama through literature, music, feature films and television—and will continue to do so for years to come.

A Note on Rural Circuits

The rural circuits of the wartime period represented something more than a special program of films designed for the interest of rural audiences. The films, packaged together as integrated programs, were brought directly to the audience by a traveling representative working on a regular monthly schedule. Thus the local representative who brought the new film program each month served as a regular contact between the audience in many small communities and the producing organization. A considerable amount of feedback was made possible. Reactions, criticisms, endorsements, and requests for other films on specific subjects came back to the production center in Ottawa from the local representatives reporting to their regional offices. For three or four years these reports provided a form of contact between audience and producers, and had their direct influence on the selection of film topics and the content of individual films.

When the system itself was dissolved for economic reasons after the war, the National Film Board sought new channels to reach the diffuse, nationwide, nontheatrical audience of film-users. Alliances with public libraries, universities, and local self-supporting film-use committees were promoted. But the problem of a total and effective 16mm film distribution pattern (as distinct from the regular business of 16mm film sales to the school systems) was never fully or satisfactorily solved before the advent of national television, with its great potential for bringing documentary films to a mass audience.

The Postwar Prospect—Excerpts from Three Addresses

By the end of World War II, Grierson had experienced some seventeen years of active involvement with the documentary film medium. During the war itself, he and his associates looked ahead beyond the victory to a postwar time when a more educated public would have a greater understanding of the contemporary world. These ideas were constantly stated in the wartime films, to force the audience to think beyond the armistice and the return of peace to a time of new responsibility and opportunity. His writings in 1945 reflect this forward-looking sense of program and objectives. Excerpts from three such pieces follow.

Education in a Technological Society*

When I was pretty young myself, I had to teach a night school in Scotland to young people who worked all day in the local coal mines. They were poor tired characters and I was supposed to teach them literature or something; the subject was Shakespeare's *Midsummer Night's Dream*. That is what they called adult education in my early days. My next experience was no better, except that I survived it, for it consisted of teaching Plato to a lot of old clerks and spinsters in the benighted town of Newcastle-on-Tyne, who evidently wanted to know about Plato, but would have been better occupied raising hell about the slums of the city, the malnutrition of its children, and its horrible schools.

I have been in adult education ever since, not so much in the matter of Shakespeare and not so much in the matter of raising hell about the slums of the cities, the malnutrition of the children and the horrible schools and suchlike matters. I have used films to do it, and I think I was amongst the first to believe that with films you could open a window on the world and stretch men's eyes, and tell people how the world went round and bring the problems of today with all their difficulty and all their drama right under the eye of the citizen. So far as I am concerned, education is about *living* and how to make it better, and so far as I am concerned it is about things like food and houses and a break for the children and clean cities and happy villages and full employment and international cooperation and to the devil with racial prejudice, and things like that.

Education is a two-way process or it is nothing. It must be about people

* From a radio broadcast by John Grierson, May 28, 1945.

and therefore must be very deeply related to the problems of people, the actual problems of actual people at every turn. Often the educator sits on his high stool or stands behind his pulpit or whatever it is and goes off the earth. It is a paradoxical thing to say, but the principal person to educate is the educator. He has forever to have his nose pushed into the actualities of living if he is to be of any good with his knowledge. The contact with reality, so to speak, is the *oomph* of the academe; he may be as learned as he pleases, but he is only a museum piece without it.

Nor should we forget what I have already, perhaps not sufficiently, emphasized, that *today all sorts of people are concerned in education* besides the professional teachers. A very important contribution is being made by the service clubs, by the public libraries, by the trade unions and the cooperatives, as well as by the larger and wiser public utilities and corporations, who are beginning to realize that private enterprise in the last resort means also public responsibility and public service. As I said, there are a lot of us milling around in the pool of adult education. We all know each other pretty well, and with that native capacity for working together which is the especial genius of Canada, we get along pretty well; but it is obviously high time that a group picture, so to speak, were taken of the adult-education forces of the country. Now, if ever, with the war in Europe over, we ought to be coordinating *all* our forces to the bright end of creating a public imagination, a public mind, and a public will worthy of Canada's spectacular possibilities.

*The Changing Face of Propaganda**

There is a paradoxical point where a national information service must become international to fulfill itself. There is a field of operation beyond those services which involve the answering of questions about one's country, concern that the nation's diplomacy shall be supported, and an adequate picture of the nation's self-importance in the foreign press. It is not self-evident that organizations like OWI, the Ministry of Information, the British Council, and the National Film Board of Canada must always pursue exclusively the interest of Britain, America, or Canada as the case may be. It is not self-evident because nations do not now, in the light of Lend-Lease, Mutual Aid, Bretton Woods, Dumbarton Oaks, and UNRRA, exclusively pursue their own national interest, but have in fact at many points sublimated their national interests to international ones and have thereby assumed an international character as real as their national character.

* From an article by John Grierson published in *Free World*, January 1945.

I am making the case that it is now within the logic of the national information services to think less of presenting their own nations to the world and more of presenting the new cooperative world to which their nations are pledged. What are we informing our citizens about today, if it is not about those problems and concerns which are the problems and concerns of all the world: food, health, housing, reconstruction, and the rest? They involve, each one of them, international relationships and dependencies. We have in the past, all too often, had to foist our national story on others, and necessarily so, because our national story was only our own. In the concern for social progress which now besets the nations, the national interest is often, and deeply, the interest of others.

The Future of the Films*

I am thinking particularly of the documentary potential of the next ten years or so. But I would guess that some of the best and most valuable sponsorship will come from city councils and state governments, from national and trade associations, from the trade unions, as well as from the big corporations and public utilities.

The classical example of public-utility sponsorship of documentary films is of course the work done by the Gas, Light, and Coke Company in England. At a time when we could not get the British Ministry of Health to support the movement for slum clearance and nutrition, we bore down on the Gas, Light, and Coke Company and found a basis of common interest which turned out to be of the greatest significance. We said in short: we are not interested in how much money you make, and we are not interested in any publicity films whatsoever. On the other hand, you are in a very tough position in relation to your competitor, electricity. Electricity is associated with the twentieth century, whereas you have not yet rid yourself of your dark and somewhat sordid association with the gaslit nineteenth century. We are prepared therefore to bring you with all speed into the twentieth century by the simple device of associating you with the most modern progressive elements of the day.

I shall say for the Gas, Light, and Coke Company: they saw the point very quickly, and more or less all the best film things done in the thirties in and around slum clearances, town planning, local administration, progressive schools, and nutrition originated with them. Of course it did their commercial interest no harm to have a bath in every room and the substitution of gas fires and cookers for coal fires in the kitchen. But I would be

* From a speech by John Grierson given at the Conference of the Arts, Sciences and Professions in the Post-War World, New York City, June 23, 1945.

accurate in saying that this particular public utility did realize the still greater value of proving its public utility to the public and of reaching a point where it could call itself public servant number one and get away with it.

I give you this instance in some detail because I see in its extension to other public utilities and corporations a very important potential for civic education.

It is the custom, particularly in the United States, to consider dangerous the educational materials emanating from corporate groups. Danger of course there is, but none that cannot be guarded against, at least in the field of technological description.

Good film producers who have the concept of public service in their imaginations should always be able to direct the path of these films along safe and constructive lines. The work of the British group with the Post Office, Shell, Anglo-Iranian, Imperial Airways and I.C.I. proves that it can be done by resolute men who serve ideals and know how to discover the creative relationship between business and the public welfare.

Doubts I know must arise in your minds, and I am as conscious of them as anyone. It has been my business for many years to be conscious of these doubts. However, I suggest this for your consideration. The first problem of education today is essentially one of understanding the technological world in which we live, and every force which directs its development has something of importance to say.

In this connection much may be expected from government, and much indeed has been done by governments. It is important to note, however, that nothing can be expected from governments beyond what I shall call the degree of general sanction. The degree of general sanction is not the degree of sanction by the party in power: it is the degree of sanction allowed by all the parties of Parliament or Congress. For example, in England the degree of sanction is left of the Conservative Party that is in power, and in Canada, it is slightly right of the Radical Liberal Party that is in power. I saw, as an old public servant, that if the degree of general sanction is accurately gauged, maximum support is forthcoming for creative work. Where, however, advantage is taken and the degree of sanction is estimated on partisan lines, ineffectiveness and frustration result.

This of course imposes a clear limit on the creative artist working within the public service, for obviously the degree of general sanction does not allow for forthright discussions of such highly controversial problems as, say, America's record with the Negroes in the South, or England's record with the Indians in the East. The creative worker must not, however, simply denounce this limitation and dissociate himself from government service. If he is a practical operator and a practical reformer he will take the situation for what it is and do his utmost within the limitations set, and this is one of the disciplines which the creative artist must learn in this particular period of society.

If he wants to pursue the more difficult and controversial themes, I am afraid he must look elsewhere than to governments, and here I think it will be well to examine in future years the sponsorship potential of authorities and associations who are less hamstrung than governments necessarily are. In particular, one expects much from the trade unions and cooperative movements. One also expects much from the associations devoted to such matters as nutrition and town planning and public health. To take one example, why should Mayor LaGuardia have a radio station and not a film unit? I can imagine no more effective center for films dealing with town planning, child welfare, public health, educational progress, and interracial understanding than a film center based on the social interests of the City of New York. I make this suggestion not only for New York but for every city in the country. City councils, professional associations, trade unions alike, are all directly concerned with the media of public observation and analysis for the simple reason that they are all equally concerned with the growth of professional and civic understanding.

Here I am not altogether guessing. Even now there are many signs of a growing use of documentary films by these bodies. In my own experience hardly a week goes by that I am not asked for advice on how to make or circulate films by groups whose varying interest ranges all the way from psychical research to stamp collecting. It is one of the phenomena of the time that there is hardly an organization that is not in, or about to be in, the documentary-film business, simply because it is an instrument by which knowledge of a functional nature can be exchanged and extended.

We ought to be clear from the first that in education we are not just concerned with mobilizing new techniques for the teaching of the same old thing. The problem of education today is not one of techniques or of visual aids or aural aids or of any other aids. These represent specific improvements in the teaching of *known* areas of knowledge and very important they are, but they do not go to the heart of the matter.

. . . In my view, the basic problem of education lies not so much in the acquisition of literacy or of knowledge or of skills, as in the pattern of civic appreciation, civic faith, and civic duty which goes with them. They mean nothing—literacy, knowledge or skill, the whole lot of them—if they do not make for *order* in the world, and today they quite obviously do not. Where I think we have failed is that we have not sufficiently realized the implications of the change which the technological revolution has brought upon us. The objective nature of that new society we understand well enough, but not its subjective implications. We have obliterated the obstacles of time and space and have made the world's riches of matter and of mind potentially available to everyone. We have become specialists, in the safe knowledge that we have the benefit of the specialization of others in a new and more complex system of creation and enjoyment. We have learned that two and two makes five, of the corporate and the cooperative.

But, on the other hand, we have become more and more citizens of a community which we do not adequately see. Under our feet go wires and pipes leading to complicated supply systems we blindly take for granted. Behind each counter of our modern buying lies a world system of manufacture, choice, and conveyance. A simple weather forecast is a daily drama of complicated observation over a large part of the earth's surface, without which men could not safely fly or put to sea. We do not see it. Messages that roll easily from the local press may have come at six hundred words a minute from Moscow or may have been relayed south from London to Africa and by complicated steps north again to overcome an atmospheric problem we know nothing about. It is a nickel buy, like an ice cream cone or a packet of chewing gum. Sleeping or waking, we are all concerned each day in an interdependency, one with another, which in fact makes us each our brother's servant and our brother's keeper. This is the fact of modern society, whatever medieval theories of self-subsistence operating in the name of art or operating in the name of religion may try to tell us. This is the fact of modern society, yet we are slow to adopt the habits of thought which must necessarily go with interdependency, if we are to control the forces which we ourselves have released. We operate in a new world, but are not yet possessed of it. We have given ourselves a new kind of society, but have not yet given ourselves the new kind of imagination or the new conception of citizenship which makes it tolerable. Like Tomlinson, who gave up the ghost in his house in Gloucester Square, we stand betwixt and between with the winds of the universe blowing through our empty spirits. We operate in a system of complex interdependency, but still like to think that we are simple souls, face to face and on the most personal basis with our Maker. We have given away our capacity for self-sufficiency, but still want to be free individuals, so called—free to go our own gait and let the devil take the hindmost. Now, when we ought more than at any time in history to be talking most about responsibility and disciplines and duties, we are talking most about freedom from controls and freedom from restraints, even when they are only our own necessary self-controls and self-restraints. This is the most paradoxical fact of our time. I think it is no wonder that we are full of frustrations and neuroses of one kind or another, for we are, in fact, in the process of trying to eat our cake and have it too; enjoying the interdependence but still demanding the privilege of independence.

This in turn places a great burden and a great creative responsibility on education, as an art, if we are dealing, as I think we are, with the intangibles that affect the imaginations of men and determine their will. It is no longer a problem of known areas of knowledge simply and directly communicated. It is a question of the images that direct men's vision and determine their loyalties, and we are concerned not only with the conscious processes of the mind but with the subconscious ones which insensibly govern the pattern of men's attention and the manner of their action.

Do we still see the world in a rectangle, up and down and left and right, or do we really, in our heart and mind, see over the world and think over the world and feel over the world in the circles of common interest and actual interdependence? That, I think, is the style of question which education and art will presently be asking itself. It involves inevitably a reanswering of Tolstoy's question as to what men live by, a reanswering which will not inevitably leave the classic conceptions in their old and honorable places. I hesitate to suggest it, but we may even have to revise our views on Plato, Milton, John Stuart Mill, and the hundred best books. It is possible that we need not take them quite so seriously as guides to the special and urgent problems of what may be, in the light of time and philosophy, a new dispensation of thought and habit—as new a dispensation as that which followed the development of measurement and perspective at the end of the Middle Ages. The key to this new dispensation may well be our use of the two words, *corporate* and *cooperative*. They represent, it is possible, a new species of measurement and perspective and therefore a new species of power and thought and habit.

Lean Years
and Full Years
(1945-65)

PERHAPS America always represented for Grierson the greatest challenge. Here was the ultimate chance to experiment and to achieve in the field of communication, in the land of true democracy where men were free and equal to begin with. Here was the place where techniques for public purpose, civic action, and community initiative should and could be mobilized within the great twentieth-century society of mass man. Grierson had found ways to promote the sponsorship of educational films, science films, useful and constructive films: big business would pay for them, government would pay for them. This had worked in Britain and in Canada, but in the United States the possibilities were far greater. New York was where the money was, where the action was, the bankers and film distributors and publishers and radio networks and advertisers. In a way, Canada had provided a protected situation; let the effort now be made afresh in a new and tougher area.

From his base at the Film Board in Canada, Grierson, during the war, had had frequent contact with influential public figures in the United States. He met in Chicago regularly with the Commission on the Freedom of the Press; he had frequent contact with American documentary film-makers, with commercial distributors, with Louis de Rochemont of *March of Time*, and with journalists and editors; he frequently had dealings with such large American organizations as the National Educational Association and the Educational Film Library Association. A number of American documentary film-makers and technicians had worked for a time at the Film Board in Canada, and the Film Board productions were becoming widely known in educational and media circles in the States. In view of all these contacts and his earlier visits to the United States, it seemed that he would find a congenial group to work with.

But complications arose. In Canada, after he had already announced his intention to withdraw and "leave the show to the Canadians," an incident of some political significance occurred and the National Film Board, with Grierson, was to some degree involved. This was the Gouzenko affair concerning Soviet espionage in Canada, outlined on pages 198–200. An investigating tribunal was appointed, a Royal Commission to determine the extent and veracity of the charges against all persons named or implicated. Grierson must needs appear and testify. So he did, with unfortunate results. His answers to the commissioners were not so much answers as broad and ringing philosophical statements concerned with freedom of thought. He felt not so much that he had outsmarted the commissioners but that he had raised issues of profound importance; he in effect read them a lesson on their responsibilities. His testimony was not considered in that light; Grierson's sharpness, his rhetoric, his unquestionable intellectual brilliance no doubt provoked suspicion of him. To the commission he seemed not so much lofty and profound as evasive in failing to supply what the commission considered straight answers to simple questions.

His departure from Canada was clouded by these events. No official recognition was given to Grierson by the Canadian government he had served so notably. Nor could the Film Board itself acknowledge his going, for he simply, quickly, and quietly left the scene of his very considerable achievements without formalities of any kind.

In New York, with some of his associates from Canada and London, Grierson established a company for independent film production under the title of International Film Associates. Efforts were made to find sponsors and to develop an effective distribution network for documentary films in commercial theatre channels, as in the manner of the highly acceptable *World in Action* series produced in Canada at the Film Board during the war years and widely distributed in the United States and Canada by United Artists. Grierson had with him a talented group of film-makers, a proven team; now he needed money and a distribution network.

Some films were begun under various sponsors, while the main effort to develop a regular and widespread distribution network in theatres continued. In the United States, there had been no widespread consistent policy of government support for the distribution of educational films. There was indeed specialized production of films—films for agricultural or industrial training or military service training—but there was no overall pattern of government-sponsored films. Commercial distribution, sale or rental of 16mm subjects, provided the basic system of circulation for educational ("educational" in the wider sense, meaning not limited to classrooms) films.

Grierson's ideas for the use of films almost invariably required some new and specialized channel of distribution in order to bring the films effectively to their intended audience. Such a channel was very difficult to come up with in the United States, since there were no coordinated means of national distribution in the nontheatrical market. In any case, U.S. sentiment was traditionally opposed to the principle of film-making or distribution by government, on the supposition that any such activity must essentially be propagandist, special pleading on behalf of the government of the day. Of course in theory television was the answer to all distribution problems, but television had not yet appeared upon the scene.

What did pop up were U.S. government agents who questioned Grier-

son's purposes and credentials for work in the United States. The Gouzenko affair had tinged Grierson's record with ambiguity. In the prevailing
American climate of suspicion and morbid anticommunism, Grierson's
labor permit was withdrawn and he was in effect denied residence in the
United States.

In 1947, Grierson went to Paris, where as it happened he had been
offered the directorship of the division of Mass Communications at
UNESCO, the cultural and educational agency of the United Nations.
UNESCO was new, seeking to formulate its own new programs on a basis
of consensus among the member-nations of the world community. Here
was another thorny problem, that of achieving consensus among scores of
squabbling states, many of them divided among polarized political camps.
As with all the specialized agencies of the United Nations, UNESCO had
to work through a massive multilingual bureaucracy. Whereas Grierson
had found single ministries of the British government approachable and
flexible when presented with new ideas, and whereas a Canadian prime
minister had given him virtually complete support for the development of a
national film policy in Canada, he found the situation at UNESCO vastly
different. The weight, complexity, and comparative inertia of the UNESCO
machinery was such that Grierson simply could not get it to work. William
Farr comments in these pages on Grierson's experience during his brief
span at UNESCO. It was for him impossible, and again he moved away,
back to Britain.

Here too were large problems to be dealt with. The wartime machinery
of information had produced material in great volume. Against this background, the Crown Film Unit had risen to heights of genuine artistry in
many of its films. Where prewar British films in the commercial feature
field were mostly artificial and lackluster, the best of the British wartime
documentaries had combined notable energy and human feeling with fine
filmcraft. Hopes for British film-making were high in 1945, in view of the
excellent achievements in documentary; there were many new young talents at the Crown Film Unit and in the abundance of independent film
groups that had sprung up to handle wartime production; there were ambitious new plans for British feature films and distribution systems financed
by J. Arthur Rank. But in government, retrenchment was the order of the
day. Whereas in Canada the Film Board had survived the postwar wave of
cutbacks in government spending, this was not the case in Britain. The
Central Office of Information, succeeding the wartime Ministry of Information, was sharply reduced; and the Crown Film Unit, representing the full
flowering of the documentary movement which Grierson himself had established, was disbanded.

It was under Grierson's aegis at the Central Office of Information that

In Wiltshire—Grierson, Golightly,
Margaret Grierson.

this unhappy policy was carried out. He had in effect returned to Britain to
supervise the painful retrenchment of government film-making and the
dissolution of the Crown Unit. It seems a cruel irony, looking back, that he
had to preside at the liquidation of a large part of the film structure built
upon his efforts.

By now in the early 1950s, the mood among film people was bitter.
Many in the documentary group felt that they had been cast adrift, for
commercial-feature work could not begin to take up the slack in terms of
opportunity and employment. Grierson had rows with many of his former
colleagues and protégés. He was discouraged by events and by the meager
goals of policy-making at the Central Office. His health was poor. His
gloomy visits to the Beehive, a drab London pub adjacent to the Central
Office, did little to improve his spirits. A great friend and longtime associ-

The Brave Don't Cry—a low-budget feature film by Philip Leacock
in the Group III program which brought a strong documentary
feeling to the account of a mining tragedy (1952).

ate, a person of infinite discretion, loyalty, and forbearance, the legendary
J. P. Roderick Golightly, was stricken with tuberculosis and became a
permanent invalid living with the Grierson household in the country.

Grierson's most positive activity during this period was as joint director
of the Group III program of feature-film production, funded by the British
government as a means to develop and stimulate increased commercial-film
activity in Britain. The commercial-film industry did not provide anything
like sufficient opportunities for young writers, actors, and film directors,
and the Group III scheme (by utilizing money rebated from entertainment-
tax earnings) helped to remedy this situation. As executive producer and
administrator, Grierson again found himself involved in actual production,
in planning, supervising, and producing new feature films: done on low
budgets, these films were free and flexible in style, with offbeat stories and
as-yet-unknown talent. Some of the young actors who had their first screen
opportunities within the Group III program were Peter Finch, Kenneth
More, Peter Sellers, and Tony Hancock.

The strongest of these films was probably *The Brave Don't Cry* (1952) by the young ex-documentary director Philip Leacock, now in Hollywood. This was a coal-mining story of forceful dramatic quality. For the most part other films within the Group III program were curiously light, gentle and whimsical in style and feeling, perhaps a reaction to the violence of the war just ended and to the still bleak and restricted life in Britain during the early postwar period.

Despite this short-term involvement with Group III and its production work (though not, again, without severe administrative and financial problems), Grierson remained restless and unsettled. Angry at the course of events, hurt no doubt by his recent series of misfortunes, he became at this time increasingly arbitrary and difficult to deal with. He abused his health quite savagely and intemperately, and at length became seriously ill. Anthony Grierson, his older brother, took him sternly in hand, told him to mend his ways or resign himself to imminent oblivion. Grierson obeyed instructions, recovered his balance, and entered upon a period of sorely needed rest and rehabilitation.

So far the postwar years had been hard and largely unrewarding. The documentary film had entered an uncertain, unstable period. Money was tight and sponsorship grudging. Television had gotten its start. The vital idealism, energy, and excitement of documentary experiments in film-making seemed to be gone. Grierson had amassed no wealth and seemed to have few prospects. He had loyal friends, but his public influence, status, and authority seemed to have eroded away. Yet in this gloomy time he set about his own program of regeneration and in 1960 turned—successfully —towards the medium that had in effect created much of the problem for documentary films—television. Grierson would still have twelve more years for new explorations, experiments, involvements. The winter of his discontent was nearly ended.

Bosley Crowther

As film critic for the *New York Times*, Bosley Crowther has enjoyed a central vantage point from which to view film affairs for many years. The whole world of films—American and European, Russian and Japanese, esoteric and popular—has passed before his eyes and (so to speak) over the roller of his typewriter. He has long been aware of the documentary film and of the affinities and differences between British and American efforts in the documentary field. He was a long-time friend of Grierson's.

In 1972 Mr. Crowther retired from the *Times* and had become a film consultant with Columbia Pictures in New York. We arrived there early one morning, drove to a midtown hotel, made contact with Mr. Crowther, and about an hour before lunch began to film him in Times Square. Broadway is not a quiet location for exterior shooting, but we felt it would be appropriate to Bosley Crowther and to the whole idea of movies in America.

In any case we filmed Mr. Crowther in Times Square willy-nilly, surrounded by a mildly curious aggregation of native New Yorkers of many hues and ethnic antecedents. A small black man with a straw hat stuck close to my elbow with great interest and persistence. We pivoted with the camera around Mr. Crowther; so did he. We backed off and moved in reverse ahead of Mr. Crowther; so did he. We doubled smartly around to the other side of Mr. Crowther with another view of Broadway in the background; so did he. It became apparent that the black man was listening closely to Crowther's words, following his comments with genuine interest. We finished filming after thirty or forty minutes; our little gallery of spectators melted away in the traffic. But the black man came up to me and shook my hand, and Bosley Crowther's, and said warmly to the latter, "I want to tell you, you ratiocinated that *real well.*" And took his leave. All of us were very pleased with this endorsement.

Crowther: I must say that I'm delighted to talk about Grierson, particularly in this environment, at this spot here in Times Square—to me at least very appropriate, because I always thought of Grierson as a man of the world who lived as much in New York as he did in London or Montreal or wherever he happened to be doing his work. He wanted to do things in New York. When he would come to New York, during the war years, he would usually call me and I'd pop in to see him. He'd usually stay at the

Warwick Hotel. John was full of conversation and always full of great enthusiasm about the whole Canadian project.

I remember one time we had an evening with Robert Flaherty. John and Flaherty got into a rather heated discussion about their particular styles. Of course Flaherty was then an old man, and they'd had a good dinner with a few drinks. Along in the evening Flaherty began to get awfully sleepy, and John kept going at him, like a little terrier going after an old bear, you know. Finally Flaherty went off to sleep completely and John continued his conversation with the rest of us in the room. I thought their relationship was delightful.

Question: Did he ever talk to you about his first visit to Hollywood, his impressions of that visit in 1924 or '25?

Crowther: He was fascinated by Hollywood. Actually I think he went out there expecting to be horrified by it, from all that he had heard and read. I got the impression that he really was quite fascinated by the people, particularly some of the directors that he got to know—Murnau, for instance, and he had a very interesting experience with Lubitsch. I know that he had high regard for Chaplin. Grierson met many people and got a new kind of feeling about Hollywood—a respect at least for the craftsmen and their skills, which of course was what he was beginning to think about at that time. He felt there was great power in the medium itself, in the way the audiences were growing. But the stuff that was being put on the screen in the early 1920s was merely frivolous, run-of-the-mill material.

At that point, he felt the potential of the Flaherty films. And this was a kind of revelation—in the humanism of the treatment, in the fact that everything filmed was *real*. This seemed to him highly exciting, and completely at odds with the existing film style in Hollywood at that time. His interest in the film craft was so intense, and his respect for the craftsmen— not necessarily all the directors by any means, but his concern for the cameramen, and later with the beginning of sound, with what they were trying to do with sound. I would say that Grierson manifested his expansive and objective point of view by *not* being supercilious about Hollywood. He definitely saw there a form of motion picture that could be expanded and made much more effective.

I felt always that John Grierson regarded Flaherty as sort of the Jean Jacques Rousseau of motion pictures—the romanticist and the idealist. He idealized man and regarded man and nature as one, against the encroachments of civilization generally. John really had no sympathy whatsoever for that point of view, or for that concept of man. I suppose it was purely a sociological difference. Grierson believed in action and in what was happening, so he wanted to capture that on film. For instance, take a film as early as *Drifters*, it's a film about the jobs that men do—nothing heroic, but tough dirty jobs. It always seemed to me that Grierson's taste was for action, for people doing things and for their relations as active people, as people who probably were in competition and angry with one another. Economics was an area of great interest to John, and he was always reaching for the understanding of economic motivations, including the war, and including the economic conflicts *within* the war. Grierson and his associates were also much concerned with using the urgencies of the war socially, so that what was done in the postwar world, resulting from the work of wartime policies and organizations, would be to the great advantage of the ordinary guy.

I do recollect very well one occasion after the war when John came to New York. I would get a telephone call and he'd be in his hotel. This one time he called me from a hotel here which was not his usual hotel, but another. He asked me to come there, so I went to the room that he told me and knocked on the door. No answer. A moment later a door opened down the hall on the other side, and John stuck his head out and said, "Come on in here." This was a mystifying thing indeed. When I got in and spoke to him, he said, "We'll have to talk very low because I'm afraid that I'm being bugged, or watched." I couldn't understand then what this meant. He believed that he was being pursued by elements that he felt were inimical to him, and as clearly as I could make out they were definitely political. He said, "You know when I was in this country years ago, the *Chicago Tribune* took a very dim view of me, and they had some editorials I recollect." The *Chicago Tribune* did run some anti-Grierson editorials. We talked for a while, but I could never obtain from John precisely what all this was about. It was the most mystifying visit with him I ever had; indeed, I never did get it clear because when I saw him in London some years later he was in a very serene and gentle mood, and when I asked him about that period, he said, "I'd rather not talk about that at all." So I had the feeling that he was worried very much at that time in New York—that was the period right after World War II. A little later when Senator McCarthy got going, Grierson was one of those who got knocked about. I recollect he told me that he was having great difficulties in the U.S.A.; his visa had been taken away from him. He had been to Washington to see if he could straighten it out, but had not been successful. That bothered me. I was waiting to hear whether something might come of it, but I never heard anything more.

He was of course very highly regarded by the American documentary people—rather, his inspiration, the kind of thing that he was able to do, the doors he was able to open for documentary. The later film group here in New York was Willard Van Dyke and Irving Jacoby and Rodakiewicz, who formed a group almost imitative of the National Film Board. I think those men were very admiring of Grierson's inspiration. I don't know that they ever thought of Grierson himself as a film-maker, but they got work for their own operation, and of course began making films for the U.S. State Department, which later became USIS, then USIA, almost a duplication of what the National Film Board in Canada was doing.

I think I was the only critic that Grierson ever saw much of. The motion-picture critics at that time were not anything like as interested as I was in these marginal uses of motion picture, such as the *World in Action* series, and all the things *The March of Time* was doing, the Frank Capra films done for the army, the *Why We Fight* series, you know. But there was a blanket of obscurity over documentary in the United States even at that time, except insofar as we would occasionally see a picture on the screen, a war picture, shot by one of our army or air force film units.

There was one occasion immediately after World War II when he called me and made a suggestion about something he would very much like to do when he left the Canadian Film Board, and that was to establish some form or continuation perhaps of the *World in Action* film series on a commercial, theatrical basis, a periodic series of films somewhat similar to *The March of Time* but one that would have his own character, his own stamp and style. He wanted to establish something of this sort, but he needed sponsorship to obtain his film material. He asked me if I thought it might be possible for him to discuss this with the publishers of the *New York Times*. What he wanted to do was get the *New York Times* to allow him to use the *Times*'s name in some fashion, perhaps in the title of his film series, but particularly to allow him to use all of the news services, all of the information that funneled into the *New York Times* every day, to use these as the basis for his dispatches and for the stories that he would prepare for the film series.

I set up a luncheon with the publisher of the *Times* (this must've been 1947, maybe '48). The publisher, with the entire operational line of *Times*'s editors and executives, through one very agreeable, delightful luncheon listened to John expound at great length concerning what he wanted to do. I must say it was a tremendously impressive suggestion, about how he wanted to develop a news film series, a documentary series. The idea of doing it then, of course, was to show it widely in the theatres on a periodic basis.

The publisher of the *Times* seemed to be very much disposed towards it, and other editors were also, but one of our top management men who had a great deal of influence said absolutely not, the *New York Times* should not be involved in anything of this sort, and so the idea was abandoned.

Later I realized what an ironic lack this was, because what John had in mind was specifically the sort of thing that was later picked up by television and became very popular as we now know from all the top news shows, a combination of views and talks. If John's idea had been embraced by the *New York Times*, I think the *Times* would've developed it before anybody else, a tremendous device for expanding its service as a medium for disseminating views and opinion.

I think the fact that John did not continue with any film series of that sort was a great misfortune. Indeed, I would say a waste, because he had a talent and a wonderful capacity for bringing together young men, enthusiasts, and I'm sure that he could have gotten generations to come along with him. I dare say he would've been, himself, very much to the fore in that sort of operation over the years, especially now, when we need that kind of communication and his kind of thinking, editorial thinking, more than ever.

Joris Ivens

Grierson chose to utilize film as a means of documenting problems and issues in the world of reality, while other film-makers seized upon it for quite different purposes. Joris Ivens of the Netherlands has been a chronicler of world events. His films, as he says, have anticipated states of crisis, great struggles between nations and ideologies. His work has been politicized in the sense that Grierson's has not; it has been more partisan, more committed, more emotional. Yet the issues and events that concerned Ivens have been very much akin to those that concerned Grierson—social justice, freedom, human dignity.

Through the good offices of Jan DeVaal, director of the Filmmuseum at the Museum of Modern Art in Amsterdam, we were able to contact Joris Ivens in Peking shortly after Grierson's death. We described our film project and the interviews we hoped to do, and told him that we would not get to China to film him. We asked if he himself could make arrangements for a self-conducted interview if we sent him film stock and a full account of our requirements. With a Chinese crew (quite unaccustomed to shooting interviews) Ivens was able to oblige us, and sent to Canada a film record of his feelings and judgments concerning Grierson.

Ivens: I knew John Grierson very well and I first met him in Europe, but I think if John would see me now, he would say, in the keen and brisk way he always talked, "What the hell are you doing here, Joris?" Then I would tell him I was making here a film about China, about the Cultural Revolution and all the accomplishments of the Cultural Revolution, and I was doing it together with a group of Chinese film-makers . . . and this film will be a documentary film about China.

Now I will go on with the question you asked me. Grierson was the man who sacrificed his profession for us. He was a real film director, but he stuck to his main work and became an organizer of work for others. He really worked so that other people could make their films, and that was wonderful from this man who also fought against bureaucracy. He got the money for the film people so from their documentary work they could live. We in Europe, we couldn't even live with our documentary film, we had to make publicity films to live. And he made this possibility, and at the same time he formed many very important documentary film-makers. What he did was make the international prestige of the documentary film.

Question: Before you met John Grierson, what was your own film work?

Ivens: I started rather different. John started, you could say, from a direction of the educational and cultural, and I started more from the aesthetic, artistic point of view. I was part of the avant-gardist movement in Europe, with Paris, with Berlin—then into this artistic movement came realism. That was the influence of the Russian film-makers such as Eisenstein, Pudovkin, Dovzhenko. And my work was also influenced by the work of Flaherty. And then with this realism I started to associate myself with the social problems of my own country and other countries in Europe, and I made a film about the coal miners' strike in Belgium. I was for the workers and for the strike. John Grierson saw this film; he was very interested and encouraged me, and he also showed this film later to his own unit. That was a very great pleasure for me that he did this. Then later this English group went on and made the film *Coal Face*. Cavalcanti made this film, but it was more observing, it was not taking part in the miner's life. You could also see later on when I went to Spain to make the film *Spanish Earth* about the civil war there, with Ernest Hemingway. And in China in '38 with the film *The Four Hundred Million*. Such films are never made by the units from Grierson but by some independent unit, that's the difference between John and me.

You could say, as I told you, that I started in an artistic and aesthetic way; then I worked more in a realistic way, and from this realistic way I started my work with more social implications. And with that I have stayed consistently. I always try to give the deeper truths, the ideological truths, of the things I've filmed, and at the same time I try to always express them in the highest artistic form. John said to me: "You are a lucky person, and I see in you that you have a unity in your work, there's a unity between what you are thinking and what you are doing." I'm trying to keep this up, but you cannot do it only yourself, you have to be helped by something, and there I can be sure that John Grierson was one of the men who helped me very much in my work at a certain moment of my life. It was a moment at the beginning of World War II. I was a professor at the University of Southern California in Los Angeles. The war started and I couldn't get a job as a film-maker. It was idiotic because I had always been fighting against Fascism in Spain and in China, and now when the war started, I was out of the game. John Grierson in Ottawa saw this and said, "You know what they say of you—you are a premature anti-Fascist, you were too early an anti-Fascist. But I don't care, I will help you immediately. Tomorrow you come to Ottawa." And there was the National Film Board, and in Ottawa they took me right on a film job to chase Nazi submarines on the North Atlantic. So John was really the man who had confidence in me and who put me right to work against the enemy I wanted to fight. And that I'll never forget. John has many, many people he has put on the right track in their work.

Question: How would you define your own objectives in the pursuit of documentary film-making?

Ivens: That's the eternal question they ask me. It always comes back to the documentary film-maker. Already many, many documentarists struggle with that for forty years. One answer I can give, because I'm an old film-maker: just look at the series of my work, you will understand what I mean about documentary film; but in the audience there will be many people that don't know my films, so I will define it a little. I have tried always to show the high points, the crisis points of history, of contemporary history, in my documentary films—to *take part* in the social and political life of the different countries. I mentioned already an example of the film I made in Spain, *Spanish Earth.* Then later in China I followed many of the revolutionary movements in Indonesia and later in Cuba, in China again, and also the war of Vietnam. I define my film, for me at least, as a film that takes part in the struggle for independence of the people, and for the freedom of people.

I would add that I take very seriously the responsibility towards the audience. The people who see my films know that I say the truth and that I have a firm standpoint when I make the film. There is an ethical and moral point of view, not just an aesthetic point of view, that is very important; then in the execution of my films, I'm always very much linked up with the people I'm filming. When I'm in the wartime situation, I live with the people under the earth for protection against the bombs. When I made a film in the United States about the farm problems, I'm living on the farm. These are not exactly principles, but they're practical things for the principles of my work. Grierson in a certain way agrees with that, but he goes less far than I do, he goes not so far as that. He's a man who was very well read, he read Marx, Lenin, Mao Tse-tung. And sometimes he was a strange man, eh? When he saw a Communist, he quoted the Bible, and when he saw Catholics, he quoted Lenin. I only say that to characterize Grierson, because he was a man who knew a lot, but who, as I said before, went less far in his work.

Question: What do you consider were Grierson's objectives in film-making? Did you agree with his policies? Or disagree? Did he influence your thinking in any way?

Ivens: He talked sometimes of evaluation, of observation. I am more for *participation* directly in my films and identifying myself with the people I'm filming. We were of the same direction, you could say, but I was more to the left than Grierson was in his work. I think I learned from him to appreciate my own profession even more. I would say, the value and the importance of the documentary film, that is what I learned from John Grierson. You must also not forget that after World War II, John Grierson took part in a lot of cultural movement at UNESCO and elsewhere. That was the time when we often met in little bars in Paris and we talked about the future of documentary film, and there our friendship became even more solid, and in that way I think of John, because there was a very strong relationship, and our love for the documentary film was really the span that joined us.

Question: What would you say were the chief influences of documentary film upon feature-film development?

Ivens: I think there was a great influence that the documentary film had on the fiction film. For example, we could see very clearly in the beginning of World War II, especially in the fiction films of England and the United States, how many of the influential and realistic subjects were taken over by the fiction film, and how many fiction-film directors became documentary film-makers. Then you can see a great influence in the neorealistic school after the war in Italy, where the documentary-film method, our method of filming, was completely taken over by the fiction film. I think cinema verité, the film of truth, was a movement twenty or fifteen years ago that was also very much influenced by documentary. And then also television. But I would also add that we of the documentaries have also learned from television—not just from television, I must say, we also learned from the fiction film. In the dramatization of our sequences I also learned much from the fiction film. So now in the last years, especially in the United States and France and in some other countries, the young film-makers don't care much if it is fiction or documentary—these frontiers between fiction film and documentary film are very vague now, so I think that's the answer I would give to this question.

Question: What do you think are the prospects for continuing production of documentary films all over the world in the next few years?

Ivens: I think that these prospects are very good, and you could say in a certain sense that Grierson has done a lot to make this prospect bright and very broad for us. I think that for the documentary film the whole field is opened—the movie houses, the schools, the universities, the film clubs, the cinemathèques. Everywhere there's a place for documentary film, as for the fiction film. The television has also broadened this field for documentary, but we have to say that it also depends a lot on the documentary film-makers themselves. If they really stay close, *connected* with the social and the political and economic life of their country, if they really feel the pulse of their people, of what happens—then their films will be exciting. The great danger of the documentary film is if it is boring. A documentary film has to be very vivid; and all the documentaries should be more daring in their work, more audacious—should tackle great things that have to do with the future of their country, and the people, and the freedom of people.

Question: What about China? How would you characterize the making and use of documentary film in China?

Ivens: This question would be better answered by the Chinese film-makers, but still I will try to tell you something about it, because they told me and I'm working already a few months here. I see that through the Cultural Revolution the artists and the cultural workers are now very close to the people, to the masses, together; and I think that will help them, because they say that art in the socialist countries should serve the people. What do they mean by that? They mean that with their art they want to assemble the people, to make them aware that they are really together building a socialist state, a socialist society. Here they take the socialism very seriously, you know; and I think that the documentary film can help a lot in serving the people. Also important is the educational work of the film, because in education you have to see very broad; education must help you to think for yourself, to solve the problems which come up in your daily life—that is one of the tasks. They find also that with their art they have to denounce the forces that would go against this development of a healthy socialist society, and that task has to be taken very seriously too, in this country.

Question: How do you sum up Grierson's achievements and influences on film-making? Do you think he failed or succeeded or both?

Ivens: I remember in the last ten years, I met him several times. He was working in UNESCO, I was working in Italy but came back to France; then I was working in China and came back to France, and we had many good times at the bars around UNESCO there in Paris. Then he was also very helpful in being the president of our organization, the International Association of Documentary Film-makers. He had a good sense of humor, so we had very good meetings where really very important serious things were decided, but at the same time John always was there to make a very relaxed atmosphere at this kind of meeting. When you ask me if John really succeeded in his work, I would say yes, he succeeded; of course nobody can succeed completely, so he too has certain fields where he failed. But years before he really made the foundations, the conditions so that the documentary film could have a healthy development, and we have to thank him very much for it. Really, many people will say it, but I can tell it really from the heart that it is so, and one other thing I want to say, I think that the young film-makers now making documentary films are maybe not aware of John's work for the documentary film, but they can still be happy that John Grierson was there, in our international film field.

William Farr

William Farr speaks as an international civil servant and as the former director of the Mass Media Division of the United Nations Educational, Scientific, and Cultural Organization of the United Nations. At the beginning of its activity, Grierson had served at UNESCO in the same capacity. In Grierson's time, however, policies were just being defined and the wide-ranging international program of UNESCO was just being worked out, amid the usual stresses generated by almost a hundred nations espousing different ideologies and different goals.

Farr recounts something of the problems Grierson encountered at the very outset of UNESCO's work, when a basic program had to be established despite the disparate pulls of opposing power blocs. In this context, the scale of operation was too large for Grierson's comfort. In one-to-one relationships with other professionals, with people in a single government, or with people in the film industry, Grierson could promote effectively and with great dash. But when confronted with large committees, a Niagara-like flow of documentation, and the processes of internal translation and communication, Grierson's ardor in fighting the good fight was much diminished.

We filmed Mr. Farr in the Japanese garden of UNESCO, at the Place de Fontenoy in Paris. He had retired from UNESCO but was still engaged on a consultancy. Sad to report, William Farr died in Paris in November 1976.

Farr: Grierson joined the secretariat of UNESCO in April of '47, as director in charge of public information and everything to do with mass communications. He was also general adviser to Julian Huxley. He left around April of '48, so he wasn't with us very long, but his influence at UNESCO had begun at the general conference, the first general conference in November 1946. And it was quite a dramatic affair. The British delegation was a very strong one; it included, among other people, Jack Priestley, Professor Blackett the scientist, Ritchie Calder, and Grierson himself as the delegate on mass communication.

The British delegation didn't at all like the program which was presented to the general conference. By the end of three days of debate there wasn't very much left of it. This was rather a critical situation, so the UK delegation undertook within twenty-four hours to put the whole program together again, and present it to the commission on the following day. And it was then that Grierson very much took over. He organized an extraordinary working party, which began at eight at night at the hotel where they were staying, and the job was finished at four the following morning. He had

William Farr, a colleague of Grierson's in the early days of UNESCO.

managed to get in all the important ideas proposed by other delegations, and he presented as *rapporteur* a report that was adopted unanimously the following day, and that, as it turned out, would set the shape for the future work of UNESCO in the field of mass communication.

I think his big contribution was that he was practical and pragmatic. He wanted to do on an international scale what in fact he had been trying to do previously on a national scale. He wasn't much concerned with the use of these media for education in the narrow sense. His proposal was the old documentary thesis. And the thing which was so abundantly clear was that, in the communication field as in all other fields, two-thirds of the world were lacking in all the communications facilities. They were lacking in trained personnel, trained staff, and so on. So Grierson said, "For God's sake, let's forget about all the political business, freedom of information, censorship—if we start discussing those, if we try to do anything in those fields, we'll simply divide the organization right down the middle. Let's get on with the immediate job, with the only thing that makes sense. There is no sense in the phrase 'freedom of information' or 'free flow' for people who've got no transmitters, who've got no newspapers, who've got none of these things." And so he initiated a survey of technical facilities, to begin first in the war-devastated countries. After he left it was extended through the whole world. So in three years, we had a picture of exactly what existed and what did not exist in every country of the world. And we drew up plans for what these countries needed in order to maintain themselves at the bare minimum.

Question: What would have been the danger otherwise for UNESCO if this policy wasn't followed?

Farr: There would have been the danger of long fruitless discussions and recriminations, and not merely between East and West in the strictly political sense, because you remember at that time the Soviet Union still wasn't a member of the organization. But there would have been recriminations; for example, there are countries in Asia, democratic countries, that have systems of censorship as severe as you will find anywhere in the world. And you felt that in their stage of development this was necessary. So Grierson says, "It's no good preaching freedom of information for people who still haven't themselves got a voice."

Question: What does one say about his time at UNESCO? Did it work or not? Was he frustrated? What was the nature of it?

Farr: I think he was frustrated. He found all the administrative paraphernalia rather more than he could take. But it did work, it *was* a success in another way, because he did inspire a whole group of people, including Mr. René Maheux, who became the director-general of UNESCO and who worked very closely with Grierson. And of course, Grierson also founded the magazine *The UNESCO Courier*. That was his idea.

Dr. Prem Kirpal

Although his time at UNESCO was brief, Grierson had a definite impact upon communications policy and development within the UNESCO program. Thirty years later, a review of communications activity among the Third World countries, those who most largely utilize the services and expertise provided through UNESCO, confirms this fact. In many countries of Africa, Latin America, West and South Asia, programs to establish film-making, broadcasting, and television facilities are used for purposes of education, literacy, and social development. To examine the current programs of UNESCO is to discover time and again requests for the recruitment of specialized media personnel, requests for the installation or expansion of media facilities within the developing nations. These situations stem from the first objectives of UNESCO communications policy. This in turn began with the effort to survey and evaluate all the existing media facilities in every country, worldwide. From that basis, from established facts, a program of gradual and systematic development in media technology and application has grown around the world. With international assistance, access to the means of production becomes possible for many small states whose industrial or economic base is insufficient to generate media activity on their own.

Dr. Prem Kirpal, a leading Indian educationist, lately Secretary to the Ministry of Education, New Delhi, has long been associated with UNESCO and was formerly vice-president of UNESCO's Executive Board. He was also a member of India's delegation to UNESCO at the time when Grierson was seeking to define a communications program. He recalls this period and Grierson's role in the direction of events. His note was written following a discussion which we had in New Delhi in 1975.

An early impression of my time with UNESCO dates from November 1947 when as an Indian delegate to the Second General Conference of UNESCO I was elected to the Budget Committee for screening of the program and allocating funds to different items approved by the Program Commission.

Among several distinguished specialists appointed by Julian Huxley, the first director-general, was John Grierson, director of the Cinema Section of the Arts Department and a pioneer of the documentary films, an outstanding person.

The communications sector of UNESCO's responsibilities has always been hazy and controversial; in the Budget Committee few attached a high priority to the program items proposed by the director-general. Indeed, some influential delegates believed that it should have only the limited role of publicizing UNESCO's own activities and concrete programs of international cooperation.

It was John Grierson's forceful advocacy and tenacity of purpose that led to a decision in favor of a wider role, comprehending programs of training, worldwide dissemination of film and radio materials for cultural understanding, and systematic inquiries for developing the media in less-developed countries. For hours John Grierson sat in the Budget Committee, fiddling with his pipe and explaining with force and lucidity the rationale of the program, answering questions tersely and effectively, courteous but unyielding, a truly dedicated specialist with strong faith in his calling and a clear vision of its immense potentialities.

It was fortunate that Grierson was at the helm of UNESCO's communications section briefly in the formative period. His creative leadership gave a new direction, specially favorable to the needs of the developing countries in the years to come.

Roberto Rossellini

Any consideration of the realist film must take account of Rossellini and his compatriots, whose films made in Italy in the immediate postwar period so greatly strengthened the place of realism in modern film-making. Rossellini, De Sica, Visconti, and a dozen others established an approach to film that dealt a heavy blow to the conventions of films produced in studios. Among these directors, concern for the reality of places and atmospheres was combined with a strong humanism. These aspects of the neorealist films were not far removed from documentary, although as Rossellini remarks, the Italian film-makers were not acquainted with British documentary work, and their own production was aimed entirely at commercial feature-film release.

Since those years during the late 1940s Rossellini had moved entirely away from the feature-film industry into television. His concerns were majestic in scale: the history of man's technology, the history of man's production of foodstuffs; biographies of great thinkers, monarchs, scientists. Rossellini was a humanist with a deep understanding of technology and science and of the impact of these upon human affairs. He organized for his films not only financial support but also a very wide audience deriving from a television pattern combining Italy and France. State-sponsored television systems of both countries joined in underwriting and releasing Rossellini's series, which dealt with serious intellectual matters at a mature level. In 1974/75 Rossellini was again into a wide range of historical material. With *Italy: Year One* he returned to the Rome of 1945 to describe the rise of the Christian Democratic Party out of postwar disorder. With *The Messiah* he undertook an account of the spread of new ideas that underlay the growth of Christian belief.

Rossellini sought to use the film as a medium to convey something of the complex interrelationships between man and his technology. He believed passionately in the capacity of human intelligence, but felt that people must be able to understand what has happened in the past and to draw the essential lessons therefrom.

We had sent off relays of telegrams to Rossellini from our locations in Scotland, London, and Paris and finally intercepted him on a location of his own at Fiesole near Florence. He was staying in an Albergo overlooking the valley of the Arno and designed (truly) by Michelangelo. The day after we arrived we filmed him, busy with his own filming of an historical television drama, in a cavernous sixteenth-century church of Fiesole. Scores of actors in velvets and furs, doublets and hose, waited their call while lounging in the square and in the church portico. Inside was a scene of great solemnity: noblemen with grave faces filing past the catafalque of a Renaissance prince; a choir intoning the solemn mass. A day later we filmed in the council chamber of a medieval town hall filled with noblemen and citizens, their faces and costumes straight from the paintings of Carpaccio. Calm and composed, Rossellini sat on a stool in a corner, operating his remote-control zoom lens through lengthy takes of complex action and dialogue, the camera moving and circling in a nonstop exploration of the single scene with its wealth of characters and movement.

Rossellini was inventive, intuitive, and resourceful. His concern was with reality, the forces and influences that shape our lives, whether in past or present time. He died in 1977.

Rossellini: I think I have learned a great deal from him.

Question: In what way?

Rossellini: Well, how to look at the truth. To take an honest and direct look at the thing.

Question: How much of Grierson's work or the British documentary work were you aware of, before you started your own film work?

Rossellini: I didn't know the British work at all. During the war we were cut off from everything. Grierson's name I knew only vaguely.

Question: Then what would be your approach, your objective, when you made your first films like Open City?

Rossellini: To see the truth. We had gone through that terrible experience of the war and were coming out from the ruins. It was important to look around and understand things. That was my only approach.

Question: Sometimes people say there is a connection between documentary work developed in Britain during the war, and your own work after the war in neorealism. Was there any real connection, or just a parallel?

Rossellini: Connection I don't see. But our work was something like the English work. The development was more or less independent because we didn't know at all what was being done elsewhere. For us, or for me, the main goal was to make filming something accessible to everybody. At that time it was impossible to consider film outside of a studio. I felt it was very important to go see the reality of the thing, not the foolishness of the romance. It was very important not to have the temptation to go indoors. It is important to go into the street and really look at the people.

We are so lost in our world, and we are trapped near the end of our civilization; in order to make something new, we must know ourselves very well. And the only way to look at yourself, and to understand ourselves, is to look back at our own history, and all around us. Because we are either mature or immature through the working of a process. If we know the process, we know ourselves better.

I think the very careful reconstruction of the thing is the way to understand. So it is really a question of understanding human beings in the historical past. I think in this sense Grierson and I were very similar. From the beginning, we never thought a great deal of our own work. When I arrived in Paris immediately after the war, Grierson had the chance to see my old films, so he got in touch with me, and we became very good friends.

Question: You are talking about the reasons why you went out of feature films and went in this direction now, of television?

Rossellini: With the feature film, you have really no freedom. Apparently you have freedom—for example, to be against the censorship—but not the real freedom of choice concerning the theme of the thing. The Italian television, the French television have a certain kind of social duty. And you can convince them to do a certain kind of work. At the beginning,

Roberto Rossellini (right), innovative Italian director of films and television and one of the founders of neo-realist film in Italy, with Blais during location work in Florence.

they were frustrated when they allowed me to start to do a certain kind of thing. Now they are successful, and I have no more problems.

We are rushing into change, every second. All knowledge was quite static in the past. In the past we had only a little knowledge in comparison with the knowledge that we have today. And in the development of science, knowledge comes up with tremendous speed and in a tremendous quantity. And on top of that we have a society of specialists; a specialist is a very learned person in one direction who is completely ignorant in the rest. So a society of specialists, more or less is a corporative society.

The only chance that we will have in the future is to put the thoughts together. So we must develop a new kind of a system of information in our education, if you want to call it that. And the *image* can be tremendously efficient in doing that kind of work because the images are always very easily and well remembered. First of all, you must learn—you must have made the effort to learn—and afterward you must remember what you have learned.

Grierson had the genius to identify what the needs were, and then to organize a system in which to develop the thought, to satisfy those needs. He was very open and full of curiosity, always searching for new things. And that is the reason why dialogue with him was very easy. As you know, to be a film-maker is already a start, it is a portion of your humanity. And he was a great human being. With a *great* capacity for film-making.

Laurence Henson

The young Scottish film-maker Laurence Henson was attached to Grierson's production team for the television series "This Wonderful World," which played on Scottish Television and throughout Britain for an impressive ten years. With the television team, Grierson exercised the same electrifying kind of generalship as he had displayed earlier among his film groups in Britain and Canada. The bond of comradeship and professional dedication in the TV unit was a strong one; Henson married his script assistant. Today, he is one of the most promising among the Scottish film directors. He wants to remain in Scotland, to work there, not to bow to the usual inexorable pressure and go South to London.

We had tried earnestly to connect with Laurence Henson during our shooting days in Scotland, but he was then on location himself and was not available. We therefore arranged to meet him in Amsterdam, where we had gone with our French crew after filming Rossellini in Fiesole and several others in Paris. We filmed Henson on a terrace balcony high above Amsterdam harbor.

Henson: I was working with Scottish television, a new thing in Scotland, just arrived. A Canadian, Roy Thomson, had got the franchise to operate in the Midlands and Scotland. Then Grierson arrived to make the program called "This Wonderful World." After about six months I joined his team making the TV program, which consisted of his view of the best short films that he could bring together from all the sources that he had built up over his lifetime. He was in a sense in retirement when he came to Scotland to make this television program. He traveled all over Europe and South America to Canada and America and Australia and everywhere else to bring the films back and show them—films that captured a moment of magic, a moment of observation.

When he came back to Scotland after a lifetime of public service for all kinds of government departments in various countries, he adopted for the first time the Doctor of Letters which had been conferred on him by Glasgow University. When I asked why, he said, "Well, the Scots, I know them well as people who would not recognize a prophet in their own country. It happens elsewhere, too, but nowhere to such a degree as in my own home country. So I am going to make them pay attention, you see, by using this title. It will impress them, and they will pay attention to me like they would to the family doctor or a schoolteacher or a lawyer." They revere the old established professions in Scotland, and Grierson's whole attitude toward the program was a throwback to his first contact as a very young man with the Scottish public, as an almost ordained minister. He set out to be a minister but cut it off very quickly. Because that was his first direction, he used his "Wonderful World" TV program almost as a pulpit, to preach and illuminate. This was very much his attitude. You could see it in his contact with people in the streets around the theatre—the policemen, the girls on the telephone switchboard, the people in the shops. They'd say, "Oh, Doctor, I saw that marvelous film about the goats jumping down the mountainside" and things like that; this pleased him enormously.

For example, Grierson would introduce a film on Reubens, the painter—a film by Henri Storck, which did an analysis of Reubens' compositions by means of moving lines and circles and diagrams—by showing a sequence of World Cup Football and explaining Reubens to the TV audience in terms of how Reubens played the corners of the rectangle of green, like the football field. After that program, a man stopped him in the street and said, "You know, Doc," he said, "that was fuckin' poetry." That is exactly the reaction he wanted.

Question: Reading the press reviews and the letters from TV you get the impression that there was a very direct relationship between him and the audiences, that they had almost a family feeling about the television show.

Henson: That is true, there was a special kind of respect. Again it goes back to his use of this term "Doc." He said, "In Scotland I'll use my title because it will identify me not as a showman but as a family consultant on the order of a G.P., or a school dominie in the old sense, and then they will listen to me."

Our first meeting was due to the fact that I had been partly responsible for making an amateur film about a drunk man in George Square in Glasgow, a subject quite close to his heart in the sense that it was observing something real. In the TV series we viewed all the material that we could find; then he could compile programs which had a kind of balance, not just one point of view. We had one interesting situation with a film about the pathetic living conditions in Hong Kong, made by the World Council of Churches. This went almost the whole running time of the program, and we didn't want to cut it down, to make it into another standard-sized item. I remembered that just that week we had received a film from Hungary with a choir singing Bach in the most glorious manner; I suggested a little bit of that. He looked at that and said, "Now that is a very good idea." So we had the Hong Kong film and finished off with three minutes of glorious Bach; somehow it all seemed to work, seemed to make a program.

I think there is no doubt about it that his first vocation was as a priest. He adopted film as a medium. He felt his mission was to be a propagandist, and film just happened, he discovered it at just the right time, when Flaherty had made *Nanook* and Eisenstein had made *Potemkin*. He talked like a priest or a minister; he talked about his job in those terms, and film was the chosen instrument, which was ready at the time when he needed it.

Question: How did you get on with him? Did he drive you, encourage you, insult you?

Henson: He could never retire. This television program became another new life in his hands, though he had officially "retired." He demanded things, and when questioned, wouldn't give answers, but would demand that you do them; then from the results, he would wait and see your own reaction to what you had done. Without actually saying anything, he would be saying: There, you see. Do you get it? As things went on, he was always talking to me in terms that would mean something to me in later life, talking to me as a person, to me as a potential film-maker, as possibly a creative person. He was saying things which sometimes even now, I say to myself, Ah, *that's* what he meant . . . and then I realize that it's ten years since I worked for him. Pennies are still dropping, you know.

Question: He made you aware that you could get much more out of yourself.

Henson: He had an attitude towards the making of films, towards the making of anything, whether it be painting, or writing, or any endeavor like that—if you had a dedication to something outside of *yourself*, you were in business; if you did *not* have a dedication to something outside of yourself, then you'd had it, and you ended by disappearing up your own arsehole. This attitude was very important to me. It made and continues to make sense as time goes on.

He was austere, he was capricious, he was funny. At times he could charm the birds out of the trees. He existed in an enormously complex manner. After three years of working with him I felt that if anyone ever wanted to attend a university in a single person, then they should do so with this man, because that is what he was. His grasp of the whole life was so good and so broad and so *industrious* that everything was worked out. It was like being at the university.

Question: He made you find your own solutions.

Henson: Seaward the Great Ships had an American director whom Grierson picked after seeing some experimental work of his at the Brussels 1958 Exposition. This director, Hilary Harris, the American, kept saying, "The man has asked me to find the *kiss* when a ship is launched, that first moment of touching the water. Grierson has asked me to film the *kiss*, but I cannot find it. The ship goes down the hill and into the water and there is no kiss." But Grierson says, "No, no, no, there *is* a kiss!" So Harris filmed about fifty different launches from fifty different angles, using all kinds of elaborate setups, to try and get this first touch of the water. Then Grierson said to take those fifty and cut them all together, and it made the most glorious opening of any documentary film I've ever seen, the most beautiful, dramatic, glorious poetic opening. So Grierson could turn around and say, "Well, *there* is your kiss." He was asking me to do that all the time. But that was the way Grierson chose to do it. He didn't *make* you do it. He led you. It wasn't pressure but rather coaching of a very clever kind, very kind and also very kindly. Exhortation, it was producership off the top of the tree, it was producership as it should be.

Olwen Vaughan

Another member of the TV production team for Grierson's series "This Wonderful World" was Olwen Vaughan of London. She was extremely important to the series, for Miss Vaughan was the chief scout and procuress of film materials to feed the insatiable maw of the program. Since "This Wonderful World" presented film selections from all over the world, the tasks of discovering new sources and physically obtaining delivery of the film were enormous. Miss Vaughan accomplished this, as she describes, by assiduous attendance at international film festivals and by many judicious scouting trips behind the former Iron Curtain.

Olwen Vaughan, who died in 1973, was a well-known personality in her own right. A great champion of film study and film culture, a former close friend and colleague of Iris Barry of the Museum of Modern Art in New York, she had taken an active role in founding and building the New London Film Society after the war. During the war period, she took an interest in the cause of the Free French, and owned and operated a dining club in London largely for the comfort of the Free French community.

Later the club became a haven for film people, musicians, dancers, itinerant Europeans, and Americans with an interest in any of these fields, and for people who enjoyed good French food at a very modest price. Documentary people were particularly welcome at the French Club (Le Petit Club Français) of Olwen Vaughan. For many years Grierson was a regular. His great confederate and financial counselor from the early GPO days, J. P. R. Golightly, would sit nightly on a high barstool and smile benignly at all the company. If there was any one place where documentary-film people from Canada, the United States, Scandinavia, Yugoslavia, Western Europe, Africa, and the far Antipodes could feel kinship and solidarity, it was at the French Club in St. James's Place, S.W.1.

We filmed Miss Vaughan in her appointed place behind the bar at her club. She had not been well and was quite crippled by arthritis. To help her through the interview, she had occasional recourse to a glass of red wine. There were various interruptions, so a good deal of wine was consumed. Finally we were done and repaired upstairs to dinner. Miss Vaughan was fatigued and drowsy and after a time began to nod softly over her Dover sole. We thought her to be asleep, so continued our conversation in low tones. At a certain moment, a low murmur could be heard from Miss Vaughan. I bent very close to catch whatever message there might be. Very faint, very slow, but very distinct, the words "The club needs a new carpet" could be discerned. This indicated the form of acknowledgment for her time and services that would be welcome to Olwen, to the club, and to the community as a whole.

Miss Olwen Vaughan, a champion of documentary and of the Film Society movement, ministered to the needs of the film community at her celebrated *Le Petit Club Francais* in London.

Vaughan: I think that while Grierson was ill he had the idea of doing this sort of television program without the BBC. The BBC was scared and the program didn't jell, so Grierson went to Scottish Television, where he knew Roy Thomson. Then he came down to London to see me and asked me to find him films. He had worked with me on the film society, so he knew I could find them. And it started from there. We went on for a happy five hundred programs. I was told to find films about people working or doing their crafts to show how other people in the world went about their work and business.

It was a pretty large sort of idea, but it worked. I remembered what I had seen in the film society and what Grierson had already done in London before, and I often went to film festivals abroad. This opened up a new world to me. We started off at Brussels at the Experimental Film Festival, where Alexeieff and Grierson were on the committee or jury. That gave me a taste for festivals. From there I went behind the Iron Curtain, and I was often the only Western woman present. So of course I got the films easily. I chose the films. If I was dead certain about them, I had them sent straight to London, because I knew certain things that Grierson never failed to buy: people dancing or making rare crafts, something very obscure. That he would always buy. If they were things that I liked but wasn't sure about, I would come home with a list and tell him, and he would always say, "Send for it." So the films would come to London, through London Transport. We edited them, eventually people were paid, and the program, made by a large unit of four, found its way to Glasgow, where the shows were taped.

It was quite easy to get a response to the programs, because if you took a taxi with Grierson, the driver would say, "Yes, Mr. Wonderful World." They had seen him, they couldn't fail to recognize those piercing eyes. They knew him, and he talked to everybody. It was absolutely a pain to go into Soho shopping with him. You never got anything done. I couldn't even get back in time to do lunch for the club. By that time we had found out what everybody liked and didn't like in the last program.

Question: Reading the press comments and letters to the editor in Scottish papers, one gets the impression that it was a family audience, that people had a kind of proprietary interest in the program.

Vaughan: It was a family audience. It was a general audience, including Ann, our waitress here. He always asked her what she thought. Once he ran a film especially for her, from Czechoslovakia.

Grierson was primarily a friend of my father, who was a clergyman and ran the biggest film society in England, in Liverpool. I suppose Grierson went up and lectured—all the film boys did. I was the eldest daughter and went along, so Grierson was a family friend. And when I was at the British Film Institute in London, he and Cavalcanti were with the GPO Film Unit.

When Grierson finally moved from Canada to Paris, to UNESCO, I was often in Paris and visited the great man in his flat, where he had the most wonderful Chinese cook. Then he came back to London, and I wanted to have some important names on the film society committee. So I went to see Margaret Grierson and asked, "Can I ask John to be on the committee?" She said, "You can as long as he doesn't have to work too hard." Protective wife. So I said, "No, no, I just want his name and his advice." So he sat on all the committees of the New London Film Society. We showed some quite good films, you know, starting from *Birth of a Nation*. And Grierson was most helpful.

I remember once when we were showing a terrible film of Kenneth Anger [*Fireworks*], which I didn't like at all. Grierson stood up and said, "Any lady who is at all sensitive and doesn't like to see things that she shouldn't will be advised to leave the room during the showing of the film." And the ladies left. I think it was this association of the film society that finally led to our formal great meeting in Paris when he said I wasn't to become French. But would I kindly bring all the films back for Chaplin's fiftieth or sixtieth birthday program. They were at the cinémathèque in Paris, and would I arrive within two days' time with them in London. Which I did, and from then it wasn't long before "This Wonderful World" started.

In the old days at the club there were the Free French, and then the film people. Friday night was a studio night, headed by Cavalcanti. And we got all the film people there—Michael Redgrave and Robert Hamer and all the people who made films in those days. Then you had people at the bar, like Terry Trench, for example, Crown Unit people, and probably Liz Lutyens, who writes music, Alan Rawsthorne, who was also a very good composer, and Basil Wright. They are all tremendous friends, they all work in film in their different ways, and they can talk to each other. Years ago they all used to meet there, and they still do, the ones that are left alive.

Lord Thomson of Fleet

Lord Thomson of Fleet, Roy Thomson, newspaper publisher, entrepreneur, media baron, was Grierson's sponsor for the television series "This Wonderful World." To some degree a bond of Scottishness connected them. Thomson was Canadian-born, of Scottish antecedents. In other respects, there is remarkably little that one could discover by way of likeness between them.

Thomson was a man who handled media in the sense of commodities. He demonstrated remarkable skill in building up newspapers and in buying and selling them to advantage. Yet his control over media remained one of ownership and management, not of editorial policy. He acquired power on a grand scale, judged in terms of ownership. He was less concerned with what the particular media he controlled were saying, what they were selling, what they represented. His thought was more for market than for message. Grierson, it is well known, had an almost perverse disregard for money and signally failed to acquire any. Thomson, as he himself says, was deeply and primarily interested in money—it was the subject he found most fascinating.

The television series enabled Grierson, late in life, to speak to millions of people. He had followers, fans, a great television family, and it seems that his audience was in many ways a family kind of audience. This was made possible not by government, but by a great capitalist patron, Roy Thomson.

It is a curious reflection that in Grierson's young days, seeking passionately to communicate to a wide audience, he lacked a truly efficient system of distribution for the purpose. And in his later days, although he was given access to audiences on the greatest scale through television, the vehicle which employed him and which he employed was concerned not with social purposes but with commercial entertainment.

Roy Thomson, a towering figure in the world of media, died in 1976. We had interviewed him for the Grierson film four years earlier, in his own office building in Toronto.

Thomson: I wasn't really directly concerned with the initial negotiations to have Grierson come with us. This was done through Jimmy Sutherland, who is our program director of Scottish Television. It appealed to Jimmy and of course to me—I thought it was an excellent idea. It was quite popular, perhaps not in drawing the biggest audience, but certainly in drawing the most intelligent audience. It was the type of program that didn't appeal to people who would be interested in comedy or musicals or extravaganzas. It was a tremendous prestige program and of its kind the very best that could have been produced. This was the type of program that would have been very, very welcome, I am sure, in the BBC.

Question: Being a Scot, do you think that Grierson preferred doing the program on Scottish TV?

Thomson: I think the idea of originating in Glasgow and being a Scottish Television original presentation appealed to him very much, but I have no doubt that John wasn't at all unmindful of the money too. He liked to make some money, and I don't blame him for that. While I am of Scottish ancestry, it is well diluted: my great-great—I am not sure if it wasn't great again—grandfather Archibald came from Westkirk in Dumfrieshire in southern Scotland in 1763, and settled in America. Then he was a United Empire Loyalist when the American War of Independence broke out, so he went to Canada. Since then all my forebears have been Canadian, so we're pretty well diluted. But I have great affinity with Scotland, it's always a little bit in my mind, but not to the extent that I would disregard other considerations or business opportunities. I left Scotland and went to London where I now live, because in order to do a business all over the world as we do, London was the place to have your headquarters. That's why I am there and not in Scotland. But I own the national newspaper of Scotland, *The Scotsman*, and a number of other Scottish newspapers mostly in the north of Scotland. I have quite big interests in Scotland.

Question: About the program, we're told that people in the street would recognize Grierson from television and often used to call him "Doc."

Thomson: It was a mark of affection and respect. While he was not a man that would command respect in the usual way, because he was not very dignified and could blow up on the slightest occasion and make some outrageous remarks, he *was* a real personality and everybody accepted him as such. In many respects he was a difficult man to get along with, and our boys in the Program Department were always scrapping with him, though not in any serious way. He would insist on this and that and all the rest of it, but it was all in the way of obtaining more perfection in his programs. At least he thought he was accomplishing that, that was his objective. Of course he was a little irascible anyway. But I must say that he certainly seemed to respect my position as chairman of the company, I didn't have any trouble with him. Though he generally didn't have any respect for anybody, he always seemed to accept that I treated him fairly. Our contact was always at the office; I didn't go to pubs to drink, which John would do, so I had no occasion to contact him outside business hours. He never came after me for more money, which he did secretly from our Program Department: he wanted more expenses or more in the way of salary.

I had a tremendous respect for his ability to procure unusual great-quality films. He seemed to get these films from all over the world. Apparently he had a great connection behind the Iron Curtain, which really was an Iron Curtain in the initial days. He seemed to go to these other countries and get films that I am sure nobody else could have gotten, and he had an unerring instinct for what was good and what wasn't. He certainly knew films, there was no doubt.

Question: Did you feel that Grierson's program was a value to your network?

Thomson: When you talk about money, which is what I usually talk about, I don't know that it produced money. But in terms of prestige there's no question at all; it made Scottish Television a prestige station in many respects. It was broadcast over the whole British network for many years, and I know that the Independent Television Authority, who were the governing body of the independent stations, were tremendously impressed and regarded it as a great feature of the whole network. They were always insistent that the stations on their network should take it, although as I say it wasn't a really popular program in the sense that it would pull in a tremendous big audience. Sometimes the other stations would sacrifice it for something that was more audience-pulling, but the ITA stuck resolutely to it, and after many years they still insisted that these other stations should take it. This is unusual, because in television nothing lasts forever. I think it was unique among British programs in that it should have lasted so long and have had such general popularity with a class audience.

Comment on
"This Wonderful World"*

The success of "This Wonderful World"—the relative success, I should say—has been quite odd and surprising to me. I was asked to work out a cultural programme. I was to be as highbrow as I liked and I was to understand that no one expected me to hit the high audience ratings.

I came away with some highfalutin pieces on Leonardo da Vinci, Rembrandt, and the like, exercises in the more abstract reaches of movie, and just to please myself, I shoved in something about boxing or bullfighting, or the like. Maybe the Scots are a lot of intellectual snobs, but when I got into my favourite low-level "locals," the word was "I liked you on that Leonardo," and not a word about Benny Lynch and my superb stentorian introduction as from the centre of the ring.

That is how it has gone, and somebody had better explain it properly to me. I have delivered homilies on advanced genetics, anthropology, archaeology and other recondite pursuits, done some difficult pieces on, say, the mathematics of high-speed flight—and it has taken me weeks to understand the stuff myself—but I still have the small boys with the glittering eyes and the old soaks with the dimmer ones keeping well up with me.

I don't suppose the programme will ever make the Top Ten, and I hope to Heaven it doesn't in case I get the bends trying to keep it in a state to which it was never meant to be accustomed. But starting from nowhere, it strings along—touch wood and cross my fingers—with decent average viewing figures.

. . .

One great difference between Scotland and England is in the matter of public criticism as distinct from private criticism. In Scotland, as I say, I don't have to bother about the private stuff. I will get it anyway—anywhere and everywhere I go.

I suppose we are more of a social democracy up there, and a man's a man for a' that, even when it comes to the profundities of the aesthetic judgment. If they think you are very good, you'll get "No bad" on this,

* By John Grierson.

"No bad" on that, with the inevitable qualification, for their own self-respect, that you were a stinker six weeks ago on so-and-so.

. . .

It is the lack of this immediacy of personal criticism which makes the public criticism by the professional critics in England so important. In Scotland I didn't have a single professional comment in a whole year.

But I hadn't been to England more than twice before I got what I call the real stuff: the evaluation of the timing, the evaluation of the impact, the estimate of what I was trying to do, with here and there, of course, my comeuppance for going too far—better still, not far enough. In other words, it's warmer in Scotland: but I am too old in the game not to want and to need the body of criticism for whatever it chooses to say.

After all, I am not running this programme simply because I know where there are some wonderful slices of film. There is a special point in dragging them out from limbo. There is a special point of fitting them out and lifting them up so that what, perhaps, was hidden in the whole is now revealed in the part. But there is, for me, a special point in indicating an attitude to what I think, one way or another, is beautiful or brave, or inventive or illuminating, or great. I haven't the vaguest intention of teaching anybody or anything. The mere indication of what you believe to be beautiful or brave or inventive or illuminating or great may be enough to start in others a chain reaction of their own. Perhaps the penny you insert today in a small boy's head will one day drop and give him, not your jackpot, but his.

That is what makes television so strangely attractive to an old operator in the field of mass communication like myself. It is no doubt a public medium like any other for, say, the dramatists, but for some of us, it looks like being much more of a private medium than we have been accustomed to. It gets you very close to where the reactions are most intimate, and for that reason, the influences may be the more lasting.

From the *London Times*, Thursday, January 28, 1960:

A Mass Medium Addressed to
Individuals

Mr. John Grierson's Way with Television
From a Correspondent

So far Scottish Television have acquired only one programme of serious value, Mr. John Grierson's "This Wonderful World," which is also the only one to be exported across the border. Its implications, though, range much farther than that. It has become one of the first antidotes of its kind to the mutually nourishing and interdependent twentieth-century phenomena, mass entertainment and the mass mind.

The programme is roughly comparable to a global tour with a leading educationist who is also the best of company; a number of flights, as it were, during which you make sudden descents on whatever portion of the earth's surface holds something that has caught Mr. Grierson's eye. It may be a dancer, an excavator, a sports meeting, or a bubble, but it is certain to shock you into attention and get some kind of emotional response.

The subjects, fruits of the picaresque background of Mr. Grierson's mental living, seem disparate enough. But a closer glance discerns a pattern reflecting his particular aesthetic; the recognition of genius, which is one, whether it is expressed by Joe Louis, Leonardo da Vinci or the latest scientific achievement.

Modern Ariel

Mr. Grierson usually divides his talks into two or three sections, each section being devoted to a short film on a specific subject which he introduces personally. Fittingly, the programmes begin with a Sputnik design, which fades into flowing clouds to the accompaniment of ephemeral music. Turning from the universe spread out before him, Mr. Grierson then looks into the camera himself, a small, grey Ariel with eyes glittering enthusiastically behind his spectacles, and promises to reveal "the rich and strange."

Lately he has shown a film on crystal formation, extending from the evil beauty of strychnine to the mystique of diamonds. Another time it was a gymnasts' meeting in Prague, with patterns of movement as intricate as ballet and even more fluent, tumblers and acrobats turning and swooping and even the simplest exercise with hoops becoming a delight to the eye. Then there was the motor race in Indianapolis, where the newsreel cameras managed to be in position to record one of the most astonishing pile-ups in sporting history as 14 cars crashed at 140 miles an hour.

The same programme included an excerpt of a dancing Negro, whose fantastic gaiety and speed, and the melancholy of the song he sang, summed up his whole racial experience. Once it was the huge machines used in the building of Kitimat, a new Canadian town, and an awesome example of modern power; again drops of water and drifting bubbles were both an essay in magic and, as Mr. Grierson pointed out, a study in shapes and texture. Sometimes he puts on what he lovingly calls "a squiggly film," almost indescribable but very good fun.

In each there is a demand for wonder, fear, delight, or pity. By analysing, isolating, spotlighting, Mr. Grierson is persuading people to look, to think, and finally to feel; to resist the sludge of mediocrity in entertainment that has submerged so much individual taste.

The Far Horizon

As a teacher he recognized the vast potentialities of the cinema in the very early days and was among the first in the 1920s to found the documentary movement. Thirty years later he found television was an even better way of communication, allowing him to reach small family groups and talk to them, as it were, by their own fireside. "Everybody appreciates the romantic and the appeal of the far horizon," he wrote recently; and "You don't often change people's interests by teaching them. You do it by interesting them in new interests." He has also another advantage in the new medium where immediacy matters so much. He has travelled extensively and intensively in different countries and moved in different walks of life; over and over again he can give an eyewitness account.

In fact television, the greatest mass medium of all of them, has been turned against itself. It has become the best way to reach the greatest number of individuals, to reinforce their individuality; and as an irony, that must delight Mr. Grierson's Scottish soul.

Grierson Correspondence—
"This Wonderful World"

Grierson's time in television was an absorbing and also a grueling experience. In the following letters written at intervals during the years 1958 to 1962 to his friends George and Mary Ferguson in Canada, Grierson comments wryly on the treadmill aspects of his program and also on his relationship with Roy Thomson (cf. the interview with Lord Thomson on p. 259).

> Calstone, Calne, Wiltshire
> 16–12–58

Dear Mary:

I'll write this one in the book so that at least we get the lines straight. The hand as you see is old and doddery, written out, not from the head but from the liver. I thank you much for your kind word about the Chaplin piece for the CBC and am glad old George grunted no great disapproval. Your PM [John Diefenbaker] blew through here spouting like a grampus, surfacing all the time and never a dive to show he was any real whale at all. He sounded pretty provincial but who are we these days to think that we are other. I have been working in Scotland, George's native land, for a year and that's the worst of the lot—wee and parochial and complaisant and hard to take going back, after all the dream life we've lived about it. I now think of Moose Jaw as positively metropolitan.

What's happened has been sort of odd. Roy T. asked me to do what he called a "culture" program—because and only because he has to, to hold his concession. I began by telling him that in his mouth "culture" sounded like a dirty word and he laughed—he has that single asset—and we've got along fine in our rough Canadian way. Only the highbrow program didn't turn out as either he or I expected. I was supposed to produce it but out of sheer laziness or snootiness or something, I couldn't stand the writers or the compères and did the whole thing myself, and there I am, hey presto, away in a new world—and I have these days not so much an audience as a bloody congregation. And the highbrow program is one of the popular, and the harder I make it the more they swallow. Nothing barred—genetics, aesthetics, mathematics I don't understand myself—the lot. You have people stopping you in the street saying, Christ, Doctor, I liked you on Leonardo, and it has sort of exploded a myth as to what's popular and what's not. Here in England they didn't believe it any more than I did, so they ran three of them down there and the same thing happened and in the

New Year I'm into all the stations with the weekly spiel—the old battered presence spewing its ugly experience on every decent hearth rug without shame. I saw Roy T. a couple of days ago on his way to Toronto. He tells me he thinks he's getting the new Toronto station and if so would I spend half the year over there. So you never know. I would like it much and Margaret very, very much. She thinks, poor woman, Canada was the best time of her life. There are limitations of course working on commercial, and Roy especially. He has all the lip service but doesn't know what he's talking about when he gets past the figures. But I've done him the curious service of giving him and Scotland for that matter, the only program they think fit to bring into England and it means a lot to him. And you can tell George that I've got him over a bloody barrel. You wanted to know what I do and I apologize for telling you. Now I send you both my love for Christmas and the New Year.

Ever,

J.G.

SCOTTISH TELEVISION LIMITED

TELEVISION HOUSE, KINGSWAY, LONDON, W.C.2. HOLborn 1331
SPENCER HOUSE, DIGBETH, BIRMINGHAM, 5. MIDLAND 9303
CHRONICLE BUILDING, 74 CORPORATION ST., MANCHESTER, 4. BLAckfriars 7621
THEATRE ROYAL, GLASGOW. DOUglas 9999
Working address: C/–Western Mail, Thomson House, Cardiff, Wales.

23rd February, 1962

Mr. G. V. Ferguson,
Editor,
Montreal Star,
MONTREAL

Dear George,

It was very good to get your Christmas letter. I was working over the Christmas holidays because I go on television every week without a break and if it isn't hard work it is at least preoccupying. So your letter didn't get answered then. At that point I hit the bottom of the barrel, meaning I got short of films and dashed off to Europe to scrape up something. I've been all through the vaults in Prague, Warsaw, Budapest and other odd places, only to find this year that they are all too happy to make good pictures any more. Two years ago it was splendid. They had to earn a

In his television series "This Wonderful World," Grierson presented films from almost every country, a worldwide view of all that is "rich and strange."

living and did. Now with Khrushchev's *nouvelle vague* washing warmly all over the boys find themselves kept comfortably, supplied with handsome flats, and with enough of a margin to buy their girlfriends silk panties. So why should they worry or even work. They don't. I am all for a return to Stalin. Nowadays the safest thing and the easiest thing is to make cartoons. Nobody argues with a cartoon and of course they don't make satirical ones. The alternative is to make nature pictures. Nobody argues with a bird. In fact, I haven't seen a good documentary picture in the last two months. So what to do? I am in fact forced over to the States at the beginning of April to see what I can dig up there. I speak at the Symposium at North Carolina University and it seems I will be with Seldes and Reston on the general subject of the Arts and Revolution. I shall of course tell them about these feather-bedded slobs on the other side of the curtain. I go up from North Carolina to speak at the Museum of Modern Art and then I am back home again quick to catch up with the TV programmes. In short I am not making a long trip this time but rather preparing for a longer one during the Summer. Where did I get my visa? Hell, I got a letter from the State Department the other day saying what was all the fuss, and I was as pure as the driven snows as far as they were concerned. Try to explain that one.

I see that the Times thinks you write like a prince. They catch up gradually.

My love to Mary and yourself and from Margaret too.

Yours,

JOHN GRIERSON

Sydney Newman (II)

Sydney Newman is one of those few associates who had extensive contact with Grierson in both Britain and Canada. In his case the contact was first in Canada during the early Film Board period. In 1954 Newman was a leading director of television drama who subsequently became head of TV drama at the Canadian Broadcasting Corporation. He next went to London and entered upon a brilliantly successful period as TV drama producer and ultimately head of TV drama for the BBC. During this period Newman saw a good deal of Grierson. When thereafter Newman returned to Canada and to the National Film Board as Film Commissioner, Grierson also reentered the Canadian scene to teach as visiting professor at McGill University.

Sydney Newman talks about Grierson's later years in Britain and Canada.

Question: What about the period in England in the 1950s when you were something of a big shot with BBC and Grierson was in rather poor shape—can you speak about that?

Newman: I don't really know how much there is to tell. I think he found a certain measure of self-respect in the down years, when Roy Thomson of Scottish Television agreed with him about a program, and he did this very interesting series called "This Wonderful World." Later, after Grierson had been doing the program for about four years on Scottish television, I saw him and he said he really thought that BBC should be doing the program. He asked me if I would bring the notion that he do the same program for BBC to some of the BBC brass. I was head of BBC drama at that stage, so I did; I brought it to a very senior person. I said, "You know Grierson and his program." He replied, "Yes, I know Grierson and his program." I said, "Well, goddamn it, I think that the BBC should be doing the program. Grierson is a fantastic guy; he brings these little revelations of truth about the cinematic experiments and notions around the world, and I think it should be part of the BBC." He said, "Sydney, who cares about Grierson nowadays? This was a wonderful guy twenty years ago, but no one in England really gives a damn now."

Question: With television he started to make a comeback, so to speak. There was a kind of transformation period. Did you know him during that period?

Newman: Yes, I did. I moved to England in '58, and I saw Grierson from time to time. I never forget in 1968 or '69 when the Film Board had made a film called *Prologue* and Grierson disliked the film intensely; he was in those days very pessimistic about the youth who were knocking traditional values, who couldn't identify with any social purpose. He also was very upset about this film by the Canadian Film Board in which the critical sequence took place in Chicago. He thought it was politically stupid for Canada, for the national sovereignty of Canada, to get involved in what was purely an internal matter in the United States, and he and I had a terrible row about it. In fact I said, "Grierson, you are becoming an old man and you are really out of touch." But he was the sort of man you could have this with; in fact he forced you into taking extreme views, it was part of his own character to do that.

When Grierson came back to Canada in 1969 and he heard about the Film Board's *Challenge for Change* program, he violently opposed it. He always had this slightly elitist thing—he thought of film as being made by marvelous people who care *about* people. The notion of the ordinary people themselves using this sophisticated means to express themselves did not come easily to him, but the moment he became acquainted with it and saw it in action, within months he became the greatest proponent of the whole *Challenge for Change* do-it-yourself expression thing. I think that for several years in England his life broke apart somewhat and it was very difficult for him to realize himself again, after the Crown unit and the Group Three program phased out in '52 or so. I think that he spent a long period in which he was doggedly hanging on to what he believed in, and nobody seemed to be listening to him. I think there were a lot of developments going on that he was observing from a removed position.

I think that things like *Challenge for Change*, the fact that film was no, longer a sophisticated reserved craft, that children could use cameras to express themselves, that ordinary people when simply instructed could express their own community problems—these were things he had at first sneered at because of a kind of elitism that was part of his Scottish educational background; also, coming down to London, being the sort of poor boy in London from Scotland trying to make it big with the sophisticates of London—this contributed to the sense that he had to make it big. I think he disliked the innovations in the use of film because he was removed from these big changes between '52 and '67. He was opposed to these developments, but the moment he got back into things and became party to the changes, he immediately foresaw potentialities far beyond the people who were practicing these techniques.

When he was offered the job at McGill University here in Montreal and began to get involved in the mainstream of Canadian thinking again, it didn't take him long, so that by the time he was seventy-one or seventy-two years old this man was in better shape intellectually—in terms of his awareness and understanding—than he was when he left the Film Board and Canada in '45.

Frankly I didn't know he was dying when he left Montreal in 1971. It never occurred to any of us who dealt with him on a day-to-day or week-to-week basis—as I did over his last year and a half—that he would ever die. Earlier I was having a board meeting and I invited Grierson to come and have dinner with the board members. He got in touch with me and said that he was terribly honored to meet the board members, and then he said, "Come on now, there is something you want me to do for you." I said, "Not at all." He said, "Well, *is* there anything I can do for you?" I said, "Yes, I haven't told my board members that when our new films appear on television, there will be breaks in the films to allow for commercials, and I am arguing with my board members that this is an essential precondition for our getting a mass audience." He said, "Don't worry, I'll fix it up." And when he turned up at the dining room he came into that room as if he were shot out of a cannon. And I introduced him around, and he propagandized each and every board member about the necessity when one is trading with the devil to learn how to trade on the devil's terms. And if they want Film Board films to be seen you had to allow space for commercials, so let them have their bloody commercials. And I remember this went back thirty years: when he set out to make our early Film Board films for the Canadian cinemas, he said, "I learned in England that when you give your films away for nothing they treat you like dirt. Charge the buggers, and then they will respect you." He said that to every one of my board members. He was magnificent.

I think he was always aware that his work rebounded far beyond the periphery of his own life. I think it pleased him very much when he came back to Canada to discover that I, for example, who was just a smart-ass kid when we first met, ended up as the Film Commissioner. I think he was terribly pleased that another offspring of the Film Board, Pierre Juneau, became head of the Canadian Radio and Television Commission. It was partly as a result of his inspiration that Michael Spencer became executive secretary of the Canadian Film Development Corporation. And this inspiration has reached out to all the universities and other such places, to all the places in this country where opinions are formed, where purposes and directions are being evolved. And this was really Grierson, he was aware of it, he was vain enough to like it, and God bless him for it.

Henri Langlois

Henri Langlois, who died in 1977, was curator of the national film museum of France, La Cinémathèque Nationale. Truly an individualist, he compiled one of the world's most extensive collections of the international film in its historical framework. M. Langlois invited us to call on him at the film museum. A recent exhibition was being struck, to be redesigned and installed as a permanent fixture. It was in disarray and carpenters were everywhere. Since the weather was fine, we went outside and walked among the chestnut trees beside the Palais de Chaillot. A stippled, post-impressionist sunshine shone upon us; we walked down the broad paths, past idlers and oldsters and children with balloons; we sat on a bench and there discussed. M. Langlois spoke a piquant English, whose meaning burnt through his syntax. In dealing with the footage of this interview, however, the film editors again found the problem of selecting precise statements within a manageable length of footage beyond their powers; M. Langlois thus appears at length in the French-language version of the film *Grierson*, but not in the English. His comments are worthy of attention for the sense of his ideas rather than for the grammar of his expression.

Langlois: He is first a Scotsman, second a Greek; third he tells me one day that it is not possible to be an artist without passing through Sodom and Gomorrah—which is only a formula, but it is a very good formula, no? It is true; it is life. Perhaps Mr. Churchill is the man who makes the war, but the man who wins the war is a Grierson because he prepares the defense of civilization, not the defense of Britain but the defense of civilization. He fights with several people, they make the quota against the American cinema, which is the beginning of renaissance of the British cinema. He is the man with Cavalcanti and others who wants the true British cinema and not just a cosmopolitan cinema. Not just international cinema, though London is an international city. But for me what is truly Grierson's is not the international city of London but is Britain, is the people of Britain, who never appeared before on film. The upper class appear in film, but never the little people in Britain. Before the beginning of the war Grierson is to make films on the British people and then around 1938 or so he changed completely the way of British cinema.

I think that Grierson was a pure bureaucrat. A *pure* bureaucrat is a man who must destroy the bureaucracy. A pure bureaucrat is a man who uses true bureaucratic methods because he is a man of the public service. But he convinced such people to make things which are absolutely outside the normal bureaucracy. And he makes this fantastic work. He saved not only the British cinema, but the art cinema around the world in the thirties. The only problem after is that he became the victim of his ideology. The first part of the work of Grierson was the artistic time.

Question: How do you define the nature of the working collaboration between him and Cavalcanti?

Langlois: Grierson gave confidence to people, to the people of money and the people of education. He was in fact a very nice man, but also very clever, very analytic. And Cavalcanti was only the artist. Grierson says to me in Canada: "What is fantastic is my mixture; I and Cavalcanti, we have made cinema because it was an aesthetic; and I am aesthetic but more practical, and he is *only* aesthetic." But the mixture of the two make a kind of fantastic cinema.

Question: Grierson said that when he started the documentary effort in Britain he was looking for "a relevant aesthetic for mass information."

Langlois: That is very clear. In that time, the world of documentary was confused with something boring. Nobody wants to see it. Then from it he makes an educative documentary, education through the documentary. And you must understand cinema is a bigger "university of the world." Because I am sure, for example, that the colonies decided to finish with colonization, because of cinema. The people who are there in the colonies, they see who walks and who rides in cars, how London is and how Paris is, and they say, "Why them and not us?" This is the beginning of the *thinking.* The cinema is the university of the people. This is absolutely true. But not the newspaper of the people, because the newspaper you are reading tells you what film you must see, what program is there, what you must think. I am sure that most of the people don't know how to read. A man who is not capable of reading must think. But a man who is not an illiterate, he reads. He doesn't think, he reads, he repeats. He *follows.* And in this time, the great period until the war in 1939 and during the war, Grierson in his documentary world wishes to think, not just to educate. It was a very strong movement in cinema.

In the beginning of the world the first man, the man which is like a beast, arrives, sees his face in the water, and says, "This is another world." A mirror at the beginning of man's living was a magic thing. After, it became just a mirror. When the cinema appeared, all the magic of this other world appeared, the screen was not just *the screen.* The cinema exists before the cinema, but it is a third world where you have no access. It is a kind of window, the screen is a window. The man with the cinema became master. Cinema is a medium for explanation between men. Cinema is a medium between the world and the cosmos.

The man lives, every man lives in his time. And suddenly the cinema can go out of time, out of space. An African who has never seen a city in his

Henri Langlois (left), curator of the national French film archive, being interviewed by Beveridge.

life suddenly sees New York. And the man in New York who has never seen Africans before sees them, how they were. They may have read about them in the newspaper, but what they *see* is completely different. They see, and it is more. When you see a Japanese and also another Japanese in the same light, you have the impression that they are the same. But when you see the Japanese in a film, suddenly you discover that their faces are the same as yours. And suddenly you see how they are similar to you, and not how they are Japanese physically. Suddenly you discover the nose, suddenly you discover all, you see the Japanese with the eyes of the Japanese. And this is why the cinema was very strong from the beginning because it began with an alphabet; it begins just with people and it finishes with very great art.

There arrives another problem, the sound track, the audiovisual. And this is another great thing achieved in the art of cinema by Grierson and the group of Grierson. They have saved the art of cinema during the time when Hollywood made films like a sandwich. In a sandwich you have bread which is one thing, butter which is another, and cheese which is another. Then it is a sandwich with three different things, and the art of cinema, the audiovisual art of cinema must be to combine them. So they make this fantastic thing. They have said the art of cinema is always documentary, they learn now suddenly a new cinema is beginning. Nobody knows that, because it has not begun. The crisis of cinema is only because the people hope the cinema will change. But they don't know how. This is a problem. And the future of the cinema is to find the way more and more *visual*, in this audiovisual art. And when you see, for example, the first silent films with sound, it is a mixture. And when you see a film like *Song of Ceylon* or like *Night Mail*, this is also a film with audiovisual, but it is not just a mixture, it is absolutely different. I'm sure that Grierson is a man of the twenties, and is influenced by those times. He is a son of Eisenstein, a son of the Russians, a son of the British cinema. He is the son of avant-garde. He knows very well what was cinema. On one side it was a man who used cinema for education. He was looking for all the things that film can do to convey these realities, open these windows to other people.

Return to Canada

DURING the 1950s while Grierson was in Britain at the Central Office of Information and at Group III with the experimental program of low-budget feature films, his old friends and colleagues in Canada occasionally sought to bring him back again. At least he might visit, lecture, comment on the Canadian scene, and perhaps provide Canadian friends with some opportunity to make amends for the graceless silence and lack of concern with which the Canadian community had seen him depart in 1946.

Once again George Ferguson took the initiative, and with the support in varying measure of four Western Canadian universities, the Nuffield Foundation, the Hudson's Bay Company, and a group of former associates at the Film Board, travel costs and honoraria were provided to cover a visit by Grierson to Canada in the spring of 1957. With Dr. Norman MacKenzie, president of the University of British Columbia, Ferguson took up the principal task of promoting and coordinating this return visit, an exercise requiring patience, tact, and resourcefulness. As Ferguson predicted in a letter to Grierson late in 1956, "You will visit your old haunts and you will also see the expanding frontier, and there will be a warmth of welcome that will make a sentimental old bastard like you break down in tears. Do, please, accept the invitation." Grierson replied:

Tog Hill, Calstone, Calne, Wiltshire   16/11/56
Dear George,
What more could be fairer? I got Larry's [MacKenzie] letter and yours together, the one raising the ante on the other with great satisfaction. I am much cheered as you will know, by the courtesy of it and by the prospect itself which will do these eyes good. At this end of Europe if the West didn't exist we'd have to invent it to ease a bowel occasionally. But now to what I once foolishly dubbed the Creative Treatment of Actuality, I shall certainly come d/v and not only for the pleasure of it. I want to see the place again. I want to stir a little. And if I can teach anything or anybody beside myself in passing, there's no harm in feeling cautiously honest about it too. . . . I shall probably have a go on the changing concepts in education for one—and for another what is coming up new in the mass media in some of the new countries. I was over at Venice this year as president of the jury and there was much that was unexpected. I think too there hasn't been enough really critical on the national i.e. deliberate and formative uses of television. . . . I must have a go, whatever I finally do with it.

It means I should range as far as practical and the Hudson's Bay lead is the best one. You will please thank the ever-blessed P. Chester and ask him to reserve my usual snowshoes. If besides I can get a look at aluminum and mines as well as oil, so much the better. The picture I wants is of where the energies lie and why and I'll skip the culture as usual. In any case, I'd sooner meet the film people and it may be the television people with a rudimentary notion of their own material, rather than get involved in the old aesthetic song and dance. The Rip Van W. act I shall certainly avoid.

However, thank them all and if you can do so politely tell them seminar is on the face of it a dirty word. . . . the Buchmanite searching of noddle and navel of the long 3, 4, 5 day sessions . . . I merely promise to earn my liquor if I can while I'm there and perhaps at the end of it I'll have something about Canada that will serve it more widely.

Yours,

J.G.

The Unwild West

A spirited and labyrinthine correspondence between all the parties ensued, and the outcome was that Grierson made an expedition to Canada, traveling from Amsterdam over the pole to Vancouver, which brought him great pleasure. He visited several universities, film groups, media and television councils, and in particular some of the new industrial developments in the Northland, an area which had always greatly stimulated his earlier interest in Canadian potentialities.

At Kitimat in British Columbia, Grierson examined the colossal new aluminum smelters and extensive underground power installations. He was less in awe of the human aspects of the new Kitimat town site and its aspect of "instant community." In an article, "The Unwild West" (1957), written for a Scottish travel journal, we have a prime example of the Griersonian essay style—marked by high irreverence and good humor, and a refusal to allow that the works of technology must necessarily smother the wayward qualities of mankind.

I spent yesterday in a town of fifteen thousand people that did not exist three years ago. Nor was it any bush town or shanty town sprawling in the forest primeval of this British Columbian coast which now shines high and handsome in the western sun. It was beautifully planned and built with a community center of theatres, municipal halls, supermarkets, landscaped avenues, and ambitiously architectured modern houses in wood and aluminum and all the colors of the rainbow. Even the idea of it started only five years ago. The mountains rise about it in a giant half-circle, staring white with the fresh snow. They run to nine thousand or so. The virgin forest of spruce cedar and hemlock goes straight up solid to the peaks at the end of every vista. The Pacific is at its feet.

This is Kitimat, the city that water power and aluminum are creating two hundred miles south of the Alaskan Panhandle. It put eight million pounds into building last year, and the pace is doubling. It will be twenty-five thousand strong in two years. Aluminum alone will make it a city of fifty thousand for a planned certainty, but the city fathers, all young, figure it will be as big as Vancouver and Seattle.

Behind Kitimat is of course the dam, the great dam, and then the smelter. The dam is sixty miles down the line which is the electric line. They

In Canada Grierson urged the film-makers to respond to a powerful
natural environment and the sense of wide spaces.

jacked up some lakes behind the peaks, raised the water three hundred feet
and backed it into the mountain. They bored a tunnel into the rock for ten
miles, then down with a forty-eight-degree drop to the Pacific. The drop of
the penstock is sixteen times the height of Niagara, with a horsepower
development of two and a quarter million. Even the transmission line is
spectacular. It comes over a pass half as high again as Ben Nevis. Last
winter a landslide wiped it out, and in the aluminum world it is an especial
disaster when the power fails and the pots cool. They built two vast towers
at each end of the slide area, slung great cables between and hung the
transmission lines under.

The smelter is now nearly a mile long and will be two and a quarter—a
long, long pack of buildings in aluminum a thousand feet long. It is quiet
inside, each building with its two rows of square pots electrolyzing away
like billyo and twenty-four hours a day. For whom it may concern, they are
"100,000 amp pots" and not the peewee picayune 50,000 jobs that lesser
men have so far been accustomed to. The point of the exercise is the
production of half a million tons a year. The bauxite comes in deepwater

right alongside from Jamaica preprocessed to alumina. The ingots go out either over the new railroad across the Rockies or deepwater again down the fjord to the sea. A third of the electrical equipment was from Ferranti and all the cranes I saw were by Sir William Arrol.

There is something odd about a town that has got itself all the managements and amenities—the councils, clubs, sports centers, art centers, theatre centers—but still seems too good to be true. Everything has been so well intended and even well done. You know to start with that the town was fixed six miles away from the smelter and in a way that the winds could not carry a fume to it. You bow before what I haven't a doubt is the most progressive and liberal exercise in community building that has happened anywhere; it is a company town that was given immediately to the people, and you know the event must be writ large in any history of the good men do for interest or by stealth but wonderfully and nonetheless. Yet you quibble. I quibbled. You think of a rose without a smell. You wonder if anyone can be private with so many organizations after his well-being and his total effort. You think of the lights they shine on you day and night in the third degree.

I met a lady who was not only full of good works but also good-looking.

She spoke much about this community-building business. She waved a hand across the sweet good town to where there was "for example" a show of modern paintings. She had an ambition to bring the watercolor painters even more urgently together. She spoke especially of a great day to come presently when they would have a conference of all the cultural interests of the town and that wonderful man so-and-so would be brought from somewhere or other to lead the discussion. I looked her straight in the beautiful eye and said, "Ma'am, how is sin getting on these days in the great Northwest?" She was unstartled. "We have no sin any more," she said. "We are now a law-abiding people." I said, "I'll lay you six to four," but she let that one go over her shoulder. She was proud to say they had international affairs at the Canadian club and aesthetic at the film council. Not only that, but they had four thousand cameras to the fifteen thousand, and four thousand automobiles to the fifteen thousand, though there were only twenty-five miles to work on and the road out wouldn't be built for a year. I said I thought that was a highly significant number of motorcars. She whipped out a list of the twelve religious denominations and the twenty-five prayer parlors.

I wandered round to the man who sold the cameras. He does three hundred and fifty rolls on a Monday and nothing worse than seventy-five by the Friday. He was already very rich. It seems that it's the Germans who are mainly responsible. They make up the main body of the new citizenry in these parts, with the Italians and the Portuguese and the Greeks after. The Scots so far as I could gather build all the fireplaces and come mostly from Dundee, but one I met was from Lesmahago. He had a spanking motel outside the town and had just refused twenty thousand dollars for a spare lot of four acres. He had another hundred and twenty up the valley "for when the road comes through and I can make a real killing." There were, he said, a lot of things to foresee, and foreseeing was his trade. You come across much of it and among all sorts and kinds, and to find hard and practical men living this way in a dream world moves you. As for the Germans and their German cameras, they had been looking at them all their lives in the shop windows of their country and could actually buy them now for a mere week's wages. They run at about thirty pounds a week and there is bed and board on the company for a fiver.

It seemed a pity to be skeptical in the world of worth and well-doing they all described to me. It was mild as any English April outside. The steelhead were flashing in the bay. Mount Elizabeth was up there over your eyebrow dazzling white in the sun. I thought I had better, as the good sociologist I sometimes pretend to be, check on the local beer hall. There were maybe six hundred potmen, welders, construction men, and lumberjacks milling around dressed in the brightest-colored finery I ever saw and far better than anything in *Seven Brides for Seven Brothers*. Check shirts and every tartan and bastard of a tartan, red hats and yellow hats in a sort of celluloid, helmets in aluminum, glengarries in red and white stripes and red and green stripes, a Tyrolean job with a pink band and a feather on a German boy, the wondrous Siwash sweaters—the kind you never wash—one with a bright knitted big salmon on the back, another with a peacock. A vast man who might have been Paul Bunyan, the mythical lumberjack, had a couple of horses. They cavorted around on the rolling muscles of his back and looked as big as Shetland ponies and yet all the time he was still.

I was disappointed. They only threw one character out all the time I was there. Maybe I have gone decadent in the banana belts of Britain and have forgotten what an honest man's capacity should be. Here they were too busy to serve you in ones and the very word now seems indecent to me. They just had a look at you and gave you the number you would have dreamed of anyway. Maybe two if you were weak and pulling and an office boy or a bureaucrat or the kind of person you get on a committee, four for a salmon certainly, six or more for a peacock. As for the giant with the horses, they wheeled in the truck. I who have been at many great fights in my life never knew so suddenly what it was to be the champion of the world. They all wore the black trousers, white shirts, and bow ties of the bouncers of old New York. It is one of the prettiest active service uniforms in the world. The handsome young German beside me who was from Tilsit said he had made enough money to go to Honolulu but when he got back he hoped to "go free" on Vancouver Island and the hell with the glory of settling down even if I liked the architecture. These big men speak of taking off for Honolulu as though it were for the wakes at Blackpool.

Now schizophrenic for both Honolulu and Kitimat I went to the local paper to look hopefully at the crime sheet. . . . Ten bucks for speeding, three tens for being found in alcohol, one tenner for fishing without a license, another for being "caught in possession," though of what was unfortunately not specified. One richer character had been given thirty days for "three times in alcohol." The only fascinating case was the man who had taken his car out over the railroad track away from the infinite future and through the Rockies, and if you know the trestle bridges over the high ravines it represented quite a trick of bravery. Now there is something about the railroad in North America which only ever belonged similarly to Siberia and Chekhov. It is as sacred as any Pilgrim's Way to Canterbury. You don't pinch the bolts to go fishing and you don't escape over it to either Toronto or St. Petersburg. This offender was remanded for observation forty miles up the line. He was a member of the Y men's club, the winter club, the snowshoe club and half a dozen others, including the water color. "I had to make it," he said on arrest.

I sat with another professional foreseer gazing into the Canadian crystal ball. The house was just built and the scaffolding not yet down and the man from Dundee had quit only three days ago. The can of condensed milk was on the table. He pulled out a map and penciled in a highway all round the New California. He established another couple of Kitimats with crosses and found minerals logically off every inlet on the Panhandle. He opened up the Skeena River for agriculture. He broke through with a road here and a railroad there and brought all the lines of future wealth down to the only deepwater port with a hinterland to build on north of Vancouver. "Hell," he said, "I don't say a hundred and fifty thousand: I say a million." In the evening a few of the local Scots dressed in tartan jackets did a farback switch from all foreseeing and sang the Twenty-third Psalm for me and Scotland the Brave. We sang:

> "Far off in sunlit places, sad are the
>   Scottish faces,
> Yearning to feel the kiss of sweet Scottish rain.
> Where tropic skies are beaming, love sets the heart
>   a-dreaming,
> Longing and dreaming for the homeland again."

The sad Scottish faces looked as if they were all doing fine and weren't heading out yet to either Honolulu or the Highlands.

I took the train out to Rupert, and it seemed eager to go. It sirened wildly to the mountains and the lovely houses and all the hundred exercises in well-doing listed by the chamber of commerce and lit out with great vigor for the beyond. There were maybe only five in the lot bound on articulate business. The rest were quite simply on their way to the bees and the cigarette trees of somewhere else. You heard the itinerant cry every time the engine whistled its way across a ravine. A trio of Indians pulled out a long thin bottle of Jigger Jones with the crystal-clear liquid you only get out of the mountains, and the big men with the fine chiseled features and the bastard tartans all looking like Bob Flaherty passed other bottles from one great face to another.

Challenge for Change
—A New Approach

IN 1968, a new experimental application of the use of the documentary film began in Canada. The methodology has steadily evolved with experience and testing and now represents what is an important or perhaps even a major achievement in the social application of documentary.

In 1930, Grierson tried to find ways and means of bringing the workingman to the screen, presenting him to an audience of his peers. By 1970, the new Canadian program *Challenge for Change* (*Société Nouvelle*) had devised a system for bringing the screen to the workingman, enabling him to utilize these media (film and videotape) on his own initiative to change or improve his own social and economic situation.

The new program embodies a number of innovations in the making and using of films. Grierson had been concerned with the role that film might play in generating social awareness, which in turn would lead to social action. In the *Challenge for Change* pattern, films or video programs would be made not *about* but *by* and *with* the people living in a particular social situation. They would (with the assistance and support of professionals, as requested) make their own films or video programs, to illustrate and analyze situations that troubled them as a group. These visual documents of their own situation would engender further study, involvement, and pressure for action. The films or videotapes could be shown to local government officers, to members of investigatory commissions, to legislators and administrators. Where experience had shown that petitions, elections, protests, lobbying, or long-suffering were ineffectual, with this method a community could define and give expression to its own deep-rooted problems.

The program began with the National Film Board, which by 1968 had almost thirty years of experience in the making and distributing of many kinds of documentary and social film. As television became widespread after the 1950s, it became oppressively apparent that information distributed via television was received in an essentially passive way. The commercial ratings for television programs were almost the only feedback from viewers. The transmission was *broadcast* to an undifferentiated mass audience of all sorts, many of whom might be totally disinterested in the content. In other words, the tremendous increase in reach meant a corresponding diminution in intimate contact with particular groups for particular purposes. The familiar flattening process—pursuit of the lowest common denominator, widest popular appeal to a mass audience—almost automatically ensued. The spread of television was phenomenal but the means of production continued to be inaccessible in terms of the community. Offsetting this were some other developments: the increasing availability of lightweight movie cameras and tape recorders; the growth of cable and community television systems; the production of relatively low cost videotape equipment that might be used by small local groups in connection with community television programs.

From these circumstances arose the theory of *Challenge for Change*, which philosophically derived almost directly from documentary film-making. The aims of the new program were essentially these: (1) to increase public awareness and understanding of social problems, (2) to examine the effectiveness of government programs designed to alleviate such problems, (3) to promote citizen participation in the solution of the problems.

The initial impetus arose within the National Film Board but financial support for the programs also had to come from other departments of the federal Canadian government. The following departments joined in financing the first five-year phase of the new series:

Secretary of State (Citizenship Branch)
Department of Labour
Department of Agriculture
Department of Health and Welfare
Department of Regional Economic Expansion
Central Mortgage and Housing Corporation
Department of Northern Affairs

A combined annual budget of $1,400,000 was provided by these departments together with the Film Board, for the first-phase operation of the program.

Some of the initial projects (series of films or video documents, rather than single set pieces) were these:

· Needs of Newfoundland outport fishermen.
· Representations by Montreal slum dwellers directed to municipal authorities.
· Problems of indigenous Canadian Indian groups on Indian reserves and in urban areas, directed to government agencies both federal and provincial.
· Conflicting claims of Saskatchewan environmentalists, local farmers, and the provincial Parks department.
· Land-use conflict in a rural British Columbia district involving farmers, building developers, and local industries.

These subjects are typical of those which have been presented in the form of videotapes or film documents by grass-roots citizens' organizations.

The Film Board has provided the necessary equipment and technical support, but has not imposed direction or conclusions upon the programs.

In this context the film director has a catalytic rather than a creative role. He makes his experience available to the people with whom he is working, and is a social *animateur* rather than a creative film director.

On his first acquaintance with the new super 8mm film cameras, Grierson was impatient with the thought of ill-prepared and undisciplined amateur film-makers "waving their cameras around" to no considered purpose. But he soon became intrigued by the possibilities in this kind of work—in particular, by the prospects for decentralizing the means of production. This interest would be paramount during Grierson's later brief exploration of India, where he foresaw the enormous potential of such equipment for educational purposes.

In the following pieces, notably comments transcribed during a forum on *Challenge for Change* held at Montreal in 1970, Grierson relates his past thinking and experience to the new potentialities embodied in the *Challenge for Change* experiment.

Decentralizing the Means of Production*

With cameras coming smaller and lighter and easier to work and cheaper to buy, the decentralizing of film-making becomes an ever more practical possibility. We see it happening with home movies, with movie-making in research departments, with teaching organizations who make their own films without benefit of clergy.

I have been watching it even more wildly manifest in the undergraduate circles of the American universities, where the young people have declared for an "8mm revolution."

Much is claimed—and rightly—for the technical range of "Super-8." But I am skeptical. It troubles me to see people loosely waving a camera around. It is like loosely waving a baby around; for the camera, like the baby, has its rights. I shudder at all catch-as-catch-can film approaches, even when they claim to catch a falling star. I find it odd that university teachers should spread the doctrine, that shooting film any-old-how absolves the student from all need to read and write.

What I hear most about in North America is that the 8mm revolution will provide a magical path to what is all too loosely called *self-expression*.

There are philosophical uses of the term which mean a great deal; but the way I hear it, it is more often a refuge from the normal disciplines of work (yes, *and* observation *and* collaboration). There are times again when self-expression means self-indulgence, and this often at the expense of others.

This matters, very much matters, where self-indulgence means public hurt. Perhaps it doesn't much matter in the midst of North American affluence, but the attitude as a public attitude may weaken the political fiber of the next generation. In poorer countries, self-indulgence, involving the selfish use of a valuable means of public instruction and expression, presents a simple and nauseous example of bad taste.

As you see, I am in a dilemma as I look on the potential of the 8mm revolution and see what, in some quarters, they are doing about it. I am all for easier cameras, lenses *et al*. I am all for the 8mm revolution, *so long as* the 8mm mind doesn't go with it.

The National Film Board of Canada, for one example, is engaged in a

* By John Grierson.

more considered effort at decentralizing the production process. They have a continuing program they call *Challenge for Change* which is concerned with social problems at the local level. What makes it special is that it represents a genuine effort to keep in contact with people at the grass roots. *Challenge for Change* makes much of cinema verité but has cured itself of one cinema-verité deviation which has always been peculiarly attractive to the provincial: the secret camera's talent as a peeping Tom, and its ingenuity in catching the embarrassed reaction to the embarrassing question. Like all harlots, the cinéaste of easy virtue is apt to run into power without responsibility; and it can go to his head.

The basic tendency of the *Challenge for Change* program is to follow decently in the original cinema-verité tradition which the English documentary people associate with *Housing Problems* (circa 1936). With that film there was talk of "breaking the goldfish bowl" and of making films "not *about* people but *with* them."

But not yet is there a real decentralizing of production. The cinéastes may make their films *with* the people and *in* the villages, but they are soon off and away *from* the people and the villages, to their normal metropolitan milieu. The old unsatisfactory note of faraway liberal concern for humanity-in-general creeps in, in spite of these real excursions into local realities. . . .

I can't for the life of me see that communities in the future will have any continuing need for those faraway cinéastes. I start on the ground that a good teacher is, by the fact itself, a good exponent and a ready talent for exposition by film. So for all other professional exponents of cases and causes. The 16mm and 8mm film and the videotape are best seen now as relatively simple tools, to be locally owned and operated within the context of local reporting, local education, and democratic representation at the community level. The cost of equipment now puts the 8mm revolution within the reach of most groups and associations—at least in North America.

The professional standards need not be lower than the standards associated with local newspapers when they were making their vital contribution to community building in, say, the twenties. These standards were very high indeed, as the memory of William Allen White and the *Emporia Gazette* testifies.

I leave it to others to say how it will operate in other countries, but I have been looking into decentralizing possibilities in India and think I see one possible great development there. In India there is a special imperative for decentralizing the film-making process. All the mass media together reach out to only a hundred millions of the population, leaving four hundred and fifty millions to word of mouth, to local educators and the itinerant entertainments of native origin. Obviously the biggest role in economic and social progress of all kinds will be with the local educators, making it necessary to add in every way possible to their local powers of persuasion. Here, with the local educators, I associate all developments involving the community welfare. The local activist front is complex.

In India, too, there are many languages to contend with, and areas distinctive in ethnic and cultural background. Film-making at the district level is, I would think, a logical development, and one to which the various Foreign Aid programs should soon be giving their attention.

This means, among other peripatetic entertainments, the appearance of peripatetic teachers of film-making, moving modestly from district to district, teaching the doctor-teachers and other local educationists how to hold their cameras steady and shoot simply, *as their own native powers of exposition direct them. That would be a real 8mm revolution, anchored in necessity.*

I submit this to the attention of any aging documentary types who may be on their way to Benares.

A Forum on
Challenge for Change*

There have been times of plague, there have been times of war, there have been times of revolution. There have been other situations far more disastrous than the miserable defeat of the United States in Vietnam, the defeat of the American spirit. That event mustn't override your sense of objectivity. It would be false to tie up *Challenge for Change* with the so-called prevalence of protest in the world, of confrontation, the desire for self-expression, for participatory democracy and all these other things. I have watched it all at McGill University for three years, and I tell you quite frankly when I hear about the generation gap I laugh, because the plain fact is that when you set aside a certain justice in the protest, you've got to take with a grain of salt the fact that all these youth are really against the establishment. They are really against the tribal law. . . . It is the duty of the social movement to make use of social instruments for change; it is the duty of those making use of such instruments to be very careful that they are indeed objective, and that they are not seeing things in a juvenile and silly way. . . .

So here you have in *Challenge for Change* a positive intention of using the film and videotape, to do what? To do things that were usually done before. You are concerned with tying up with cable, but you are also concerned with tying up with all the other forms in which film can be used. You are concerned with tying up with the libraries. I see the library as the great coordinator of circulation, over and above the circulation represented by cable.

Now what are you dealing with? You are dealing with a prospect of using *Challenge for Change* on various levels. First of all, I suggest that you analyze the community to yourself. The community represents the age-old pillars of society represented by the state government, by the provincial government, by the municipal government. Not only politically but also managerially. The politics are concerned with the debate between one viewpoint and another. The managerial efficiency is also of concern. But you are further concerned with representation of the educational authorities, which have become the most powerful growing force in the North American continent. They have become a political force, because the edu-

* By John Grierson

cational system is the key to the *loyalty* of the future. You see, one thing is certain about the teaching profession—it is bound to teach a coherent future. Otherwise it is certainly not doing its duty to the young of the country. *You cannot teach defeat.* That is an impossible thing, you see, so the educators must teach a coherent future. And of course they must inevitably be concerned with this question of what is objective, and what is merely passing. . . .

But these are not the only forces—the forces of the state—forces of the municipal council, forces of education, forces of the church. They are not the only ones, because all kinds of specialized interests in every community have been organized from ancient times. In other times it was the farming community, on the land; or it would be the crafts or the guilds, in the towns. But today what have you got? You've got chambers of commerce. If there are big industries in any town or community, they have their own public-relations problems, and these big organizations should be challenged every time to give an account of their stewardship. You have very specialized representative units like rate-payers associations, consumers associations. You've got, for example, people concerned with the ecology, with the environment. At every turn your community is already organized. It is for *those* people who want to get on to their soapbox, to get up and find power *within* the machine. . . .

One of the greatest things that the Film Board could do in this country is to do what we have suggested for India. They should start planting acorns all over the country, instead of just spending all the time working in one community, providing expression for that community. The Film Board has not given the community the means of production so that they could express themselves; the Film Board has butted in at all times.

. . . I want you to teach these local people to *report* so they can report to themselves and report to the community. Plan to give *other people* the knowledge. Stop being so damned professionally arrogant, and stop making films for yourselves, and instead teach *other people* how to run cameras or run videotapes. Then they can make their own pictures. Don't *give* them the videotapes, for there's enough money in the community to buy a videotape machine. There's enough money among the local industries to buy videotape. There's no question of having access to the means of production. . . .

I think you've simply got to help people to express their own point of view, and above all you yourselves have got to take a highly objective viewpoint, and not regard the establishment as the enemy. If the establishment means Socrates, how can it be the enemy? If the establishment means the laws of Thomas Jefferson and the principles of the American Constitution, how can that be the enemy? I've been fighting the establishment all my life, but I had to have the establishment to fight *against*. And this is the thing that we have to restore. We've got to restore a feeling that there is a continuity in democracy, and that whichever side you take, you still have to preserve the older values, to fight for the new in terms of the continuing good of the community and people.

I would start very modestly, with a whole new renaissance of reportage. Also I would start with a whole new renaissance of news in depth. You have done some very wonderful film portraits at the Film Board. You are the people who can really teach other people how to make poetry. . . .

But reporting you will have to teach people, and you will have to get out from under and not try to kid yourself that *you* are going to be the reporter for the nation. Nobody wants the Film Board to do that, but everybody would want the Film Board to teach. The Film Board, apart from the teaching that it could do, must do a lot of writing; it must have also a creative body of criticism about all this. . . .

Another thing that the Film Board should be thinking of: In itself, it's got a big stake in the development of the libraries, not only its own film libraries, but its own relationship with all the local public libraries. I believe the local libraries could be reconstructed as libraries for all manner of videotapes, all manner of local videotapes, all manner of local films, as well as the usual library functions. Because it has a national distribution system, the Film Board ought to become a member of the *national* association of community leagues. I look forward to something like a community league in every place where there is cable TV, plus a national association of community leagues, to which the Film Board should really have something to contribute. They can contribute technically, and by teaching. All the time they can be helping local expression by giving people *examples* of local expression, by *making* examples of local expression. Altogether I think this is a very big role to play; but the fundamental thing I have to say about *Challenge for Change* is, it must look at itself very clearly as being *not* just a reaction to the present fuss and bother or a yell for participatory democracy. It should be something for the articulation of the community on democratic lines, and a restoring of the community's sense of duty and respect for the problems of today.

In India

(1970)

D URING his time at McGill University (1969 through 1971) Grierson developed a compelling interest in India, its philosophy, culture, and society. One of his seminar students, Rashmi Sharma, talked with him at length during this period. According to Miss Sharma, his extensive previous reading had given him a general broad awareness of Indian philosophy, but he became particularly interested in the comparison between Judeo-Christian belief and Hinduism, particularly in its Shaivite aspect.

In 1970 the Canadian International Development Agency contracted to send a team of Canadian communication specialists to India to consult on a broad plan for the intensification of educational campaigns on behalf of family planning. The Indian government had already planned and carried out extensive national educational programs in this area, but it was felt that more effective campaigns must still be developed. Grierson was selected to head the group.

The party flew to New Delhi and undertook a three-month tour of India to assess the nature of the task and the problems presented by both the physical and social conditions of India. The group of consultants came to certain broad conclusions and submitted their report to the Ministry of Health and Family Planning. The major emphasis of the report was on decentralization. In essence, the consultants suggested a decentralized pattern for the production of information materials, a network of local centers where such materials might be produced and used within the regional or local context, with regard to the special language and local conditions of each area. Lightweight, low-cost, easily accessible and operable equipment for making film, slides, filmstrips, and other simple visual aids was recommended. The involvement of local officials, medical personnel, teachers, and village-development workers was urged.*

Grierson was greatly excited and stimulated by his journey. He pro-

* For administrative and cost reasons, the report as submitted in 1971 has not been taken up. But at the other end of the spectrum, the government of India initiated a Satellite Instruction Television Experiment (SITE) in August 1975 with daily telecasts to a broad sample of 2,400 villages grouped within six population "clusters" and representing four distinct language areas. Programs on family planning, health and agriculture were designed specifically for village audiences, and special receivers were installed in each village for direct reception of the satellite signal. School programs were offered for two hours each morning, and adult programs (for group viewing) for two hours in the evening. Extensive feedback and evaluation studies have been commissioned.

foundly wanted to visit India again, but died in February 1972, within a year of his return to Canada. During his progression through India, Grierson did not hesitate to speak his mind on many subjects. There is a kind of fury of communication on his side, at the scale of the problems, the complexity of the task. His thunderings at the film people of India, the communicators, were not muted. In a sense, some of these outbursts (as to the Films Division staff in Bombay) were less than fair and just. But as always, he spoke and thought in the context of the broad problems as he saw them; no temporizing, no diffusion of effort could be allowed in face of the heavy human needs and tasks at hand.

A talk Grierson gave to the National Institute of Design at Ahmedabad, excerpts of which are quoted in the following pages, is eloquent of his feelings for India. Also quoted are interviews in the Indian press which give a clear account of Grierson's impact upon the film community, and the way in which his views were received in the Indian context.

Grierson
in India.

Indian Press Comments

From a column, "Cultural Causerie," by Bikram Singh, in *Evening News of India*, May 26, 1971:

The Films Division ought still to be in a daze from some hard knocks it has recently taken from no less an authority on the documentary film than John Grierson.

He was visiting India as the head of a Canadian delegation to study the utilization of short films and other audiovisual aids in the promotion of India's family-planning program and to explore the scope for Canadian assistance in the promotion effort.

Waste of Funds

Mr. Grierson, after an exposure to Films Division films, felt it ought to be paying more attention to the villages, "where the heart of India beats," instead of laying great emphasis on urban problems and events, which he felt it was doing in its films.

In what was perhaps the unkindest cut, he attacks the Division for its "attempts to gain renown by competing for awards in all sorts of festivals," some of the festivals being unknown even to a man like him. . . .

Classic

Though one doesn't know the shades and details of Mr. Grierson's sharp criticism of the Films Division, it seems to be only sound advice when he suggests that the rural scene and rural problems should find more place in F.D. documentaries.

But there is a very real danger that his scornful remarks regarding F.D.'s "attempts to gain renown" at international festivals may be interpreted as a call for reviving the bad old days of the Films Division.

All that mattered then was the "content"—which mostly meant the crudest and dullest ways of communicating a given "message"—and aesthetic values were all but nonexistent. . . . Mr. Grierson's criticism must be taken as an impatient gesture to prod the Films Division into a great awareness of the urgent need to provide to the country's teeming masses information and instruction on the numerous important problems of a developing country.

But it would be sad and retrogressive to use the Grierson indictment as an argument against striving for excellence in the medium.

John Grierson, the "tough-minded Scot" in the words of Arthur Knight, has always been a staunch advocate of the role of the documentary film as a medium for public information and instruction.

But we mustn't forget that Grierson, who wrote the "main theory of British documentary," once also said: "Most professors are a dreary warning of what happens when the informationist fails to become a poet."

From the *Sunday Statesman* (Delhi), May 9, 1971:

Grierson: The Reluctant but Angry Guru
By Our Delhi Film Critic

The Father of the Documentary Film. The inventor of the very term "documentary" and also of that classic definition of documentary as "the creative interpretation of actuality." Yet at seventy-three, Dr. Grierson refuses to be any sort of father figure or guru. "I am only an academe," he murmurs with that reversion to the Greeks which punctuates a good deal of what he says.

Small-built and outwardly very much the dour Scotsman and certainly in his burred speech, Dr. Grierson sticks doggedly to his Scottish woolen cardigan underneath his neat suit and beneath that cardigan beats a heart of pure gold. His youthfully nonconformist views, teamed with what I can only describe as a canny Scots instinct about hypocrisy in people and institutions, must have made him a holy terror. But his natural kindliness and generosity shine through his outer fierceness and a puckish sense of humor softens even his most scathing judgments.

But let John Grierson speak for himself.

ON THE FILMS DIVISION:

They win obscure prizes at obscure festivals, then talk of mass communication. They are using public money for self-indulgence, which Socrates deplored. A public purse for private pursuits. Their standard is very high, but they haven't got very remarkable films like those that come from Poland, Czechoslovakia, Canada and Holland; they haven't hit the level of Bert Haanstra. They are rather inclined to make films as laid down by departments, there is not enough creative urge, they do not reflect the spirit of the country lyrically and dramatically. I am tired of films on Indian music and carvings. I think cultural India had better be forgotten. Mrs. Gandhi talked of India on the march, going forward in terms of social revolution. The Films Division should be more reflective of the overwhelming story of India, its new economic and social programs, the new life for the people.

I am an authoritarian and don't believe in self-indulgence. If a man takes money from the government to make a film, he must have the responsibility of an editor, who can go to jail.

The Films Division should develop news in depth, they need great reportage not in the sense of the Indian newspapers which are out of date in

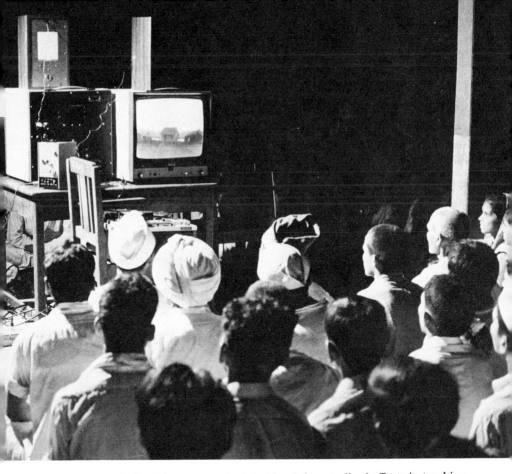

In India Grierson preached that local decentralized efforts in teaching
and information were essential to deal with overwhelming social
needs on a national scale.

manner, style, and approach. Even good reportage is not good enough, it
should be inspired reportage. The columns in India are reaching more for
news in depth and quality. I hope I'm not being arrogant, but our academic
background in documentary was far better than it is today. We knew our
geopolitics, our scientific world. I was offered jobs on the *Times* and the
Manchester Guardian. This is what film people here must think of. There is
no final blessing in being a film-maker, it is not sufficient to be a poet, but
an inspired poet. Documentary must have so much of today and what is
going to happen tomorrow.

What we need is a dramatic sense, the oomph behind the news. Look at the
Hindu religion with its chain reaction of creation and destruction. You have
to show how Lord Shiva operates today. But the information must not be
slanted. I mean real freedom of speech, what the Greeks called "Consensus
of the Congregation."

ON THE FILM INSTITUTE OF INDIA:

I tore them to pieces, blazed away at the staff and students. They asked me to speak about "the art of the film." I spoke about "the service of the film." For film is a disciplined medium and must have inborn respect for expression of public opinion. Film cannot be dissociated from service of the people. Most artists, the moment they get into the film industry, have to conform to the laws of show biz. There is no room for fun and games, least of all in the Indian film industry. They will get cut down to size, especially their technical exhibitionism, which does not make for box-office success.

ON CENSORSHIP:

I believe in censorship. How can you have a revolution unless you defend it? There is the question of maintenance of loyalties. In this country you can't allow so much to the enemy. That is the law of all social revolutions. But censorship has to have priorities. It is not a question of moral choice but social, political, and national priorities. Censorship is the central institution by which national priorities are maintained. No censorship is laissez-faire in spiritual affairs and a *reductio ad absurdum* in a dedicated society and in a religious society, which you presumably still are. And I will not compromise about film societies. They belong to a minute minority and now they show only sick films. I don't want India to be infected with false aesthetics of defeat preached by sick films. It does not belong to you. You Indians are under very great examination. You have pledged to do better than the British. You had better. You can't do worse.

CINEMA AS THE ART OF MOVEMENT:

Most movies are theatre and 90 percent of the history of movies is cinematic theatre. I watched the double helix, that double spiral, the twist in the axis of those gorgeous cookies, the peasant women, their natural sense of balance —from the train going to Poona. Cinema is the art of movement, participation in movement, as described by the Greeks. Visconti and Rossellini have it in some films and Satyajit Ray in *Aparajito* in his use of movement up and down the steps of Banares—Ray is a true poet. Dovzhenko and Pudovkin had it too. Eisenstein did not except in sequences. The Odessa steps were the steps of theatre, the Banares steps were natural, like Greta Garbo, like Bogart, like horses in Westerns. We had it in *Night Mail* and *Song of Ceylon* and in *Corral* and *Nahanni* of the National Film Board. Bert Haanstra had it in *Glass*.

ON VISITING INDIA (with a chuckle):

I object on principle to visiting great countries like India—I prefer the small ones. And, of all things, I have come to India in the name of family planning. It all seems surrealist.

An editorial from the Indian publication *Star and Style*, September 9, 1971:

KEEPING ALIVE THE SPIRIT OF EXPERIMENTING

The Indian feature film, but for a few occasional exceptions, has taken such a rigid, crystallized form that any sort of true and mature experimenting, in style or technique, gets automatically ruled out. The term "experimental film" has come to be loosely applied to efforts of all sorts, which either make some small departure from the trodden paths or try an entirely eccentric muddle in the name of new wave or avant-garde. The real worth of an experiment, as an individual creator's exploration in a totally new direction, is not being realized at all. Experimenting being not possible in the expensive sphere of feature films, run by private sources concerned only with their own monetary gains, it can find a rich pasture in the field of short films, especially since it is almost totally under government control. Though the experimental nucleus in the Films Division, initiated first by Jean Bhownagry and followed up faithfully by Pramod Pati, is still on a small scale, yet a new path has been opened in making documentaries more artistic and having a direct participation of the people, instead of being just dry diatribes. In the purely technological sphere, a remarkable beginning has been made with *Explorer* [1968] followed by other films.*

Here too, the question often arises whether a government department should indulge in the luxury of experiments with the taxpayers' money. In this connection, the views expressed on his recent visit to India by Mr. John Grierson, considered to be "the father of the documentary," appear strangely reactionary. Castigating the Films Division for making experiments and for trying to gain renown by competing for awards in the world fetes, Mr. Grierson seemed to advocate the type of propaganda-filled and rural-oriented product that earned a bad name for the Films Division not too long back.

Mr. Grierson's opinions gain further importance, since there is news of his coming to head a mass media program on family planning for the Indian government. Perhaps Mr. Grierson forgets that his own early documentaries were in the nature of experiments promoted by his government and they had to earn "renown" for the movement to gather strength. If John Schlesinger had not

---

* A film made by Pramod Pati with other collaborators at Films Division, *Explorer* created a great deal of controversy and violent argument among Indian film-makers and audiences. For virtually the first time in India, the film made use of subliminal imagery, synthetic and orchestrated nonmusical sounds, a very free use of traditional visual symbolism plus contemporary objects and activities, and a complex sound track without narration. This, added to the percussive rapid-fire rhythm of editing and abnormally loud level of sound reproduction, created a near-riot response in many cinemas. Withal, the film had a coherent and serious theme: the search for values and directions by young people within the complex contemporary society of India.

experimented and gained fame with [the documentary film] *Terminus,* perhaps he may not have made such a big breakthrough with features.

The flickering fire of experiment has to be perpetually fanned by recognition that brings it to public notice. In a country like India, eminently lacking in foundations and funds for research and with the private sector not touching anything useful unless it is profitable, it is only the government that can encourage and aid experiments. To oppose it is to shut out the last hope for its existence.

Address to the National Institute of Design, Ahmedabad, India

It's interesting that in India you are being very much infected by some rather crazy influences which have nothing to do with the urgency of your tasks. I was talking to the Film Institute of Poona, which had just finished a student strike, and there was much concern about the business of self-expression. My own view is that *if the public good is involved*, self-expression is not permitted to a private person, and certainly personal indulgence is not permitted to the private person, with the spending of government money. And any technical exhibitionism that doesn't have a function in society cannot be allowed in a country like India, which is in the process of a social revolution. You must be committed or you're against the revolution. A revolution must be defended, a revolution must be proceeded with, there is no other thing than to be committed, and in being committed you are committed to a public thing, a public responsibility, and not to a process of private indulgence.

Of course experiment has always got to be allowed for. Nobody will say that in my shops—the National Film Board in Canada, the GPO unit in Britain—we didn't experiment. I think sometimes we experimented more than most people, but I don't think we ever lost sight of the *line*. . . .

There is a tie-up between documentary and yourselves, in this sense of commitment and the sense of national duties to be done. . . . Outside the comforts of the town, the clubs and secretariats and coffeehouses, beyond the deeds and perhaps misdeeds of the politicians, a whole world waits to be explored, to be illuminated and interpreted by serious endeavor. This is the world of Indian life in the raw, the whole complex and interlocking web of economic activity, the catalytic forces, the agents of change, the forces unleashed by technology and industrialization, the tides and undercurrents of social change, the momentum of urbanization and its impact on politics, society and religion—in short the countless facets of the total dynamic Indian reality. Now that is something. I personally feel that when you have a social revolution going on, you must be very clear as to your priorities.

Now we, in our little family planning study unit, are thinking very seriously of restoring the "magic lantern revolution," by introducing filmstrips
at the village level, the making of filmstrips at the village level. I think of
course all you genius people in graphics might do worse than give three or
six months of your life to help *teach* people at the local level to make their
own filmstrips, and bring the best out of their own graphic sensibilities,
which I assure you are there because all over the place we've seen talent
that could be used in the making of filmstrips. Under the guidance of
people who know about camera work, people who can teach about continuity, under the influence and guidance of people like yourselves who have
graphics training, we might be able to *decentralize* communication in a
very vast way in India, in a way that's never been done in the world before,
beginning with the filmstrip and only then moving up to 8mm film possibilities. But the future doesn't lie with the film industry as such, it lies with
something in which you can *all* participate at the village level, at the block
level, at the district level. The film industry of course and the Films Division in particular have great work to do, all kinds of lyricisms to develop in
relation to the life of India, so that the picture abroad is not the gloomy,
gloomy picture that Mr. Mao gave, which does very serious harm to you.

A picture of lyrical belief in the future, you must develop that, you must
develop *The March of Time* idea, which has been so valuable in the past.
You must develop a sort of *India in Action* outlook, so that every two
months or so there is a report to the nation, and to other countries, showing India in action—what is happening in your progressive society. There
are all kinds of things to occupy you, but my own thinking and that of my
colleagues is that the decentralizing of communication may be the great,
great thing in this country, and maybe the revolutionary use of the new
technologies represented first of all by cinema verité, and second, by the
technical application of the super 8mm camera, and of course the filmstrip,
which is just your old magic lantern invented here in India and China
2,500 years ago. It's still a very valid and important thing to have your
village visitors carry with them, illustrating all kinds of subjects, beginning
with family planning, taken up by the agriculturists, by the health people,
and so forth. The other thing one thinks of is that there's a future for the
cassette player—not the cassette recorder, but the cassette player—so the
villages can really be given items they're not now being given, an intimate
contact with particular plays or particular speeches on radio.

Note you, all the time I'm thinking not only in terms of decentralization,
but also in terms of the difference between the communication that secures
collaboration, and the communication that shouts through a sort of loud-
speaker, a giving of orders in a bullying manner from *us* to *you*. This won't

do. We've got to think of communications involving the sense not only of family planning but of belief in the future. But belief in the future is not *imposed* from the top, it is *assumed* from the bottom, so the leaders of the villages are themselves in the forefront of the whole exercise in persuasion.

McGill University, Montreal

IT seems fitting that Grierson's last activity was teaching at a major university. His life was spent in the study of communications. He exploited the capacities of film and television for the purposes of education, of teaching. Education itself, as he states in these pages, is the ultimate communication, the ultimate mass medium. To it he brought a lifetime of study, experience, and human insight. Moreover, he brought a value system and a philosophy seldom found in these days in the last quarter of the twentieth century. He taught about standards, excellence, integrity, responsibility. He taught against self, against egoism. His teaching in many ways ran counter to the ideas and attitudes current during the 1960s and 70s. But his students understood his message and responded to the abrasive goading that came out of his affection and concern for humankind.

His seminars at McGill have left a deep impression on many students. His small hotel room in Crescent Street was the scene of many an energizing interchange. He loved young people, students, apprentices, film-makers, whom he scolded and heartened and imbued with his own intense sense of mission.

Donald Theall, Head of the Department of English at McGill, wrote about Grierson at the time of the memorial retrospective program given in London at the National Film Theatre in 1972; he is quoted in part below. Following this are comments by Grierson's students, whom we filmed in a classroom at McGill University. In their own language, wholly of these times, we hear the impact of Grierson's views and his spirit upon the young people of today.

Donald Theall

All his work in documentary film and the establishing of national and
international agencies was an extension of teaching, as far as he was concerned. Even propaganda he saw as the instrument of the teacher confronted with massive problems at times of crisis, and although many of us
are not too ready to admit it, in a deep sense he was right.

But while Grierson was always a teacher in his own mode and always an
intellectual, the extent of this manifested itself only in his last years when
he made a formal commitment of teaching and intellectual work here at
McGill. Many of his virtues from the film business and government work
informed his teaching. He lectured to groups of five hundred, holding them
involved by his wit, his cutting insights, his tirades against cheapness and
tawdriness and the enfeebling of moral, aesthetic, or intellectual values.

                                    .   .   .

He viewed teaching as personal encounter, just as he viewed all of the
multifarious activities of his life as personal encounters. It was this that left
the highly personal mark of John Grierson on the National Film Board, but
it is also the same personal mark that has been left on a variety of faculty
and students at McGill. He arrived at McGill during the height of the
student problems. This was a time when everyone seemed hyperconscious
of the gap between the generations. For Grierson in his seventies and his
students there was no gap. They disagreed with him at times, but they
respected him for the disagreements and they often came to see his point of
view. He had been strongly sympathtic to the left, associated with causes of
the left, but just as he could not tolerate "8mm minds," he could not
tolerate people whose commitment to revolution or to social change was
marked by a lack of discipline or the capability to think through intellectually and emotionally the implications of their positions.

To the student too committed to the aesthetic he would violently assert
the primacy of politics and propaganda in the world. He would insist that
they read works such as Trotsky's *Literature and Revolution* and understand the significance of the way the world and the artist are interrelated.

To the overpoliticized he would insist on the fundamental aesthetic nature, the solid morality and essential importance of the aesthetic standards,
in craftsmanship and making. He could show a deep sympathy for the
clowning of Charlie Chaplin and also an understanding of contemporary

film-makers like Dusan Makavejev, with whom he stayed up a whole night excitedly discussing new film ideas.

．　．　．

He shared that true commitment to the humanities which recognizes the best of everything is in the word and speech of man. Literature, in the broad sense of learning, and philosophy were the first prerequisites of the intelligent person; and then the person could become a film-maker or a civil servant or a teacher. In fact, properly viewing their role as human beings Grierson saw them all as teachers. In many ways universities exasperated him as much as he loved them. He could one day speak of McGill as an intellectual slum and the next day wax eloquent about its international status and that it shared with other major universities the role of being the major source of standards and principles for man. If he saw a close alliance between the church and university, or rather the university with its literature and philosophy becoming a kind of Arnoldian substitute for a church, it was again because of his tradition rooted in Glasgow University and in Scotland. The same roots gave him his personal commitment to students and to learning. Day after day when visiting him I found his apartment filled with new books. He knew more about structuralism in a real sense than many university professors of literary theory; he was a perpetual challenge to the narrow specialist whether among his students or among his friends. Yet he always respected the ideas of others; in fact, he seemed, along with a firmness and the ability to argue endlessly, to have a genuine humanity and respect for anyone's thoughts or creative work.

Mcgill University Students—
Grierson as Teacher

A Student: The first time I heard him I couldn't stand him. He was about the most pompous—like he was out to really get you going. Like my reaction was, I can't stand this guy. This guy is really upsetting me and I'm really reacting violently against him. After a while I got to know him. I took two years of classes with him, and after a while I understood that he was pushing you to get you to do something, to get you to produce, to get something out of you. But I know people who didn't even take his courses because he challenged them the first day and they backed down. The first day he always asked why people wanted to take one of his courses. Some-one said, "Because I want to. I enjoy the subject matter." So Grierson said, "That's not good enough. What are you going to do with the course?" The person repeated, "Well, I might enjoy it." Grierson said, "Get out of here." He wanted people to go out in the community, to use film in the com-munity, to do something with film as a communication means, but he didn't want us to take the course because of him, or just for the subject.

A Student: I was really perturbed about the whole course. I didn't know what he was trying to do. When we started the seminar last year we went for about five weeks with no idea what the aim of the course was going to be. I just thought it was really interesting listening to him. It took a long time to get the hang of what he was trying to do. Once you did find out that he wanted us to do something concrete, then things sort of smoothed out. I think people loosened up. He wouldn't let anybody talk for the first six weeks of the course. He didn't consider anything we had to say important. We weren't even allowed to ask questions. We just had to sit there and listen and watch. He was really strange.

A Student: I think he was younger than most of my contemporaries. In many ways I felt his mind was more agile and he was more energetic than most of my friends. In other ways he sort of had the stamp of his upbring-ing, the age when he went through school, but in terms of quickness and versatility I would say he was younger than most of my friends.

Question: Did you think his ideas were rigid?

A Student: I think he sort of had a standard. I mean he wanted everyone to live up to some standard of their own. He didn't impose it on you, but he wanted you to find out where you were and what you really believed in. A few people didn't understand what he was doing. Sometimes it just seemed that he was being obnoxious.

A Student: He'd keep questioning everything about any statement you'd make, so you had to make sure it was really what you believed in.

A Student: Or you could make a small point and he'd take it and expand on it so much that it wouldn't be your point any more. You wouldn't recognize it and you'd say, well wait a minute. Well, no, you couldn't say wait a minute.

Question: Did you find in his lectures that he brought in a lot of material, a lot of references beyond your own field, beyond your range?

A Student: Always.

A Student: Classical references I found really impossible to keep up with, and philosophy too.

Question: So what did you do?

A Student: I didn't. I just went along and assumed that it was something that I should know.

A Student: He also had a list of books you could read, and he would mention them in his course. If you wanted to fully understand his seminar group, you had to go to the sources, to the foundations of what he was talking about. It was usually rooted in Plato or Socrates or something like that. And then he would have people prepare reports. But it was all voluntary. Someone might do some work on Trotsky and bring it in and explain it to the rest of the class. Everyone always understood in the small seminar group anyway. The big lecture group got out of control because there were too many people and it was sort of difficult to take the time to explain. So he left it up to them to do as much as they wanted.

Question: What about his ideas on films? Did he say the things you wanted or expected to hear him say? Did his ideas about films irritate you?

A Student: Seemed to me he didn't talk all too much about many films, and he did do a lot of talking about philosophy and concepts and ideas. He had sort of graduated from criticizing films to the ideas behind them.

Question: Did he put concepts to you that were new to you?

A Student: All the time.

A Student: More than concepts. He gave us a whole new perspective. I have met very few people, much less teachers, that have had some kind of global perspective on what they were talking about. He was talking about India as much as he was about Montreal.

Question: How about law and order? Some people said he was very authoritarian. How did those ideas seem to sit with you, with students—the idea of ordered freedom, responsibility to the community, of the citizens?

In Montreal with students (1970).

A Student: I think a lot of people at first were taken aback by some of his tyrannical stands on things, and by the fact that he was such an authoritarian. This responsibility to the community doesn't tie in with some socialist student views.

Question: Do you think there was any antagonism amongst the students to these views?

A Student: Oh, yeah. I think the line was just too strong not to antagonize a lot of people. He was saying that in order to change the system, you work within the framework—ordered freedom. This fit in with my ideas. A few people were sort of grimacing.

A Student: I don't think anybody ever challenged his ideas.

A Student: I think he made a point of trying to get to people individually. He made everyone in the small seminar participate, and we had to write two or three essays for him during the term. I wrote a satire on his course and he was delighted. After that my involvement was a personal sort of writing involvement; he encouraged me to write and had a tremendous influence on me, because I've been writing ever since I graduated. Otherwise I might not have done that. And I know there are other students who were in our small group who are still doing poetry. He took a very determined interest in our poetry, invited us down to his little gatherings on Crescent Street, and said, "We're going to have the poets here. We're going to have the writers and the artists and one day I'm going to invite a football player so you can see!" And he fed us all; he had a very personal interest.

A Student: But later there was a complete change in emphasis. He wanted people who were going to teach. He wanted people who were going to be politicians. He wanted activists. He didn't want to have anything whatever to do with the so-called artists. He wouldn't hear it mentioned.

A Student: One day I told him what I was interested in and what my field was going to be, like history and teaching art somewhere, I wasn't quite sure. He just completely slashed my whole future. I was practically in tears when I walked out of the class. Somebody walked out after me and patted me on the back and said, "It's okay. You don't have to worry about it." But he came across with this strong attack at first, and then sort of supported me later on. It was totally contradictory, and he sort of stood behind me all the time, encouraging me and prompting. He was really good.

A Student: But it was strictly on an antiart, antiaesthetic kick.

A Student: Also writing had to be a public service for him. We weren't just writing for the sake of writing or for our own amusement or for the sake of the stories. You had to be doing a political or social satire, something that was going to make an impression on other people or change their attitudes. He strongly insisted that it had to be functional.

A Student: The very last seminar he gave, he really got into a whole new thing, decentralizing media. All the discussions were centered around the idea of people going out into the community.

A Student: The year before, he had said that it was a lot of nonsense to give everybody cameras and let them go out, that shooting should be kept within some sort of professional framework. But then he really changed his ideas a lot because of that Indian experiment.

A Student: But that's what was really amazing about him; he wasn't so set in his ways that all of a sudden he wouldn't say, "Well, yeah, maybe that's possible . . ."

Question: You're studying communications. What did you think finally about these courses?

A Student: I think they changed just in the two years that I had him. Especially because of this Indian experiment that he was so involved in, the decentralization and training of people to go out in the field, that sort of thing. But what always impressed me was the eminent practicality of every-thing. Everything was purposeful film, purposeful writing, purposeful talk, everything.

A Student: And also you weren't allowed to be negative. If you men-tioned anything that had to do with a negative, he'd just say, "Well, you're only saying something negative. You have to give something positive."

Question: All through his life he was quoted often by people who got bruised as coming down very hard on art and the pursuit of art for aes-thetics' sake. And yet as you say he would help you out or give you encouragement. Some people do believe finally that he was against art and aesthetics. What do you feel?

A Student: I think he was hostile to precious individualism more than art, and I think art is one place where you find precious individualism, more than, say, in teaching.

A Student: I remember reading in one of his books something he said: "Art is a byproduct of doing something well." And I remember him saying that he made that film that he talks in, *I Remember, I Remember,* to show people that he *was* interested in aesthetics.

A Student: In his small seminar courses he stressed the fact that during the ten years he'd had a television program in Scotland he could always find something to talk about, he could always find beauty. He told us that you could find beauty in some very strange objects, and also that the architecture of a city can have certain beautiful or characteristic elements. That there are shapes in an environment that can form your own perspec-tives of things, and in that sense he was very conscious of aesthetics.

Question: Did you have a sense of his being a contemporary man who was with the times, with the scene? Or was he speaking from another time?

A Student: He was either outside it or oblivious to it. He had his ideas, and whether these ideas conformed to the times or not didn't seem for him to be important.

A Student: When he first came to McGill, he said that his main function in coming here was to find out firsthand from the students what they were all about. He thought there was a revolution taking place on campuses across Canada and across the United States, all over the world. And he wanted to find out from us what exactly this involved. So right up until the end he was keenly concerned with everything that was happening around him. And very aware of it, plunged right into it.

A Student: He was probably disappointed that he didn't find a real revolution here too.

A Student: He wanted to find out what was going on in the environment, but he was concerned with universal things like revolution, rather than minor things like daily life. He was really interested in the things that change men's minds.

A Student: But that's not being outside our times. That's being right in them.

A Student: But it's also being *above* them—you know what I mean?

A Lifetime in
Communication

AT the end of his life, Grierson could take pride in the many direct and indirect ways he had influenced the field of film in his roles as theoretician, producer, promoter, innovator, distributor, and teacher. He had developed new possibilities for the effective use of film outside the cinemas. He had directed and produced a major seminal film in 1929. He had persuaded ministries of government and large public and private corporations to take up the use of film for public education. He had recruited and energized many young film-makers. He had persuaded film distributors to open up the industry to documentaries. He had worked with the feature-film format and by direct or indirect means had helped bring realism into the entertainment film. Late in his professional life he had entered television, and although he did not participate directly in the initial phase of TV development, he became a spokesman to a wide television audience on behalf of the unique qualities of the film medium. His television series about films ran for an astonishing ten years. Later he taught about film, but more importantly about philosophy and ethics, in a major university. And near the end he voyaged to a new territory—India—and saw there a huge potential for the purposive use of the newest aspects of film technology in the most urgent areas of education.

In an interview with Ernest Betts* shortly before his death, Grierson defined two broad periods in the history of the documentary. Phase I was the organization of film for reportage, for creating social awareness, in a situation outside the cinemas and with finance from outside the film industry. Phase II was television, which took over the principle of documentary and embodied it powerfully in the form of TV news reports and TV analyses of the broad social and cultural movements of our times. Grierson still saw a distinction between the making of films destined to be used *as films*, and the making of television films or shows destined to be broadcast *as television*, whose "undue pursuit of the immediate does not permit the more patient pursuit of excellence."

In another analysis of documentary history, talking with Elizabeth Sussex,† Grierson defined four principal chapters of the documentary story.

---

* "The Last Word," an article by Grierson (1972) done as a tape recording in reply to questions put to him by Ernest Betts, and appearing as an appendix to Mr. Betts's book *The Film Business* (George Allen & Unwin).

† "Grierson on Documentary" (the last interview), from a conversation with Elizabeth Sussex shortly before Grierson's death in 1972. The interview appeared initially in an article in *Film Quarterly* (Vol. 26, No. 1, pp. 24–30, © 1972 by The Regents of the University of California, quoted by permission of the Regents). This interview is also included in the book by Elizabeth Sussex, *The Rise and Fall of British Documentary: The Story of the Film Movement Founded by John Grierson* (University of California Press, 1975).

t was the simple travelogue, at a very early stage in film history. Second was the insight into human life and qualities provided by Robert Flaherty. Third was the effort (led by Grierson himself) to bring workingmen and -women, "ordinary people," onto the screen as dramatis personae no less rewarding or valuable than the characters of conventional drama. Fourth— the present phase—represents another shift in the function of films, the making of films *with* people rather than *about* people. In this context we are confronted by the greatly expanded use of film-making and film-using, as well as videotape recording, for the most practical and urgent purposes by every kind of group and community. This is the area exemplified by the Canadian series *Challenge for Change,* and by all those present-day efforts to exploit the media—film, video, sound tape—in order to deal with the social problems that we face in this century. In his last months, Grierson was fully aware of these new possibilities.

In the following brief comments, Grierson states his position on certain fundamental matters, comments made near the end of a very active and productive life.

From a videotaped interview with James Beveridge, York University, Toronto, 1970:

Grierson: I do not believe that the exclusively important media is television or film or that sort of thing. I believe that the first great mass medium in the world is conversation, word of mouth, and it is about time somebody reminded us of that because it is by word of mouth that all values are exchanged, all loyalties exchanged, all political loyalties in particular are created. Setting that obvious fact aside, the master medium is education itself.

Education, if you conceive of it as the process by which people not only are given information, but are given the sentiments, loyalties, and other attitudes to living, then you have got to think of the family as an educative location; and the church and church hall; and the Rotary and Kiwanis and all these other groupings of a community, as having a bearing on education. Of course, the school is the important center wherefrom children are given a sense of direction, not only in the matter of information but in the matter of character, in the matter of loyalty to their country, in the matter of loyalty to their fellow-men.

You have the thought that education is the master medium of all media and, of course, when it takes over as I hope it will take over much of the television process, a good part of the film-making process. I want the teachers to take the damn thing over, take it away from the experts, who call themselves professional communicators. I want the real professional communicators to be the teachers and the givers of law, and the givers are the people who can address the people properly, grammatically or otherwise. I leave you with the thought that the most important thing in this world, the one priority, is *Who chooses the teachers*, who chooses the teachers of the teachers? If you ask me in what quarter I would want to seek power in another existence, I would say that I would want to be the guy that chooses the principals of the universities exclusively.

Question: In Canada we have the national, federal agencies of information, and recently we have an educational TV–communication complex in some provinces. Do you see any danger in this?

Grierson: Not as long as the teachers take over the film-making.

Question: How literally do you mean this?

Grierson: Absolutely as I said it. The teachers must become film-makers, it is not for the film-makers to become teachers. You have got to be a born teacher in the first place, and then be an artist.

Question: Then the teacher presumably has to learn film-making?

Grierson: I have been a political animal and I have been a film-maker. I was a political animal first, and a film-maker relative to being a political animal. I think you must be a teacher-animal first, a creative animal in terms of teaching, and a technician second.

Question: You don't see this necessarily as a matter of teachers going through formal courses in the methodology of making films or television shows?

Grierson: No, for God's sake, you aren't going to get many of them, if you get a hundred good film-makers in this country—I would doubt it, that is a great number of good film-makers. But you have got to find in the teaching profession that nucleus of forty or sixty, whatever it may be, who will be the givers of life in terms of film, and to this all children are exposed. I am scared to death of photographers pretending to be teachers.

From an interview with Grierson in the *Sunday Post*, Glasgow, December 4, 1966:

You're approaching your seventies. What's your secret of living to a ripe old age?

First, I learned to forgive others their mistakes. Then, more important, I learned to forgive myself my own mistakes.

What has been your narrowest escape?

Once I was coming in to land in one of the early Comet jets. Suddenly we were told the undercarriage had failed. Next we were told two of the engines had cut out. We flew around New York till we used up all the fuel—then we belly-landed. But there was no fear inside the aircraft. The crew were well organized. And the airways had a stroke of genius when they put lassies up as stewardesses. If they didn't seem to be afraid, how could we men?

Are you a religious person?

Every person is. No one can fail to believe in the finite and the infinite. It's inevitable, therefore, that we're bound to believe in the fact of religious faith.

If you could live your life over again, is there one particular pitfall you'd avoid?

Pitfalls are the spice of life. And young folk should know that. But there's never a pitfall that the human spirit can't dig itself out of. Probably the most dangerous pitfall is the loss of faith in the human spirit and its infinite variety. If that happens, remember—it's you that's at fault.

About the Film
GRIERSON

THE film *Grierson* was finished in the winter of 1972. We had shot a very considerable amount of 16mm footage—40,400 feet of original location filming quite apart from compilation film. The problem for the film editors was severe. By the terms of its television showing, the film was necessarily restricted to 57 minutes and 50 seconds. We had to presuppose an audience mostly unacquainted with Grierson.

We had footage of Grierson in interviews, from videotape, and from a very limited but useful coverage of the twenty-fifth birthday celebration of the National Film Board. There were excellent candid photographs made by a student at McGill, a gallery of revealing studies showing "the Doc" in many of his characteristic moods: cantankerous, skeptical, pitying, quizzical, impish, and stonily disapproving. There were private photographs contributed by his wife, Margaret. There was newsreel and stock-shot film from various archives, to sketch in the time frame and the important world events of the period. There were film excerpts from some of the major documentaries of the past and from some of the influential "landmark" feature films that pointed the way to new film methods. All of this had to be edited together, so the group who did the filming retired and the editing group took over. An experienced film writer joined the editors and helped order the diverse materials. A two-hour version was completed, followed by a series of screenings, assessments, disputes, and decisions. Sequences were cut out, reshaped, shortened, merged. The shape and the impact of the film changed from one version to the next. Certain key scenes, statements, and juxtapositions survived the reduction process and remained as points of reference.

Finally it was done. The decisions were all achieved by consensus. Everyone involved was dedicated to the film, to the importance of giving a truthful, fair portrait of Grierson. His own voice, taken from taped or filmed interviews and speeches, contributed greatly to the sense of a living personality. The voice itself was a splendid one—the fine diction of a highly educated Scot, with its unique phrasing, cadences, and rhythm.

Inevitably, some things were a disappointment. I regretted the minimal nature of the statements by each person interviewed on camera. The average statement by one of Grierson's former colleagues or friends has been edited down to less than one minute, an absolute minimum if any coherent framework is to be maintained. I felt the text spoken by the film narrator was disappointing—certainly clear but somewhat lumpy, brusque, insensitive. Yet subtlety would have served no purpose, because TV viewers, the audience for whom this was intended, by and large knew nothing of Grierson and therefore all statements must perforce be brief, sharp, and unequivocal in their meaning.

At the end of the film is a scene in which the camera pans across distant somber hills beyond a Scottish loch. Prior to this are landscapes photographed near Ben Nevis, mists and distant waterfalls among the high hills. Over these scenes, Grierson's voice:

I've spent a wandering life, and the paradox of getting around is that you hold closer in the mind to where you come from—it is your first and original power of attorney. No, your national affections will not stray much, and distance will lend enchantment, and all the dreamers will behold their Hebrides. But as you come up against other horizons, other peoples, other conditions of life, you do find yourself examining more and more the attitudes to life your country gave you.

Under the voice is heard the music of distant pipes, the symbol of Scottish feeling. End-title credits come on the scene, the many people who took part in making the film or otherwise contributed to it. They too are part of the effort.

They—we—have done our best. It must stand or fall on its merits, such as they are. It is a record made under pressure of time and emotion, of a man's life and his aspirations. It will no doubt stand for some years as a useful, well-known record, a reference vehicle. But far beyond the range of the particular film, like ripples on the pond, Grierson's influence widens across the years.

Appendix

The Grierson Series

Further to the production of the Grierson film, and as a result of the large accumulation of interview footage and related stock-shot film material, it was decided by the National Film Board in Montreal that a supporting series of short study films might usefully be made for communications students and others. After thorough assessment of the interview transcripts and collected film footage, plus the voluminous texts of speeches, broadcasts, and writings by Grierson himself, a series of six short films dealing with basic Grierson concepts of communication was proposed for production in 1975–76. The subjects are as follows: The Public Servant as Film-Maker; The Common Man in Film; The Unit Formula (Collective Film-Making); Propaganda and Film; Education as Activist; Decentralization. The theme of this series would be Grierson's Social Philosophy of Film.

Each film contains clips from the interview footage shot for the original *Grierson* film, plus stock-shot footage acquired for this same subject. Commentary in each film links it to others in the series. Each film has an individual structure of its own, but all fit into a general framework. They follow a chronological order so the film work done in England will not be confused with that done in Canada.

Each film is directed towards a special audience in an area of the humanities—sociology, political science, communication or film education. The series as a whole, including the original *Grierson* film, can then be used to depict the role of film as a tool of social education.

Awards Won by the Film Grierson

Bronze Reel Award and winner in the "Personality" Category, Seventeenth San
Francisco International Film Festival, October 1973.
Etrog Award for best documentary film, Canadian Film Awards, Montreal,
October 1973.
Robert Flaherty Award, Society of Film and Television Associates, London,
1973.
Best Profile Documentary, Ninth Hollywood Festival of World Television,
Hollywood, December 1973.

GRIERSON *Film Credits*

Research coordinator	Marjorie Saldanha
Location research	Louis de Rochemont III

Unit manager	Ian Ferguson
Photography	Eugene Boyko, C.S.C.
	Lewis McLeod
	Michel Thomas d'Hoste
	Magi Torruela
	Jacques Fogel
Location sound	Bev Davidson
	Colin Charles
	Gildas Le Sausse
	Ron Seltzer
	Hans Oomes
Stills layout	Pierre L'Amare
Animation camera	Raymond Dumas
Voice	Michael Kane
Film editors	Les Halman
	John Kramer
Sound editors	Bernie Bordeleau
	Andre Galbrand
Music editor	Don Douglas
Rerecording	Jean-Pierre Joutel
Original material directed by	Roger Blais
Special consultant and commentary	Donald Brittain
Advisor	James Beveridge
Producer	Roger Blais
Executive producer	David Bairstow

Definitions—Answers to a Cambridge Questionnaire

The task of the film and of this book has been to provide an interpretation of Grierson, a complex man who during his lifetime was active in many fields. As a recapitulation, it would seem useful to provide a framework of definitions by Grierson. An astutely designed questionnaire prepared by students of Cambridge University was presented to him late in the 1960s. In filling this out, he gave terse answers to specific questions, and these answers supply in unusually complete and compact form a chart or even a manifesto of his policies. All along the line, from the 1920s to the 1970s, Grierson's critical writings and speeches exhibit his single-minded loyalty to certain goals—self-discipline, personal and social responsibility, concern for our fellow-men. In order to put all this into clear focus, the following statement is attached as a summing-up of the story.

Question I. As a director and producer, do you see yourself as an educator, an artist, or a philosopher?

Rather than answer your questions in personal terms, I think it would be more useful to remind you of:

1. the nature of the documentary idea.
2. the development of the documentary idea on various levels, e.g.
    a. reportage.
    b. reportage in depth.
    c. dramatization of the actually observed.
    d. poetic interpretation of the actually observed, etc.
3. the development of the documentary idea in its *uses,*
    a. in the theatre for its ancillary entertainment values.
    b. by governments in the presentation of the nation's image to itself and others, i.e., propaganda in the larger, long-term interpretation.
    c. by governments for its more immediate instructional and propagandist uses (as in many emergent countries today).
    d. by commercial and industrial organizations for
        i. local instructional purposes (including, in some areas, instruction in nutrition, health, etc.).
        ii. the improvement of its public image in depth, i.e., the larger

public significance of its operations (Shell is a good example in both categories).

Even this analysis does not give anything like a complete picture of the many various developments of the documentary use of film. You have to take note of that development against the various political and economic backgrounds of the different countries (socialist and nonsocialist) who, largely from the example set originally by the U.K. and Canada, have developed the documentary film as a deliberate instrument of public policy.

Above all, you should be guided by the inalienable fact that film is a relatively expensive medium, even at the single-minded amateur level. Contrast the position of the free poet, free painter, free writer, with the would-be free film-maker, from an economic point of view. He must depend largely on personal wealth or access to personal wealth. For the most part, and you must take it as an invariable rule, he has to come to terms with the economic and political realities from which access to the means of production and distribution derive. In some cases (France and French Canada provide amusing examples), he will make his deal with the political and economic realities, then proceed to double-cross them in the name of freedom of expression, etc. But he will not get away with it often.

On the other hand, he can, in all fidelity to his public undertaking, emerge with a film far beyond the expectations of his sponsors in the matter of aesthetic quality. He may even, in certain ideal personal relationships with his sponsors, establish an aesthetic expectation of his public work, and further establish the long-term advantage of it. This is what happened to the British documentary movement of the thirties, and at the Crown Film Unit during the war. The National Film Board of Canada is probably the best example, because its relationship in depth with its public contract (including aesthetic depth) has lasted longer than anywhere else and is in very good health today.

Holland is a good example of this higher sponsorship, partly due to the personal powers of persuasion of individuals like Bert Haanstra, but partly also from a correct reading by both the Dutch government and the larger industrial sponsors, of the English example.

In all the socialist countries, public sponsorship is permissive of aesthetic achievement, but there are many, many variants—from the U.S.S.R., at one end of the scale, to Yugoslavia at the other—dependent on factors other than the powers of personal persuasion on the part of the documentary film-makers, and the personal imagination of the responsible public officers, e.g., national or sectional emotions overcoming the doctrinaire party line in Poland, Czechoslovakia, Hungary, Rumania and Yugoslavia, with interesting new signs from the outlying studios of the U.S.S.R.

You will conclude, I hope,

1. that access to the means of production and distribution being paramount, the political and economic factor in documentary development has been the key to its worldwide development, and that it was this basic assumption which made the United Kingdom the paternal source of the whole process;
2. that the many various forms of documentary construction and use will inevitably emerge;
3. that even within the limits so set, an aesthetic result of the greatest quality is possible;
4. that what emerges in quality, especially in the more obvious aesthetic categories, will depend on

    a. the powers of persuasion of the documentary producer vis-à-vis the political and economic reality,

    b. the imagination of the ministers and public officers who provide the authority and, as a last resort, the defenses for experiment and adventure,

    c. ideally, a personal relationship on the highest level between a and b.

From all that, you may get some sort of an answer to Question I. I could say briefly

1. I have been associated with some large exercises in national and international education (in the widest sense of the word).
2. I have been associated with the making of many good films.
3. My basic academic origin was in political philosophy, but I would rather note that I have been a highly practical operator in the field, in the sense that the original analysis of the documentary potential was largely mine, and its management in the original key situation was my responsibility. A point worth noting is that at all times I was both the producer in charge and the public officer with the necessary government authority—worth noting because the development in some places of a gulf between the public authority and the production process has diminished the quality of the "movement." I shall return to this in your Question IX.

I shall do that last piece over again because of a new question suggested. Consider the development of a "movement" like documentary. You had better call it a "movement" or a "drive" or something, because it was a considered effort to mobilize an economic place for the serious film-maker within the politico-economic framework (first in the capitalist-socialist framework of the West, thereafter in the more self-conscious socialist countries). To make it work, it involved

a. a theoretical analysis of the possibility,
b. a promotion of the idea,
c. an involvement with the politico-economic power and a certain participation in its management,
d. a production and distribution process and organization of the machinery therefor.

Item a means that you are an analyst of some sort, of the political condition and of the relations of the artist with the community and of the conclusions and arguments that must arise on that score:

i. in fast-moving revolutionary periods like, say, the eighteenth century or the nineteenth century of industrial Britain,
ii. the contemporary period of mass management and mass communication and absentee landlordism in the biggest way.

Items b and c above mean that you will have to be a bit of a propagandist for the idea vis-à-vis the persuaders (e.g., in my case, the *London Times* and influential individual supporters like H. G. Wells); and vis-à-vis the powers that be (e.g., in my case, ministers like Walter Elliot in Britain and Mackenzie King in Canada); and vis-à-vis civil servants and accountants-general, not least. This in turn makes you incidentally something of a teacher, or even a preacher; certainly a fellow traveler in the national and international business of communication; certainly also a bit of a politico.

Consequent success on these levels might leave you *tout simple* a propagandist for the powers that be. But watch. In the process of promotion you have built up an idea because it has public worth and public value for the powers that be. In the documentary story, this hinged basically on its dramatic educational potential in the field of communication. You will not have said much about the aesthetic potential, not to mention any personal aesthetic ambition you may have. It is not of primary concern to the powers that be. This you will only reveal to individuals who natively appreciate the aesthetic factor in mass communications and in public management, and have a personal concern for the personal contribution which the aesthetic factor supplies. But when you talk politically of "bringing England alive to herself in the modern world," or "filling the Canadian mind with such images as will give its citizens a more vital appreciation of Canada's individuality as a nation, and so *condition* their mind to a greater will for the future," you have involved yourself not only in the propagandist implication of the world "condition," but also in the aesthetic implication of the phrase "bringing alive."

In other words, I cannot answer Question I as you put it in your subdivisions. Your subdivisions are all part of the same thing so far as I am concerned. One thing you may find interesting is this. Except under the special circumstances I have noted, you do carry a *secret* intention (the aesthetic one). You will find an excellent presentation of this in Trilling's essay on Isaak Babel. That "secret" intention cannot always be revealed, but there will be much sensing of the fact that you carry it. So you will always be subject to a certain mistrust and even a certain inarticulate opposition, at many points of your bureaucratic journey. After all, you *are*, from many a point of view, taking the wooden horse of aesthetic into Troy. The story of the documentary movement is in part the story of how, not without a scar or two, we got by. Maybe you win more or less for keeps, as in the case of the National Film Board of Canada. Maybe you lose, though never altogether, to the bureaucrats and the other boys behind the woodwork (e.g., the Crown Film Unit and the present Central Office of Information in the U.K.).

The fact is that there are many real sources of opposition to the idea of art (activist) in the public service: and they will only be overcome where you establish a most manifest need, and secure a measure of imaginative indulgence on the part of the powers that be.

Ordinarily one must expect opposition arising from the following factors:

1. the genuine old-fashioned disbelief in a government's indulgence in an instrument of propaganda (this is now altering greatly in the general acceptance of the idea of ministries of "information");
2. political fears on the part of opposition parties, at the initiatory stage, that the government party is giving itself an advantage;
3. jealousy between ministers as to who will control the power; sensitiveness to the dangers of ministers using the new power for their own political ends;
4. the opposition of routine bureaucracy to any operation which is interpretative and involves a quality judgment;
5. fear that the artist will occasionally be too adventurous for easy defense in parliament;
6. a genuine attachment to the "quietist" approach to culture and a positive dislike of the idea of art-in-action.

These sources of opposition have been demonstrated in most countries but vary according to the feeling of manifest need, and indulgence to the aesthetic factor, in high quarters. Obviously the sense of manifest need must be established more firmly than can be done by individuals, however powerful in their persuasion. The manifest need of art (activist) in the management of society must, I think, be given a deeper base in academic teaching of the highest order. In other words, the future of art (activist) in modern society will come, not from the artists, but from the academicians. This means that the teaching of political science, etc., must be brought up-to-date to cover the relationship of culture, in its new powers and formations, with the nature of the modern state in its new powers and formation.

Question II. Should a documentary record its subject with the greatest possible verisimilitude, in the belief that the subject is the meaning, or is it a case of the true interpretation?

Question III. You mention the importance of Claude Lévi-Strauss for people thinking about films today; could you say just what this importance is?

In any creative treatment on any level of penetration of the given phenomena, you seek the noumenal, which is variously described by the philosophers. "Meaning" is the least evocative word; the "thing-in-itself" does more for you; *"sub speciae aeternitatis"* does a lot; but "reality" is the basic word you arrive at, as it was at the beginning. So observation in depth will always lead you to some significance or some "meaning" in the subject. You will always be referring somewhere along the line to a larger context of social significance or to dramatic or poetic or other forms which makes the subject more deeply communicable to others (who are likewise concerned in finding the meaning or more ultimate shapes for their own observation and experience). I know there is a good deal of concentration just now on observation as such ("cinema verité," "the non-film," the "non-novel," etc.). One understands it as representing a revolt against the established shapes of social observation and aesthetic forms. But it is, a priori, a cul-de-sac, and even the imagination of Freud does not provide a very solid foundation. As Ivan Karamazov's Grand Inquisitor demonstrated, the cult of the person has always been wide open to authoritarian takeover, and in its crudest forms. This is not accidental. Consider the comment by Lévi-Strauss in his essay on Sartre ("History and Dialectic"):

A *Cogito* which strives to be ingenuous and raw, retreats into individualism and empiricism and is lost in the blind alleys of social psychology. For it is striking . . . that the situations which Sartre uses as a starting point for extracting the formal conditions of social reality—strikes, boxing matches, football matches, bus-stop queues—are all secondary incidentals of life in society; and they cannot therefore serve to disclose its foundations.

Another consideration: technical adjuncts to observation carry their dangers. It is noticeable that an otherwise simple character with a pair of binoculars can become a pretty conceited fellow—the more so when you add to your otherwise simple fellow the multiple adjuncts of a movie camera. He can now see every which way, up and down, and all around, and near and far and slower and faster, etc., etc.; and no wonder the wonders of the possibilities on the mere observational level were celebrated early by Vertov* with his "kino eye." But all this does not necessarily take us far in the field of comprehension. When I first got interested in these visual possibilities of the movie camera (around 1919) a friendly professor said: *Be sure you are not pursuing the shadow instead of the substance.* I thought it a pretty jest about the cinema in general, but I don't laugh at it any more. The fact is that the multiple visual aids given by the movie camera have turned out (in simple fellows) to be not an aid, but an actual barrier to comprehension. The pursuit of the cinema-of-the-subject as a cultural pursuit is too easy, providing as it does the illusion that by seeing a lot interestingly, you see much. I sometimes wonder that students at great universities give it so much consideration, so much more than they give to, say, architecture, painting, and sculpture—which have to stand up, and for a long time.

So an interest in the nature of comprehension is for me fundamental to all interest in the creative process. Philosophy is obviously vital in one or the other or all of its disciplines (pure, political, social, aesthetic, etc.). So too is history in all its disciplines (political, constitutional, social, etc.). (The trouble with historical discipline is that it is damnably tied to a sense of time.) When anthropology becomes a study in the nature of comprehension in the "savage mind" (as in Lévi-Strauss), it becomes enormously interesting to anyone concerned with the extension of observation into comprehension because it is, in the "savage mind," notably based on direct observation (of sky and land and water, of the seasons, of meteorological phenomena, flora, fauna, etc.). If, in fact, the deepening of the art of observation in the cinema involves many perspectives of comprehension, you would have to consider with the social, the historical, and the psychological, the perspectives suggested by that very same "savage mind" which is, equally, in all of us. Among other things it might add to the art of the cinema a sense of "in time" or, if you like, "timelessness," which is sorely lacking in its present concentration on observation for observation's sake.

Having said this I will now cheerfully appear to contradict myself. I am all for subject enjoyment. Some of us get a unique kick out of what we think of as "movie"—movie-as-such. We say: *that's movie*—and we mean just that. We also have a notion that we are in the same sort of minority of

---

* Dziga Vertov, Soviet director-cameraman, in the 1920s brought a new degree of perception to the use of the cine-camera as a means of recording actuality.

appreciation as those who have their immediate recognition of architecture, painting, or sculpture as such.

I here remind you of Kant's odd aesthetic category involving "purposiveness without purpose." Oliver Wendell Holmes has the interesting phrase "lazing busily." The French have their conception of *"bricolage."* There are contexts in which the "inconsequential" is enjoyed or admired. This "purposiveness without purpose" gives you, among other things, the pleasures associated with games, carpet designs, and the abstract arts of various sorts, as well as the immediacy of enjoyment involved in standing and staring and spitting over a bridge. Maybe you spoil the experience, or lack a sense of humor or something, when you get to considering perspectives of meaning for, say, the fact that infants and animals are liable "to steal a picture."

Personally, I never accepted the "purposiveness without purpose" judgment as categorically different from the "teleological" judgment, but never wanted to make much of it. If pressed, as I don't want to be, I would have a shot at putting the whole lot in some perspective or other of comprehension, including the most abstract of the abstract arts. Why, for example, their differences of focus?

Question IV. Is there any director working at the moment whose work you particularly admire, and if so, why?

Many, but the only ones I would be primarily interested in are the men who have broken through to economic viability in progressive modern terms and are sharing the opportunity with others, and particularly with younger people. It is difficult to put names to them at this time of great fluidity. Many individuals have broken through on their own personal account. I leave them out of the argument. I obviously do not share the interest in individual work which one comes across in film societies and other *in* circles. Most of the once-good things look a bit amateur today, and certainly not as significant as once was claimed. One thinks more of Sennett, though you can't exactly nail down anything he did. One thinks more of the wave that was Chaplin, and Laurel and Hardy, than of individual pictures. One thinks more of the wave that was Eisenstein and Pudovkin than of what evolved. No, today the significance I'd expect would be in nailing down the people who are responsible for the different waves of film-making. For names I would think personally of Joris Ivens and his influence on the young film-makers of the socialist countries; of Tom Daly in Canada and his influence over the many films at the National Film Board; of Arthur Elton's influence on the scientific-educational front; of Anstey's sponsorship of young film-makers; of Bert Haanstra and his influence in Holland; and of Storck's influence in Belgium. I wish I could name the individuals who have swung things in Czechoslovakia and Yugoslavia, for many good things are growing there because of one persuader or another. We know the important work that Bossak and Toeplitz have done for Poland. As you see, I am not interested in single films as such, only as they contribute to the larger thesis—and individuals likewise. Film cannot of its nature be a purely personal art, except, as it were, in miniature and on one's own money. A few have managed it, but they are not significant. The nature of the cinema demands collaboration and collusion with others, and with many variant purposes; and its significance derives from those who can operate and command purposively and aesthetically within these conditions. Ask yourself who is *actually* the most commanding producer in the United Kingdom. Well, on first principles he is bound to be at the BBC, whence the biggest and best creative visual flow derives, and one must assume that he is Wheldon.*

Question V. Do you think that images on the screen have a psychological force that words spoken or written do not have?

No, except in the fact that film has an automatic audience of millions, on screen or television. Nevertheless, there is such a thing as "movie" *sui generis*, much beloved by some, including myself. But I am not sure by how many, though I have had some odd experience of appreciation of movie *sui generis* amongst my own TV millions. I have done much, for example, to spread the knowledge of abstract films, and find I have built up an audience for them in the most unexpected quarters. Here is an unknown territory for inquiry.

Question VI. Can a fictional film compete in depth and profundity with a novel, or should it be aiming for a completely different effect?

I wouldn't think any film you and I have ever seen could compete in depth with, say, Tolstoy, Dostoevsky, Balzac, etc. Film for the most part is addressing millions, and at the same time. Its economics prevent the same consideration of depth. Perhaps the technical complexity of its manufacture also does.

Question VII. Your work in films has been mainly with documentary, and production and organization, with little attention to fictional films. Is this a matter of talent or conviction?

The answer derives from my premises. Who, in his senses, *except in the socialist countries*, could pretend to share and manage (in order to further public ends), the economic costs and hazards of fictional film production? I have been associated with the production of a score of fictional films, but only under the guise of providing employment and experience for young

* Huw Wheldon, formerly managing director, BBC Television, retired 1975.

directors and actors, etc., and under the protectorate of the Board of Trade under Harold Wilson. The BBC achievement in this field is worth keeping an eye on, but its funds are limited. With the fictional film, I trust only where public trust is associated with it. The future for fictional films in the U.K., so far as I am personally interested, is with television under public authority of one sort or another, or, alternatively, with the development of the National Film Finance Corporation in its public responsibility.

Question VIII. Documentary today seems to lack some of the energy and idealism of the 1930s. Whose fault is it?

You must be provincially referring to the United Kingdom, because documentary flourishes greatly in some countries overseas, and with similar ideals. The fault in the U.K. is partly in the changing, more inward-looking context of national politics. But don't forget that the BBC has taken over much of documentary's original work, and is doing excellently by it, and will do better when it transcends its present reportage complex. The real documentary center in Britain today is at the BBC. That is where it is to be judged, and if necessary, criticized: and called to, and financed for, the larger horizons.

Question IX. You have been an advocate of a dramatic process of education, using films and other methods of propaganda to teach people "citizenship." Has this been done?

Yes, all over the world, spectacularly so, and not least in the emergent countries. See also the above reference to the BBC.

Question X. In spite of your efforts, Britain seems to be less conscious of a purpose or a destiny than ever. Do you think this is true and what can one do about it?

This is too big a question. Britain has hard economic changes to make and tends to be inward-looking at this period (economically-in-the-short-run-preoccupied). But I doubt if its "destiny" is any less manifest than that of, say, France or Germany. America is all mixed up about its "destiny," and much of its imaginative creative work is not too obviously involved in the pursuit of national ends, and making them manifest. But consider: creative effort in defiance of popularly declared national ends may in the long run reflect the labor pains of discovering the more real national "destiny." In fact America must be (in English) the most exciting field for the study of the aesthetic-community relationship: and it is a big and difficult field of "destiny" to get into focus. The more so with the U.S.S.R. and China.

Ironically, the countries most clearly sure of "destiny" are often too poor to give a creative form to it (e.g., Egypt). Others are too hamstrung by entangling alliances to give it a clear individual character (e.g., Canada in one sense, Poland in another). On the other hand, I look to all three for a progressively good flow of pictures, because the artist is—in spite of all—being positively treated as an ally by the powers that be, and a relatively free ally.

Remember among other things that national "destinies" are out of fashion—and after Buchenwald have every reason to be. Set against this the recent invitation by the American J. K. Galbraith to the British government "to think strategically instead of tactically . . . to accept the full implications of the goals the government sets itself . . . *and to do this publicly and with fanfare.*" In that latter context, there would be ample creative opportunity for the documentary film to be busy about "destiny." In fact, I cannot think of the British government, considering what Galbraith proposes, without remembering that the documentary film was from the very beginning dedicated—*and by the British government itself*—to this very same analysis and this very same end.

When we see the documentary men doing a Lazarus outside the gates, as they now are in England, it simply means that they have got into servile ways and forgotten what it originally was all about. *Documentary is a way of observation and thought: a way of creating the imaginative forms in which action is rooted.* As such, it is a necessary consideration of government. To me the task of the documentary men is plain enough. They have need to reassert and reestablish—academically, politically, and otherwise —their right to sit above the salt.

Index

Index